Advance Praise for Janet Penley and MotherStyles

"I still reflect and draw upon what I have learned in your class from three years ago (has it been that long)? All moms should know about their mothering styles. How lucky I was to know. . . . I feel like you were my mentor and teacher to help me be a confident mom."—*Lizzy*

"What a wonderful tool the concept of type is! . . . I can't tell you how wonderful it feels to have this new paradigm in my head and to feel its implications seeping in, slowly filling reservoirs that have been empty for as long as I can remember. Thank you."—*Irene*

"I now understand exactly why so many activities I have tried to enjoy did not work, why particular interpersonal frictions have occurred, and why I generally feel like a misfit with most people. . . . I now have a tool to make better choices in my life, to avoid being swayed by *other* people getting enjoyment from something."—*Wendy*

"I learned this information when my children were about ten and it was like the Red Sea parting. I could see my own preferred path to take through mothering. It showed me how to be happy with myself and gave me the confidence to go with my strengths. Instead of saying, 'I can't' or 'I don't,' now I say, 'I'm very good at . . . '"—*Joan*

"This information has helped me to understand the differences between me and family members (and friends and other mothers at my kids' school, co-workers, employers, employees, and—fill in the blank) so that my relationship with each of them is better/smoother/more forgiving/better communication/more successful."—*Mary*

"I come from a family where the mom is one type, and one of the children is a completely different type. If only both were aware of the MotherStyles 'method.' I truly believe they would have a much closer relationship. I also believe that my sibling would be a much more confident person."—*Anne*

MotherStyles

Using Personality Type to
Discover Your Parenting Strengths

Janet P. Penley

with Diane Eble

Da Capo

LIFE
LONG

A Member of the Perseus Books Group

Many of the designations used by manufacturers and sellers to distinguish their products are claimed as trademarks. Where those designations appear in this book and Da Capo Press was aware of a trademark claim, those designations have been printed with initial capital letters.

Myers-Briggs Type Indicator, Myers-Briggs, and MBTI are trademarks or registered trademarks of the Myers-Briggs Type Indicator Trust in the United States and other countries. The self-rating checklist included in *MotherStyles* is not meant as a substitute for the Myers-Briggs Type Indicator instrument, nor is it endorsed by the owners or publisher of the MBTI instrument.
Mothers of Many Styles and M.O.M.S. are registered trademarks of Penley and Associates, Inc.

Set in 11.5-point Goudy by The Perseus Books Group

Library of Congress Cataloging-in-Publication Data

Penley, Janet P.
    Motherstyles : using personality type to discover your parenting strengths / Janet P. Penley with Diane Eble.—1st Da Capo Press ed.
        p. cm.
    ISBN-13: 978-0-7382-1045-2 (pbk. : alk. paper)
    ISBN-10: 0-7382-1045-5 (pbk. : alk. paper) 1. Typology (Psychology) 2. Myers-Briggs Type Indicator. 3. Motherhood—Psychological aspects. I. Eble, Diane. II. Title.
    BF698.3.P46 2006
    155.6'463—dc22

                                                                                2006004430

Published by Da Capo Press
A Member of the Perseus Books Group
http://www.dacapopress.com

Da Capo Press books are available at special discounts for bulk purchases in the U.S. by corporations, institutions, and other organizations. For more information, please contact the Special Markets Department at the Perseus Books Group, 11 Cambridge Center, Cambridge, MA 02142, or call (800) 255-1514 or (617) 252-5298, or email special.markets@perseusbooks.com.

1 2 3 4 5 6 7 8 9—09 08 07 06

This book is dedicated to good mothers everywhere
who are perfect in their own gloriously imperfect way.

Contents

Introduction

Breaking Through the Myth of the Ideal Mother

W HEN I BECAME A MOTHER, I SO WANTED TO DO IT RIGHT.

What "right" was, I didn't exactly know. So I turned to others for advice.

Almost everybody around me had some to give. The hospital nurse showed me the right way to fasten a disposable diaper. Later, when I brought the baby home, my next-door neighbor advised me to use only cloth diapers. The pediatrician told me that the right way to feed a baby was every four hours at the breast for at least six weeks. My mother-in-law advised me to supplement breast-feeding with formula.

I read dozens of parenting books. One book said I should teach my baby to fall asleep on his own. Another touted the emotional benefits of sleeping together in a communal family bed. As my children grew, I went to how-to parenting classes about toilet training, language development, and building self-esteem. I provided a stimulating environment, validated my children's feelings, actively listened, and disciplined with logical consequences. I bought the right stroller and enrolled my children in the right nursery school. I volunteered in their classrooms, taught Sunday school, and planned PTA programs. In order to do all of the things a "good" mother should do, I cut my marketing career to part-time.

I believed if I just got up earlier or stayed up later, read my son one more story or fastened a bow in my daughter's hair, I would finally be the ideal mother I so wanted to be.

Then, one Saturday morning, I had an "Aha!" moment. While I was carefully arranging the matching plates and napkins for my son's six-year-old birthday party, he bounced in to inspect the decorations, upsetting my beautiful work.

"Get out of here!" I shrieked. "Can't you see I'm trying to make a nice birthday for you?"

The irony of my words hit me immediately. I had tried to do everything right, yet instead of moving closer to being the ideal mother I wanted to be, the gap seemed to be widening. On the outside I was "doing it all." On the inside I felt inadequate, overwhelmed, and teetering on the edge of mother burnout.

In that moment, I saw my situation clearly. I had to reclaim myself in my mothering. It was time to stop turning outward for answers and start tuning in to who I was as a person. Right or wrong, I had to muster the courage to raise my children in my own very personal and human way.

When I shared my "Aha!" moment with other mothers, I discovered many of them grappled with the very same issues.

As mothers we are bombarded with advice from well-meaning "experts," each one telling us the right way to parent—as if there were one right way. It can end up making us feel conflicted (*Which way is right?*), isolated (*Everyone else knows the secret but me*), and inadequate (*Mothering would be easy if only I were somebody else*).

Scientific studies over the last century have clearly established the importance of the mother/child relationship. In fact, in the early 1900s, psychoanalyst Sigmund Freud put forth the idea that a person's own failings might be the fault of how he or she was mothered. Over time, that notion caught on and became twisted into the idea that you can produce a perfect child through perfect mothering. Therefore, many of us expect ourselves to be good at every aspect of parenting and worry that any imperfection on our part may end up causing our children psychological damage.

Perhaps you are not as vulnerable to these messages as I was as a mother, but I believed that a good mother should be good at every aspect of mothering, whether it be baking cookies, answering children's whys, or playing hide-and-go-seek in the backyard.

Do you think a good mother should help her child to socialize and experience the world? Understand her child in-depth as an individual? Keep her child clean, fed, rested, and warm? Look for each child's unique potential and encourage creativity? Be objective, fair, and foster independence? Be warm, sympathetic, and encourage a close relationship with her child? Provide structure, consistency, and order? Be tolerant, flexible, and go with the flow?

If you said "yes" to all of these, the myth of the ideal mom is alive and well for you, as well.

Yet, can you as a mother be both structured and go with the flow *at the same moment*? No. At any given moment, you must choose one or the other. One or the other approach will probably feel more comfortable for you, and you will gravitate toward that more often. It is also likely you will consider it one of your strengths. But, overall, most mothers expect themselves to be both consistent and flexible. This is good in theory, but not so easy in practice.

Mothers of Many Styles

I came to believe that mothers needed less "do-it-this-way" advice and more support in finding their own way. I still wanted to be a good mother, but I wanted to do it based on my own strengths and values, instead of trying to live up to every parenting expectation and comparing myself to my next-door neighbor.

Thus Mothers of Many Styles (M.O.M.S.) was born.

I developed M.O.M.S. as the antidote to my own perfectionism and self-doubt, and yet it has proven helpful to thousands of other women as well. Mothers of Many Styles began in 1988 as a series of programs about the strengths of different mothering styles. This unique philosophy and body of information, developed by mothers for mothers, is the foundation of this book. M.O.M.S. utilizes a framework of personality type that is already used by 25 million people for self-understanding, management development, and career counseling.

My son is 25 now, my daughter, 22. The information in this book was developed from almost two decades of observation, study, and interactions with mothers in more than 550 workshops, qualitative research with a sample of 600 mothers, and in-depth personal interviews with more than 100 mothers. I've spoken at hundreds of schools, parent organizations, churches, hospitals, and corporations and listened to countless mothers tell their stories. To supplement my understanding, I've also interviewed dozens of fathers and children.

I bring to this book the perspective of a veteran mother. A mother, who, having come through it all, has a better sense of what really matters in mothering when the Cheerios are swept from the floor and the last high-school football jersey is sent off to Goodwill.

In addition, I have teamed up with a younger mom to help with the writing of this book. Diane Eble attended a Mothers of Many Styles seminar early on and has used this information throughout her mothering career. She's still in the thick of it, too, with a fifteen-year-old son and a ten-year-old daughter. This book is written in my voice—when I use "I" it means Janet—but Diane's perspectives are included as well. In fact, a few of her own stories are sprinkled throughout. Between the two of us, and the mothers I've worked with over the past two decades, we have put to the test every aspect of the material you'll be learning, in countless different situations, over decades of cumulative mothering experience.

Most of my research has taken place in the Chicago area, but also in California, Massachusetts, Louisiana, Kansas, Virginia, Iowa, Minnesota—and even Paris, France. Through all this work with mothers, two key truths have emerged. These core ideas can help you break free of the myth of the ideal mother, move you through "one-right-way" thinking, and give you empowering new perspectives on yourself as a mother. In fact, many women say this information has, quite simply, changed their lives.

Truth No. 1: Good Mothers Come in Many Styles

There is no one right way to be a good mother just as there is no one right way to be a good human being. As mothers, we each bring different strengths, interests, and values to the job of mothering. Strengths we do as easily and naturally as breathing. Strengths we don't have to read books or go to classes to learn. Strengths that make our children lucky to have us as their mothers.

The strengths of your mothering style are partly determined by your unique personality, and you will enjoy the most success and satisfaction when you turn your attention to your strengths rather than your shortcomings.

When you notice differences in how other mothers approach childrearing, you don't have to feel defensive or worry about which one of you is doing it correctly. There are many right ways to raise children. You and your next-door neighbor might mother differently, but that doesn't mean that you both aren't good mothers.

Think of your image of the perfect mother and all the qualities she embodies. Each and every mother has been blessed with *a part* of this perfection. No one mother has it all.

The good news is this: You no longer have to covet your neighbor's mothering style. You have your own style of mothering and your own strengths.

It turns out, motherhood is more like a marathon than a sprint. Discovering how to be a good mother based on your own nature instead of trying to fit yourself into some mold of what a good mother *should* be is the only viable approach for the long haul. It may be eye opening to walk a mile in someone else's shoes, but walking in them for the twenty-year duration of raising a child is apt to produce a bad case of blisters.

Truth No. 2: No Mother Is a Perfect Mother

Believe it or not, no mother does all of the right things and none of the wrong things. No mother has the inside track on how to raise perfect children. Every mother, no matter how good she is, is a mixed bag. She has an undeniable human side comprised of limitations, needs, and vulnerabilities.

Fortunately, this is as it should be. Children don't need perfect mothers because, as human beings, they themselves will never be perfect either. Children need human mothers who can model for them how to make the most of their strengths, come to grips with their limitations, and manage their humanness to become the best they can be.

So many women try to be perfect in mothering, but perfectionism is not very nurturing—to your child or to your spirit. We all want to give our children the best. In the case of being a mother and raising a child, our best involves embracing what it means to be human.

Sometimes we interpret the concept of wholeness as being without flaws. So we try to erase the parts of ourselves that seem lacking or broken. The irony is, being whole means embracing those inadequate parts as well as our strengths. Wholeness involves getting to know your limits and vulnerabilities, including them in your definition of who you are, accepting them just as you accept your eye color or having two hands instead of four. That's the only way to feel whole as a human being.

The reality is that the very qualities you perceive to be your personal shortcomings are the flip side of the wonderful strengths that make your children lucky to have you as their mother.

Be Yourself

These two truths add up to one overall message: Be yourself.

Much of mothering is sprung on you when you least expect it, when you are just coming out of the shower wrapped in a towel, or it's 3 a.m. and you're roused from a deep sleep. In those situations, it is hard to avoid being yourself and nearly impossible to remember how the "experts" say you are supposed to handle the situation. Unless you mother from your own perception and judgment, it's hard to improvise as you go along and react effectively in every new situation.

The experts don't tell you that every parenting technique has an upside and a downside. Using logical consequences, for example, does keep discipline objective and calm, but when overdone it can seem uncaring and uninvolved (and may be ineffective for certain children anyway). My natural discipline style is more relationship based. I show caring and involvement and expect my children to follow the rules out of their consideration and commitment to our relationship. Whenever I used logical consequences, it didn't feel like I was standing on solid ground and my lack of confidence made me less effective.

My approach, however, also had its downside. When tempers flare, it's easy to be overly punitive and harsh. Or, the fear of appearing like an ogre and wanting to avoid conflict might lead to permissiveness and indulgence.

Once I realized there was a downside to any parenting approach, I decided it was much easier to just go with what came naturally to me. Instead of making someone else's mistakes, I would take responsibility for my own.

Remember, good mothers come in many styles and no mother is a perfect mother. Being yourself is the meat and potatoes of mothering, and if you are forever copying someone else's way you are apt to lose touch with your own truth.

Mothering and Personality Type

In order to make these truths of mothering most helpful and understandable, they need to be customized to you. Every mother has strengths and struggles, but what about *your* strengths, *your* struggles? That's where knowing your personality type can help.

It's almost impossible to get an objective perspective on yourself as a mother. Those that are close enough to see you in action day in and day out are too young or too biased to be objective. And those with a more detached perspective—the saleslady watching you handle a temper tantrum at the toy counter or your child's teacher on a field trip—don't really know what goes on at home behind closed doors.

Understanding your personality type in mothering can help you be yourself and provides you with an objective tool to help you better understand your way vis-à-vis others. It can also help you custom-tailor your mothering to the needs of your unique children. When it comes to parenting, one size *doesn't* fit all.

The core of my teaching on mothering styles is based on a theory of personality type introduced by Carl Jung in his 1923 book *Psychological Types* and built on by an American mother-daughter team—Isabel Myers and Katherine Briggs. Myers and Briggs developed their own assessment tool, the Myers-Briggs Type Indicator® personality inventory, to help people identify their individual personality types, and it is the most widely used instrument of its kind.[1]

I chose this framework of personality type as the tool for understanding different mothering styles because it is grounded in more than sixty years of use and research in a variety of settings. It is popular in business for leadership development and team building. Career counselors use it because there is a great body of research that indicates different types self-select into different careers. It's widely used in marriage counseling because many of the rough edges in a relationship can be attributed to personality issues. Educational professionals use it to help identify students' learning styles. It is even taught in churches and synagogues because recognizing one's unique gifts and the differing gifts of others is spiritually enriching. Because of its broad applications in both public and private spheres, it also appeals equally to both employed and stay-at-home moms.

But perhaps the most important factor in choosing Jung/Myers-Briggs personality type theory as the basis for my work with mothers was how positive and affirming it is. It is one of the few psychological assessments developed for use with healthy, normal people. It isn't designed to measure pathology, and all personality types are considered equally valuable. It helped put my own experiences as a mother in a more encouraging light, but it also provided an impartial and more forgiving way of understanding other mothers—my own mother, my mother-in-law, my sisters-in-law, and the mothers in the neighborhood.

Through it, I experienced a paradigm shift. My core belief in one "right" way to mother changed and I could begin to see the "rightness" of many different approaches. Although I've pursued many other avenues of self-growth, learning about personality type has had the most significant impact on my self-esteem and relationships. Knowing my type has helped me manage my personal energy, find a balance between work and play, and stay true to myself in decisions as minor as whether to be room mother for my daughter's fourth-grade class and how much was I willing to travel for work.

It has given me an objective framework to value my own uniqueness and at the same time, appreciate the uniqueness of my children and my husband. My son's personality type turned out to be the opposite of mine, and without type knowledge, I doubt our relationship would have succeeded. By knowing personality type he and I were able to get beyond the misunderstandings and power struggles of who's right and who's wrong and build a respectful and loving relationship.

Once I grasped personality type, when I saw another mother at the grocery store looking happy and relaxed as her four young children helped her shop, running through the aisles hunting for their favorite cereals and snacks and piling them into the overflowing cart, I could acknowledge how challenged I would feel in the same situation. But instead of sinking into self-criticism, I'd remind myself that that mom is probably energized by action and stimulation and I need calm and quiet. She gives her kids the gift of flexibility while I gave my children the gift of structure. And even though I was privy to her strengths as a mother in that moment, I knew that hidden from my view were the times when she struggled—perhaps over a missed permission slip or a messy living room. I'm OK, she's OK, I would remind myself, and there are many ways to be a good mother.

Mothers Can Change the World!

You, as a mother, hold so much power and influence over the people you care for. A mother's love can be transforming—for you, your family, and even your community.

You want to give your child the best and you'll do whatever it takes—get up earlier or stay up later, sacrifice a career or learn a new one. I'm hoping, for the sake of your child, you may even be willing to live closer to your own truth.

Growth is what being a child is all about, but it is also what being a mother is all about. Mothering is so hard, so draining, and so confusing that it makes mothers naturally receptive to new ideas—ideas that might replace the ones that aren't working so well, whether they are in our relationships, our world, or our own minds.

There are lots of books about the how-tos of parenting and the needs of children. Maybe you have read them all in trying to do your best as a mother. But for all those hundreds of books, there are very few books about you—as a mother.

You can read a thousand books about the growth and development of children, and end up ignorant about your own personal development. Yet nothing could be more important to your children than dealing with your own personhood issues as they arise in the mothering experience.

Using personality type as a framework, this book begins by focusing on you. Armed with increased self-knowledge, you will move outward to your relationship with your child. You will get new perspectives on compatibility, differences, and what each child needs to flourish. Next, you will take a look at the interactions within your whole family: between you and your partner, between the two of you as parents and your children, and finally, between you and the larger community. Throughout, you will hear the voices and stories of real life women as examples.

My sincere hope is that by the time you finish this book, you will:

- trust your innate strengths and gain confidence in your own natural, unique approach to mothering.

- be more realistic and accepting of your struggles (we all have them).

- undo stress and guilt about not measuring up to the stereotypes of a "good mother."

- learn how to re-charge and guard your energy using your unique personality as a guide.

- understand and minimize conflicts with a child or spouse who is different.

- strengthen parent-child and co-parenting relationships.

- optimize the work/family balance for your individual needs.

- and foster acceptance and appreciation of differences . . . within your current family, your family of origin, among other mothers, and in our society.

A tall order, perhaps, that I believe we can deliver. Now let the journey begin!

Notes

1. The self-rating checklist included in *MotherStyles* is not meant as a substitute for the Myers-Briggs Type Indicator instrument, nor is it endorsed by the owners or publisher of the MBTI instrument.

part 1

. . . .

Discover and Embrace
Your Unique Mothering Style

"Some are kissing mothers and some are
scolding mothers, but it is love just the same,
and most mothers kiss and scold together."

—*Pearl S. Buck*

chapter 1

Your Unique Style

Think back to a time, a moment, an incident, when you felt you were really on top of this mothering game. An instance when you felt you were in tune with your child, when you were giving him or her exactly what was needed, when you thought with a contented sigh, *This is what makes it all worthwhile*.

What was going on in that moment? What was happening? What was your child doing? What were you doing?

Chances are, in that moment you were operating from the strengths of your unique mothering style. You were giving your child what you are best equipped to give.

According to many psychologists, we are happiest and feel most fulfilled when we are using our strengths. Understanding your personality type can help you identify your natural strengths as well as your personal path to success in mothering and in life. This chapter introduces you to the basics of personality type and gives you an opportunity to guess your own type.

If You Think You Already Know Your Type

More than 25 million people have taken the Myers-Briggs Type Indicator personality inventory, so it's likely you may already know your type. Maybe you were introduced to personality type theory through a seminar at work or a psychology course in college.

When people learn that I use the Jung/Myers-Briggs theory in my work, I either hear, "I love type, it's wonderful!" or, "Oh, that funny four-letter thing?"

That latter comment tells me that person's introduction to type was probably less than ideal. If type isn't explained well people tend to reject its value and may never give it a second chance. If you have attended a Myers-Briggs workshop before, consider the next section a review of the basic concepts. If your previous experience with personality type left you feeling skeptical, then I'd like to un-do some of your misconceptions.

Introduction to Personality Type

Appreciating your mothering style and making the most of it begins with self-knowledge.

Personality type helps us understand ourselves and how we operate by focusing on four key areas:

- Where do you focus your attention and get your energy?

    EXTRAVERSION   INTROVERSION

- What information do you attend to most?

    SENSING   INTUITION

- How do you make judgments/decisions?

    THINKING   FEELING

- How do you like your outer world structured?

    JUDGING   PERCEIVING

These four dichotomies and eight preferences—Extraversion and Introversion, Sensing and Intuition, Thinking and Feeling, and Judging and Perceiving—are the basic building blocks of personality type. Each of these words designates a certain innate mindset and approach to life, and their meanings vary from conventional definitions used in common language. According to Carl Jung, Isabel Myers, and Katherine Briggs, within each of these four pairs, people are born with a preference for one over the other. This *preference* is a lot like your natural preference for using your right or left hand. Even though we depend on and use both of our hands, one feels more comfortable and trustworthy. So it is with our type preferences. We use all eight preferences day in and day out, but in each pair one feels truer to who we are.

In fact, the analogy to being a righty versus a lefty is a great way to deepen our understanding of what I mean by type *preference*. As a right-hander, when I write my name with my right hand, my preferred hand, it seems automatic, effortless, and refined. When I use my left hand, my nonpreference, it often feels awkward, requires more conscious attention, and produces less impressive results. Imagine if you had to write with your nonpreferred hand from 9 to 5. Would you feel exhausted? Headachy? Impatient and irritable? Perhaps that's exactly how you often do feel at the end of a day. If so, much of your everyday mothering exhaustion comes from having to overuse your nonpreferences in the course of taking care of children and outside demands. Almost every day we are required to use our nonpreferences, as well as our preferences. Consistently overusing our nonpreferences makes mothering difficult and draining.

Your preferences can be your guide for maintaining your personal energy and customizing mothering to best fit your strengths. Knowing my preference for Introversion, for example, helped me say no to teaching Sunday school (interacting with large groups of children). Instead, I offered to write an article for the nursery school newsletter (better use of my preference for Introversion).

One more thing to keep in mind about preferences is illustrated well by Diane's recent experience. When she had rotator cuff surgery on her right shoulder, Diane had to learn to use her left hand and arm for many tasks. Since she is right-handed, this was difficult at first. But the more she used her left arm and hand for certain things, like wiping down the shower stall, the more natural it began to feel. However, once her arm was completely healed, she gratefully reverted back to wiping down the shower with her right hand. Your years of mothering might be like those months of recovery this mother experienced.

There is nothing like motherhood to stretch you in every conceivable direction. If you were used to planning your day to the half hour before you had children, now you'll find yourself pulled to the max in the direction of flexibility. On the other hand, if you were a free spirit before children, getting the kids to school or soccer practice on time may feel overwhelming. Because a particular situation demands it, you learn to use your nonpreferences to fit in and succeed. Although you adjust your behavior, your basic preference remains the same. When the situation changes, you will likely fall back to what feels most natural.

So when you read these descriptions, try to think of how you are naturally, not how you think you should be, or how your parents wanted you to be, or how you've learned to be. I want to get at your shoes-off self—the alternative that you gravitate toward without conscious effort. If you think, *Well, I can be this way if I try*, then likely this is not your natural preference.

Another tip is to think back to how you were as a child. Often we are a more pure form of ourselves before we begin to go through adolescence and experiment with different identities or before we become young adults trying to conform to how to be successful in the world.

If you don't feel from these descriptions that you can guess your preference in each area, don't worry. There will be plenty of information in the following chapters that will help you pinpoint your particular type.

Energy: Extraversion–Introversion

The first dichotomy of personality type has to do with *where you focus your attention and get your energy.*

Do you tend to turn outward to get energy? Does the world of people and things and external experiences energize you? Do you learn by doing and tend to think out loud? Do you need many people interactions to feel connected and like you belong? Then you probably have a preference for Extraversion. Extraverts prefer action and want to contribute to the action.

If you are energized more by turning inward to the world of ideas and reflection, you prefer Introversion. Introverts like to do most of their processing internally, thinking things through and emphasizing reflection rather than action. To others they may seem contained, reserved. It's not that they don't like or need other people;

they do. However, many favor interactions with just a few people, and they relate best one-on-one. They prefer solitude and calm to activity and noise, and prefer to work alone. They like to process things internally, to think things through before presenting their thoughts to the world. Whereas the Extravert seeks to experience the world through a wide range of experiences, the Introvert seeks to understand the world and prefers a narrower, more in-depth focus. Extraverts bring breadth to life while Introverts bring depth.

Let's take an initial stab at guessing your preference for Extraversion or Introversion. After you read the characteristics and key words below, place an X on the continuum to express which words resonate with you the most right now. Just give it your first, initial response. You will have plenty of opportunity later to verify and refine this initial guess.

Extraversion	**Introversion**
Energized by other people and things; external experience	Energized by the inner world of ideas and reflection
Expressive, easy to know	Contained, reserved
Prefer activity; want to contribute to the action	Prefer solitude and calm; like to work alone
Like to process externally, talk things out	Like to process internally, think things through

Key Words

Outward	Inward
Go and do	Stop and think
Many	Few
People	Solitude
Action	Reflection
Breadth	Depth

Where I see myself:

Extraversion �—————|—————————— **Introversion**

"Life of the Party" or "Pooped by the Party"?

The words "Extravert" and "Introvert" in the context of the Myers-Briggs personality type framework have different meanings than they do in everyday conversation. That's one reason most literature on Jungian and Myers-Briggs theory spell "Extravert" with an "a." In type theory, Extravert means someone who turns outward for energy and focus. Webster's definition for "extrovert" is someone who is "gregarious and unreserved." The Extravert may act like an extrovert, to be sure, but some Extraverts can be quiet or even shy. Indeed, Introverts can be very extroverted and social when they are in the right mood or if they think the situation requires it.

Type professionals often say that the Extravert may or may not be "the life of the party," and the Introvert is not always the party pooper—but most Introverts *are* pooped by the party. Being with large groups of people is draining after awhile for the Introvert, who will want to go home to be alone and recharge.

Parties are actually a very good context for illustrating the difference between Extraverts and Introverts. Sam, the Extravert, and Joan, his Introverted wife, attend a party. Both mingle with others just fine and make lively conversation. However, they may have different objectives for the interactions. Sam wants to talk to as many people as possible and moves around the room. Joan is looking for more in-depth conversations and is happy to sit down and talk at length with one or two people she finds interesting.

At around 10:30 p.m., Joan feels talked out and ready to retreat to the quiet of her home. She nudges Sam and whispers, "I think we should think about leaving. Let's stay another ten minutes, okay?"

Sam, whose batteries have been charged up by all this people interaction, responds, "Leave? The Joneses have invited us over for Pinochle afterwards. The night is just getting started!"

However, because Sam and Joan understand personality type, they come to a compromise: They leave at 11:30. On the way home, Sam processes his evening by talking about all the conversations he had. "Did you hear the Smiths are moving? The Browns are getting a divorce. Ted Jones got a great new job." Joan is quietly looking out the window. She, too, is processing the evening by replaying conversations and interactions, but it's all going on inside her head.

Without knowledge of their personality differences, Sam could feel shut out by Joan's silence and Joan might feel irritated with Sam's "unnecessary talking." Instead, Sam experiments with not talking, and after a while, Joan restarts the conversation with an interesting observation from the party.

The Misunderstood Introvert

Recent studies seem to indicate that Extraverts and Introverts are equally represented in the American population.[1] However, as a society we tend to overvalue the gifts and lifestyle of the Extravert, and undervalue those of the Introvert. Students' grades are partially determined by class participation. Presidents win elections based on their ability to speak in front of cameras and crowds. Sports and entertainment attract millions of dollars, while libraries and schools are typically underfunded. Extraversion is our societal norm, and in many cases, our ideal. Because of this, many Introverts experience a sense of being "a fish out of water." Especially if they were raised in an environment in which Introversion was seen as "wrong" or strange, Introverts may grow up feeling uncomfortable about the way they are.

My preference is for Introversion, but for most of my life I have pushed myself to fit in with Extraverted norms, raising my hand to answer questions in school when I'd prefer to be silent and introducing myself to strangers when I'd be more comfortable hanging out in the background. In fact, people who don't know me well can't believe I'm really an Introvert. Yet sometimes I feel like a turtle in a world full of hares. Even with awareness of type, I am prone to overriding my Introverted limits by trying to keep up with the more active and outgoing pace of my Extraverted friends.

Introverts also don't express who they are as easily or openly as Extraverts. With Extraverts, "what you see is what you get." With Introverts, there is always "more there than meets the eye." Isabel Myers said being an Introvert was a lot like wearing a fur coat with the lining facing out and the fur hidden on the inside. Introverts are often underrated or overlooked until you get to know them on a deeper level. They tend to be misunderstood, even by themselves.

Information: Sensing–Intuition

The second dichotomy of personality type concerns *information*—what kind of information you pay the most attention to and trust the most.

Do you attend to and trust information you get primarily from your five senses—things you can see, feel, taste, hear, smell, and measure? Do you trust concrete and down-to-earth information, and prefer to focus on the facts, the practicalities, the details, the reality of a situation? Do you favor a step-by-step approach? Do you pay more attention to "what is" rather than "what could be"? Then your preference is Sensing.

"I think the hardest thing I struggle with is being an Introvert. Until I learned about personality type, I thought there was something wrong with me. My mother would always say, 'Get your nose out of that book and find a friend to play with!' But being with people drained me, while reading filled up the well. Once I understood personality type, I was able to give myself permission to 'fill the well' in my own way.

"As a mom, I still struggle with Introversion to some extent. I have to remind myself not to compare myself to other (Extraverted) moms who seem to be able to handle so much. I also have to remind myself that the need to be alone is not selfish on my part, but a way of making sure I have something to give."—*Diane*

"I now know I was an Extravert raised in a family of Introverts. I always thought there was something wrong with me for needing to be with people. The 'peace and quiet' of home drove me nuts. My parents thought there must be something wrong with me for being so loud and active."—*Fran*

Or, do you consider the five senses a jumping-off point, placing your trust more in information that comes primarily from your "sixth sense"—hunches, reading between the lines, looking for hidden meanings, symbols, analogies, associations, patterns, relationships, theories, and abstractions? Do you live with a focus toward the future, anticipating what might be? Are you imaginative, preferring the abstract over the concrete, the possible over the actual? Do you usually proceed by leaping around, by bursts of energy, rather than a step-by-step approach? Do you focus more on "what could be" rather than "what is"? Then your preference is Intuition.

About 75 percent of the population are Sensing types and 25 percent have the preference for Intuition.[2] At times, Intuitive types may feel as out of step as Harry Potter among Muggles. In a way, though, this proportion of Sensing and Intuitive types in the population may be the perfect balance. It correlates with the saying that any good idea is 1 percent inspiration (Intuition) and 99 percent perspiration (Sensing). An Intuitive type might come up with an idea in a minute that will take hundreds of people years to implement, refine, and maintain.

Read the following descriptions and again place yourself on the continuum. Remember—this is just an initial guess at your type.

Sensing	Intuition
The five senses	The sixth sense, hunches
Live in the here and now, enjoying what's there	Live toward the future, anticipating what might be
Concrete, what is real	Abstract, what could be
Take a step-by-step approach	Usually proceed by leaping around; bursts of energy

Key Words

Common Sense	Imaginative
Details	Patterns
Present	Future
Realism	Theory
Facts	Innovation
Practicalities	Possibilities

Where I see myself:

Sensing ▥▥▥▥▥ | ▥▥▥▥▥ **Intuition**

The Missing Rug

My mother has a preference for Sensing and I have a preference for Intuition. Whenever she comes for a visit, she asks me questions that leave me dumbfounded. For example, does my weekly lawn service take the grass cuttings with them or leave them for garbage pick-up? It may sound odd, but as an Intuitive type, I just don't notice. Once she gave me a small brown rug she no longer wanted, saying, "If you stop using this rug, be sure to give it back to me." On her next visit, she asked me to show her the rug. I knew I wouldn't have thrown it out or given it away, but for the life of me I didn't know where it was. When I returned later from doing an errand, she greeted me at the door with a smile. "Come with me," she said. I followed her into my living room, and, much to my surprise, there was the rug under the piano bench.

Sensing types may consider Intuitive types flaky (and based on this story who would blame them!), and Intuitive types may consider Sensing types to be small-minded and picky. But knowing type can put these differences in a more positive perspective. Sensing types focus on the details and practicalities. Intuitive types focus on the big picture and possibilities. Most situations require some of both, making each important and equally valuable.

Decisions: Thinking–Feeling

The third dichotomy of personality type concerns how you prefer to come to decisions and conclusions. There are two equally valid ways of deciding.

If you prefer to base your decisions on logic and objective analysis, trusting your head to make a good decision, then you have a preference for Thinking. Words like *logic*, *objectivity*, *competence*, *justice*, and *fairness* resonate with Thinking types.

If you prefer to base your decisions on more personal and subjective criteria, giving primary consideration to the impact of decisions on people, including yourself, then you have a preference for Feeling. Feeling types tend to trust their hearts in decision-making, seeking compassion and harmony.

Thinking Types Can Cry, Feeling Types Can Think

Again, "thinking" and "feeling" are words we use every day, but in the context of personality type, these terms refer solely to how you tend to make decisions and judgments. Make no mistake: People who prefer Thinking do feel! They can get angry, cry, laugh, fall madly in love, and care deeply. And Feeling types do think. They can get As in calculus, become electrical engineers, and earn doctorates in physics.

But when it comes to *decision making*, Thinking types tend to look at their feelings objectively, as one factor to be considered among others. They are ruled by their head. Feeling types are likely to be ruled by their hearts. It's not that they always let their specific feelings (anger, fear, etc.) rule their decisions and judgments, but that they take a more subjective, personal approach to decision making ("how will this affect the people involved?" versus "what principles should govern this decision?").

Thinking-Feeling is the only dichotomy with a gender bias. No matter what your natural preference, our culture expects men to represent Thinking and women to express Feeling. In fact, much of the traditional battle between the sexes can be attributed to Thinking and Feeling differences in relationships, not gender differences. Based on cultural stereotypes you might expect all women to be Feeling types and all men to be Thinking types, but approximately 75 percent of women prefer Feeling and 60 percent of men prefer Thinking.[3] So, it is not uncommon for men to have a Feeling preference. Thinking women, a 25 percent minority, often have well-developed Feeling sides because they have been encouraged to tend to relationships in traditionally feminine ways. If you think you are close on this dichotomy, ask yourself who would you be without the traditional cultural pressures to be a certain way.

First Impressions

For many years, I co-led workshops with Diane Stephens, who was instrumental in the development of Mothers of Many Styles. She prefers Thinking and I prefer Feeling. One day when we entered the conference room to set up for one of our presentations, I was pleased to see what a sunny room it was and that each table had a little vase of flowers on it. "This is lovely, thank you for doing such a nice job!" I complimented our sponsor. Diane was quiet. I took her aside and asked her what was wrong. She pointed out that the requested slide projector was missing and that the chairs were placed in rows instead of a circle.

Our different preferences had led us to two different first impressions. Thinking types, like Diane, tend to have a more critical eye. Upon arrival, she immediately noticed the flaws in the situation. As a Feeling type, I had spontaneously focused on the positives. But when we gave the room a second look, sure enough, I noticed the items we had requested were lacking, and Diane appreciated the beauty of the space. When you are trying to discover your true preference, consider not only which alternative you use most often, but which alternative you use first.

Which do you think you are?

Thinking	**Feeling**
Decide with the head	Decide with the heart
Concerned with truth, justice, fairness	Concerned with relationships, harmony
Skeptical, take nothing for granted	Affirming and accepting
Value and trust logic	Value and trust gut feelings
Asks, "What do you think about . . . ?"	Asks, "How do you feel about . . . ?"

Key Words

Head	Heart
Firm and fair	Compassionate
Analyze	Empathize
Justice	Harmony
Objective	Subjective
Critique	Compliiment

Where I see myself:

Thinking ▓▓▓▓▓▓▓▓▓ | ▓▓▓▓▓▓▓▓▓ **Feeling**

Lifestyle: Judging-Perceiving

The fourth dichotomy of personality type concerns lifestyle—how you like your outer world structured.

Do you like a planned, orderly lifestyle with schedules and limits and structure? Do you like to start the day with a plan, and then follow the plan? Are you in love with your to-do list and the pleasure of checking things off? Do you like to organize, get things done and settled? Do you aim to control and structure what happens, trying to do the right thing? Then you have the preference for Judging.

Or do you prefer to go with the flow, play it by ear, keep your options open, wait and see what happens? If so, you have a preference for Perceiving. You may start the day with a to-do list and plan, but it is more of a back-up plan in case nothing else comes up. Your pleasure comes more from the process and the doing rather than the finishing and getting things done. Instead of aiming to control or structure life, you may prefer to live life as it comes, experiencing and adapting to what happens.

Although just over half (55 percent)[4] of the population prefers Judging, our society has traditionally been based on Judging values: structure, order, consistency. Yet, to keep up with technological advances and our ever-changing world, the flexibility and adaptability of Perceiving types (45 percent) are just as essential.

Once again, take an initial stab at rating yourself in Judging-Perceiving.

Judging	Perceiving
Plans provide comfort and security	Plans cut off unexpected opportunities
Aim to structure your life	Aim to let life happen
Like to do one thing at a time	Most productive doing several things at once
Want to be prepared, not caught by surprise	Like to take things as they come; respond well to the unexpected

Key Words

Structure	Flow
Closure	Openness
Planned	Spontaneous
Organized	Flexible
Control	Adapt

Where I see myself:

Judging ▓▓▓▓▓▓▓▓▓ | ░░░░░░░░░ **Perceiving**

Getting the Buns or Having Some Fun?

My son Dan has a clear preference for Perceiving and I prefer Judging. Knowing type has helped us transform irritation over our differences into amusement.

One summer evening, I was cooking hamburgers on the grill when I realized we were out of buns. Dan was about nine at the time, so while I finished making dinner, I sent him to the convenience store two blocks away to buy buns. I didn't tell him to hurry because I thought it was self-evident. It takes about 10 minutes to cook hamburgers and about 15 minutes to get to the store and back. If dinner was going to be on time, he'd have to hustle. Even at his age, I would have set out on this errand with one thought in mind: "Buns, buns, buns, I have to get those buns. I have to get those buns so dinner can be on time." Naturally, I assumed he would approach the errand in the same way.

When he wasn't back in twenty minutes, I was irritated. After half an hour, I was worried. I started walking down the block to find him. Just then he came around the corner holding the buns in one hand and staring intently at the palm of his other. Along the way he had discovered a furry caterpillar and as he walked, he was letting it crawl over his hand and up his arm.

"The hamburgers are already cold," I said. "I didn't expect you to take so long." As he showed me his fuzzy friend, my precocious son replied, "Next time, estimate how long you think it should take a boy my age to do something, then multiply by two, and I'll always be on time."

As a Judging type, I expected him to be singleminded, time-conscious, and task-focused. As a Perceiving type, he approached the errand as an adventure, open to the unexpected and a chance to have fun. Therefore, it took him longer. From then on, I learned to factor in playtime whenever I asked him to do a chore.

Guess Your Type

Your preference in each of these four pairs determines your personality type. I have a preference for Introversion, Intuition, Feeling, and Judging, so my type is identified by the four letters, I N F J. In type theory, the letters refer to the first letters of each alternative, except that N is used for Intuition, since the letter *I* already refers to Introversion.

There are sixteen different combinations of preferences, hence sixteen different personality types. For each of the personality types there is a dynamic interaction between the four preferences. When those four preferences combine they create a unique identity. Each of the sixteen types has unique strengths and differences. In terms of mothering style, each of the sixteen type mothers does something better for her children than any of the other fifteen type mothers are likely to do.

Look over how you rated yourself on the four continuums in the previous sections and write the letters of what you think your type is here:

_____	_____	_____	_____
E or I	S or N	T or F	J or P

If you are uncertain about any particular dichotomy of type, it may help to read "Brief Descriptions of the Sixteen Types" on the following page and see which one fits you best. If you are sure about preferences for NFP, for example, but too close to call on E-I, then read the descriptions of ENFP and INFP and decide which one most resonates with you. Or if you are undecided on two different preferences, you might need to read four descriptions and see which seems truest for you.

When I attended my first workshop on type, I guessed myself to be either an INFJ or ENFP. When I read the thumbnail description of the ENFP, I thought, *Hey, I can be like that*, but already my shoulders were tensing up as I imagined forcing myself into someone I wasn't. When I read the INFJ description, my shoulders relaxed and I thought, *Ahh—I could be like that in my pajamas*. One of the sixteen types should fit you like a glove.

The Myers-Briggs system is the only theory I know that is based on sixteen categories. Most typing systems use four categories, and some use nine or twelve. A system with fewer categories may be easier to learn, but because they are less specific, I don't think they are as helpful. I think of my type as the coat rack of my life, a structure on

Brief Descriptions of the Sixteen Types*

ISTJ
Analytical MANAGER OF FACTS AND DETAILS; dependable, decisive, painstaking and systematic; concerned with systems and organization, stable and conservative.

ISFJ
Sympathetic MANAGER OF FACTS AND DETAILS; concerned with people's welfare; dependable, painstaking and systematic; stable and conservative.

INFJ
People-oriented INNOVATOR *of ideas*; serious, quietly forceful and persevering; concerned with the common good, with helping others develop.

INTJ
Logical, critical, decisive INNOVATOR *of ideas*; serious, intent, highly independent; concerned with organization, determined and often stubborn.

ISTP
Practical ANALYZER values exactness; more interested in organizing data than situations or people; reflective, a cool and curious observer of life.

ISFP
Observant, loyal HELPER; reflective, realistic, empathic, patient with details, gentle and retiring; shuns disagreements; enjoys the moment.

INFP
Imaginative, independent HELPER; reflective, inquisitive, empathic, loyal to ideas; more interested in possibilities than practicalities.

INTP
Inquisitive ANALYZER; reflective, independent, curious; more interested in organizing ideas than situations or people.

ESTP
REALISTIC ADAPTER *in the world of material things*; good-natured, tolerant, easygoing; oriented to practical, firsthand experience; highly observant of details of things.

ESFP
REALISTIC ADAPTER *in human relationships*; friendly and easy with people, highly observant of their feelings and needs; oriented to practical, firsthand experience.

ENFP
Warmly enthusiastic PLANNER OF CHANGE; imaginative, individualistic; pursues inspiration with impulsive energy; seeks to understand and inspire others.

ENTP
Inventive, analytical PLANNER OF CHANGE; enthusiastic and independent; pursues inspiration with impulsive energy; seeks to understand and inspire others.

ESTJ
Fact-minded, practical ORGANIZER; assertive, analytical, systematic; pushes to get things done and working smoothly and efficiently.

ESFJ
Practical HARMONIZER and worker-with-people; sociable, orderly, opinioned; conscientious, realistic and well tuned to the here and now.

ENFJ
Imaginative HARMONIZER and worker-with-people; sociable, expressive, orderly, opinioned, conscientious; curious about new ideas and possibilities.

ENTJ
Intuitive, innovative ORGANIZER; analytical, systematic, confident; pushes to get action on new ideas and challenges.

---

*From *People Types and Tiger Stripes*, 1993, by Gordon D. Lawrence. Used with permission. Center for Applications of Psychological Type, Gainesville, FL.

which to hang my different roles, skills, and life experiences. Many other people have described identifying their type like a light bulb going off; suddenly they felt understood and affirmed for who they were.

The theory clicks with some people better than others. Yet in my work with thousands of mothers, usually something about the theory hits home and is useful, if not all four dichotomies, then at least one or two. Even if you are still unclear after reading your brief type description, things may become clearer as you read on and consider personality type in the context of mothering.

The Limits of Personality Typing

Categorizing people according to some inborn set of characteristics and predispositions has been around since Hippocrates espoused the four temperaments: choleric, phlegmatic, melancholic, and sanguine. We all like to do it—whether it's astrological signs, Enneagrams, body types, or gender. It's often a helpful shortcut to understanding people in a world made up of billions of unique individuals. It gives us a common language for describing a cluster of personal characteristics, whether our own or others'. It also provides a way to be more aware and appreciative of other people's differences instead of assuming everyone is just like you.

However, when typing turns into *stereotyping,* it has gone too far. Any category system simply does not explain everything about a person. We are always more unique and complicated than our type, no matter what system we're using, and every human yearns for those differences to be understood and honored. Personality type is best used as a starting point for getting to know a person better and opening the door to a deeper, less biased, more compassionate connection. Stereotyping uses categories as an ending point for understanding a person, and cuts off further intimacy and understanding.

Remember, too, that type doesn't dictate what you can and can't do. It doesn't limit you. It helps you understand what you do naturally and whether what you do energizes or drains you. But it should never be used as an excuse. You may have a preference for Introversion, but that's no excuse for not returning phone calls. A preference for Extraversion doesn't give you permission to talk, talk, talk, and never listen.

As I said, learning about personality type is like learning a new language. But be careful where and when you speak this new language. You aren't going to win points for politeness or relationship building by speaking a different language with people who don't know that language, whether it's Polish, Chinese, or typology. People hate being excluded. They are likely to react by rejecting what they don't understand, and maybe they'll reject you along with it. So don't go around telling your husband he's acting so N or telling your best friend she's a perfect example of an ESFJ. You can't speak alphabet soup to the uninitiated and then expect them to be open to learning the wonderful insights of personality type!

If You Can't Decide . . . ⁵

Often people have very clear preferences on two or three of the dichotomies but feel like they are some of both on one dichotomy, like Extraverted or Introverted, for example. First, let me assure you that no matter what you choose as your preference, it does not mean that you aren't some of the other as well. Everyone is a mixture of all eight preferences. In the case of E-I, every Extravert needs an inner life for depth and good judgment. Every Introvert needs an outer life to get their ideas out into the world.

There are many reasons why it might be difficult to determine your type just from the information you've read so far.

- *You grew up in an environment that didn't value your preferences.* If you're an Introvert and were constantly told to "go out and play with friends," you may have learned to act extroverted and may think that's how you are. Or perhaps you're really an Extravert but you were always told to be quiet and go read in your room. If your preference is for Perceiving but you grew up with Judging parents who always told you to "get your work done before you play," you may have developed the habit of planning your day and working your plan. So when deciding between two alternatives, ask yourself if there's one you feel you should be, and who told you that.

- *Cultural biases.* Our culture tends to overvalue some preferences and undervalue others. The active, doing, product-oriented, bottom-line culture of business and practical science—ESTJ—tends to be over-valued in our culture. Traditional, experience-based, concrete, practical, logical, and structured is what wins kudos. Everything on the opposite side—INFP—tends to be undervalued by American culture. It represents the contemplative, process-oriented, personal focus culture of social service, psychology, journalism, and the clergy.

  If you're a woman in the business world, you may have developed the ESTJ side of you, even if some of these are not your natural preferences. That too would make it difficult to determine your "true" type.

- *Your current situation.* Who are you living with now? We often compare ourselves to the people we are closest to. For example, when compared to the rest of the world, my husband and I are both Introverts. But if we were just comparing ourselves to each other, it would be easy for me to think I was an Extravert and he was an Introvert. Or perhaps you're a Perceiving type in a household of a Perceiving husband and Perceiving children. To achieve some sort of balance and functionality, you might feel forced to act like a J, despite your natural preference.

- *The disorientation of motherhood.* The early years of mothering especially can be so disorienting; you hardly have any time or energy to think about yourself and who you are now. In many ways becoming a mother is like going through adolescence. You are becoming someone new and experimenting with new identities.

As you read through this book, you should find your sense of identity solidifying.

Notes

1. Charles R. Martin, Ph.D. and revised by Allen L. Hammer, Ph.D. *Estimated Frequencies of the Types in the United States Population.* Center for Applications of Psychological Type, Inc., Gainesville, FL, 1996, 2003.

2. Ibid.

3. Ibid.

4. Ibid.

5. If you would like to take the Myers-Briggs Type Indictor instrument to confirm or clarify your type, contact us at http://www.motherstyles.com. We will help you find a qualified professional who will administer the instrument and give you appropriate person-to-person feedback.

chapter 2

Plug into Your Personal Energy Source

Extraversion or Introversion

O<small>NE MORNING MY FRIEND</small> P<small>AULA CALLED ME FROM HER CELL PHONE</small>. S<small>HE AND</small> I share three out of the four letters of type; she is an ENFJ, I am an INFJ. (To refresh your memory: that means she has a preference for Extraversion, I prefer Introversion, and we both share preferences for Intuition, Feeling, and Judging.)

Paula was in her car on her way to watch her niece in a school dance performance. I was in bed writing in my journal. Paula wondered if I wanted to keep her company as she drove downtown to return a lamp she had bought. We spent a few minutes trying to work out our schedules. As Judging types, we already had a rough plan for the day.

My schedule looked like this: write from 10 to 12; eat lunch, walk the dog, meditate, do yoga, make dinner, and spend the evening watching a favorite TV show with my husband and high-school daughter. Paula's schedule: watch niece's dance, play tennis, come home for a quick shower. "If we leave at 1:20," she told me, "it would give me time to come home, pick up Lucy after school, and buy tickets to the daddy/daughter dance tonight at the high school. Then I have to take Emily to soccer. . . ."

Note the difference just the first letter (E or I) made in how we each approached the day. We both had lists; we were both attracted to creative endeavors (writing for me, and attending an artistic performance for Paula). But as an Extravert, Paula could handle lots and lots of places to go, people to see, and things to do. All of that energized her. I, however, would be drained by the end of a day if I had a schedule like hers. Likewise, she would be drained by the solitude that so rejuvenates me. I could live Paula's life for a day or two, and she could live my life for a day or two. But over the long term we would each find the other's life very draining.

What about you? With whom do you identify? Do you tend to pack lots of things in, as Paula did, or does the very idea of a full schedule drain you? Do you find yourself needing alone time to regroup, or do you feel "cooped up" and bored when you're home alone for too long?

If you easily identify with either Paula or me, you're well on the way to understanding your own preference. If not, in this chapter I'll describe in greater detail the typical characteristics of Extraverted and Introverted moms. Plus I'll give you tips on how to make the most of your natural mothering style in this area and how to maintain a high energy level.

Energy: The First Key to Good Mothering

When do you do your best mothering? Isn't it when you are full of energy? And when are you more likely to do or say something you'll regret? Isn't it when you're feeling drained and tired? Do you turn outward for energy (Extraversion) or inward (Introversion)? Understanding and accepting this aspect of your nature is fundamental to developing your personal mothering style.

When asked to name their strengths, many Extraverted mothers mention "energy." In fact, many describe themselves as "high energy." Because motherhood is synonymous with people and action, Extraverted mothers are more likely to have the energy to keep up with their children most of the day.

Introverted mothers, on the other hand, tell me they have to guard their energy. They have a natural rhythm of interacting, doing, going, and then retreating to their inner world to re-energize. Introverted mothers tend to tire out during the day without some alone time. Many Introverted mothers tell me that knowing they are drained by too much external focus and energized by quiet time alone is the most valuable lesson they learned from knowing their type.

Remember, taking care of yourself is the first and best way to take good care of your children. As you understand yourself, you will also understand your children (and your partner) better, allowing each of you to be your best selves.

What Would You Do with a Whole Day?

Imagine you were given the gift of twenty-four hours to do whatever you want to do. All of your responsibilities are temporarily canceled. You have absolutely nothing you *must* do, only what you want to do.

How would you spend those precious twenty-four hours? What would you do in the morning? For lunch? In the afternoon? For dinner? During those last few hours of the day?

Or, put another way, what would the worst twenty-four hours of your life look like? Sometimes it's easier and more effective to start with what we know we *don't* want.

When I ask moms these questions in workshops, almost all, Extraverted and Introverted alike, say they would start their day enjoying the peace and quiet of an empty house. Because mothering is such a people-intensive job, even Extraverted moms need some time alone. Many mothers say their ideal day would begin with a carafe of coffee, a chocolate-chip muffin, and time to read the newspaper beginning to end.

The difference in type often shows up, however, in how mothers would spend their afternoons. By noontime, the Extraverted moms might be looking at their clock and thinking, *It's time for lunch. I haven't seen my friend Julie for a long time. I wonder if she'd want to grab a bite to eat and go with me to that new shop that just opened at the mall.* An Extravert will have satisfied her need for solitude after just a few hours and will find herself naturally wanting to connect to people and the external world to recharge her batteries.

The Introvert, however, is likely to unplug the phones, pull down the front shades and bask in solitude for the whole day. She might decide to rearrange her lingerie drawer, plan a trip, or watch a video that only she would enjoy. She may in fact feel that twenty-four hours hardly scratch the surface of what she needs to really fill up her gas tank.

When I was home all day with preschoolers, I would hire a babysitter once or twice a week so I could have a break. At first, I used that time to do errands, have lunch with my friends, and go shopping. But when I came home, I felt more impatient with my children than before I left. It was as if I hadn't had any break at all. When I discovered my preference for Introversion, I finally understood why. The next time I needed a break, I asked the babysitter to take the kids *out*, to lunch or the park, and I stayed *in*.

A Tale of Two Mothers

A good illustration of how the preference for Extraversion or Introversion works itself out comes from the stories of two mothers, both with twins.

One Extraverted mom, Jessica, said, "After being home alone with sleeping babies for a few hours, I feel drained, ungrounded, even a little shaky. I begin to wilt, like a flower without water. I feel like I'm losing it, staring at the four walls. I've found the cure for this is to dress the babies in matching outfits, pack them and the double stroller into the van and head to the mall. There's nothing like pushing around a stroller with twins to get a little attention from strangers. People will come up and ask, 'Oh, are those twins? How adorable! You certainly have your hands full.' With each conversation, I feel myself getting pumped up more and more, like a balloon."

Tori, an Introverted mom, however, had a very different story: "I don't mind being home with the sleeping babies. I use the time to read, putter, or write in my journal. But when they wake up and need attention, I like to take them out for a walk in the stroller. I hope to not only quiet them down and give them some stimulation, but to allow myself some time to let my mind wander.

"However, I find that too often, people come up to me and say, 'Oh, are those twins? How adorable! How on earth do you keep up with them?' It's so annoying to have to stop and talk to people, and I find myself coming back from a walk feeling drained."

Minivan Moms

One Extraverted mom explained why she bought her family a minivan: "I love going places with people, and we used to take two cars. This van seats nine people, so now we can all go to the museum or zoo together!"

When I heard that remark, my first response was, "Now I know why I'll never buy a minivan. I would never want to be in a position to drive nine people anywhere!" Not only would it be draining to have all those people in the same van, but carrying on a conversation with them while driving through traffic and navigating directions, all external tasks, would be too much for me. By the time we arrived at our destination, I would already be spent.

But another mom said, "I have a minivan, but I'm an Introvert, too. Here's how I use it: I put my child in the back and I'll sit in front; we'll go somewhere and I'll have my space and quiet while my child is happily occupied with looking out the window as the world goes by, or watching a video if it's a longer trip."

So you see, not all moms who drive minivans are Extraverts! And you can come up with creative ways to deal with your preference, no matter which one it is.

Verify Your Preference

These stories should have given you some pretty good clues as to where you get your energy. Now let's verify your preference by looking at the following characteristics as they relate to mothering.

For each of the following characteristics, circle the number that best describes how you relate to that point:

0—This does not describe me at all.
1—This describes me somewhat.
2—This describes me well.

Of course, this checklist is not intended to be a reliable and validated psychological measurement, like the Myers-Briggs Type Indicator instrument. Nevertheless, many women find it helpful to rate themselves as they read along.

Strengths of the Extraverted Mother

If your preference is Extraversion, you may find yourself gravitating toward the following:

- *Getting out and taking young children along to experience the world.* For Extraverts it's a great, wide, exciting world out there, and it's important to get their children "into it." Extraverted mothers say they get antsy if they're not out and about with the children each day. "I read the Sunday newspaper with a scissors, cutting out ideas for places to go and things to do with the family!"—*Debbie*

    0   1   2

- *Being on the go, involved in a variety of activities, thriving at a busy pace.* For Extraverts, a rich full life involves plenty of people, action, and variety. Juggling children's activities, her own volunteer work or paid employment, homemaking, and leisure can make the Extravert feel alive and connected to the world. Extraverts seem to be able to "do it all." "My friends wonder how I can get so much done in a day and still have time to watch *All My Children* on TV"—*Mary*

    0   1   2

- *Providing your children with opportunities to be with people.* Because being with people so energizes her, the Extraverted mom naturally wants her children to be involved with people. She'll sign up her children for Brownies and Cub Scouts, ask another family to join them on vacations, and invite the sports team over for a pre-game carbo-loading buffet. One Extraverted mother likened the sounds of people in the house to music.

    0   1   2

- *Teaching your children the importance of social skills and graces . . . so they can get along in the world.* The Extraverted mom helps her children both implicitly, through modeling, and explicitly, through teaching and coaching, how to get along with people. While visiting my Extraverted girlfriend, a neighbor boy came over to play with her seven-year-old son. Scott opened the door, looked his visitor in the eye, smiled, then said, "Hello, I'm so glad to see you; you can put your shoes over here and hang your coat on this hook." As he guided his friend into the family room, I overheard him say, "Do you know what I was just doing? I was 'greeting' you. My mom told me that's what we do to make friends feel welcome."

0   1   2

- *Enjoying casual conversations with children; feeling free to ask them questions.* Interacting with children, her own and other people's, is easy and natural for the Extraverted mom. Often her house is where the neighbor kids choose to hang out. She likes to get to know her children's friends when they come over and might maintain relationships with them even after her child has moved on to other relationships.

0   1   2

- *Connecting with and tuning in to the world beyond home; being "in the know" when it comes to community, school, volunteer organizations, and the neighborhood.* The Extraverted mom keeps up with what's going on, and needs to feel connected to the outer world. She usually is involved in at least one volunteer activity, sometimes several, and likes being part of various organizations. She's the one to call for an update on neighborhood "news."

0   1   2

- *Providing the spark to get things going and keep things moving; serving as an example of get-up-and-go.* Not one to sit on the sidelines, the Extravert is the mover and shaker who makes sure things happen.

0   1   2

- *Connecting with the people and high energy of large family gatherings.* Family reunions, get-togethers over the holidays, and parties are important to the Extravert. It's one of the ways she "makes memories" for her children and reminds them that they are part of an extended circle of family and friends.

0   1   2

Add up your points here: _____

Struggles of the Extravert

When verifying your preference, it's just as helpful to know what you struggle with as what you gravitate toward. So continue to rate yourself in terms of how you relate to the following struggles of the Extravert.

If your preference is Extraversion, you may struggle with . . .

- *Being isolated at home with babies and preschoolers.* Being alone for long periods of time with no social interaction drains the Extravert, causing her to feel restless and even depressed. Many Extraverts say they survived the early years of child-rearing by listening to talk radio and carrying around a portable phone. "Being at home with an infant felt like being in prison."—*Mary Ann*

   0   1   2

- *Tuning out social and other external expectations.* The Extraverted mother's external focus makes her especially susceptible to trying to be "all things to all people" and being one of the crowd even when it goes against her individual values and priorities.

   0   1   2

- *Worrying whether your children have enough friends and/or activities.* This is especially true for the mother of an Introverted child. She may tend to project onto others her own need for people and stimulation, even if their needs are different. "It's important to have a lot of friends in life," says Gretchen, "because friends come and go." Her Introverted son sees it differently: "I like having only a few friends, but ones I really like. If one moved away, I'd be sad, but then I'd find another one."

   0   1   2

- *Overextending: not limiting your children's and your own involvement to meaningful activities.* Again, in our busy world of unlimited options, it's easy to go overboard in an attempt to help children experience as much as possible. Constantly drawn to action, variety, and people, Extraverts struggle to draw healthy boundaries for time and energy.

   0   1   2

- *Respecting a child's personal space; not being intrusive.* Her own need for interaction and connection may blind her to her children's need to create some distance so they can become their own persons, especially if they are older.

    0   1   2

- *Listening rather than talking; not dominating a conversation with a child.* Because the Extravert likes to think out loud and talk things through, when she interacts with her child she may tend to talk too much and listen too little. Her child may find it difficult to interrupt the conversation and be heard. "We are a family of talkers; at the dinner table everyone fights for airtime. Sometimes it's hard for my Introverted son to jump in."—*Leslie*

    0   1   2

- *Understanding, accepting, or encouraging a child's need for alone time, particularly an Introverted child.* Because solitude drains her, the Extraverted mom may not understand a more Introverted type child's (or husband's) need for alone time. She may experience a child's going off by himself as rejection, or it may simply not occur to her to provide adequate quiet time for others. "I have burned myself out trying to get my Introverted child to get out, join up, and meet others," one Extraverted mom commented to me in a seminar.

    0   1   2

Add up your points from this section: _____
Now add up your points from both sections (page 29 and above) for Extraversion. Write the total here: _____

Proceed to the following section. You should find that you rate yourself higher on either Extraversion or Introversion. Once you know your preference on this dichotomy, you can find the tips and suggestions that will help you make the most out of your preference while minimizing the struggles.

Strengths of the Introverted Mom

For each of the following characteristics, circle the number that best describes how you relate to that point, with 2 being "describes me well," 1 being "describes me somewhat," and 0 being "doesn't describe me at all."

If your preference is Introversion, you may find yourself gravitating toward the following:

- *Being observant of and reflective about your children in an effort to know each child in depth.* When asked to name their mothering strengths, Introverted moms consistently claimed to really "know" their children. They focus on each one as an individual with an identity rather than focus on the collective family unit. Natural observers, they like to stand back and watch children, reflecting on what they see and hear. "I am keeping a journal for each of my children, and plan to give it to them on their eighteenth birthdays," reported one INFP mom.

    0   1   2

- *Encouraging your children not to overextend by providing the time and space for a child's "down time."* Because she craves breathing space between activities to re-energize and re-orient herself, she naturally wants to provide that for her children. If it's been a very active week, she's the one who will put on the brakes and say, "This Sunday will be our home day."

    0   1   2

- *Respecting and understanding a child's need for time alone.* She isn't likely to interpret a child's need for personal space and time alone as a sign of rejection, being anti-social or depressed. In fact, she may choose homecare instead of daycare for her child because being with people all day while she is at work seems to deprive them of the personal space they may need.

    0   1   2

- *Respecting a child who's not one of the crowd.* Because she's used to being the "different" one (remember, Extraversion is the cultural norm), the Introverted mom is more likely to feel okay about a child who is a loner or who doesn't fit in with the crowd. It's easier for her to encourage her children to be their own unique selves rather than being like everyone else.

    0   1   2

- *Providing a quiet and calming presence (although inside you may not feel calm).* The Introvert's slower, reflective style has a way of tempering interactions and bringing peace to charged situations. But an Introvert's calm exterior is sometimes deceiving. Inside, her mind may be racing. I watched a video clip of my Extraverted son and me sitting on the sofa together. He was jiggling, jumping, and flipping upside down. I was amazed to see how still and serene I looked through the camera's eye because I remember what was going on in my mind at the time. Although my body and mouth were still, my thoughts were tossing and turning, and I was about out of patience. No wonder an Introverted mom's outbursts seem to come out of nowhere and surprise everyone!

    0   1   2

- *Tuning out distractions, concentrating on one child or one thing at a time.* The Introvert is gifted with depth and single-mindedness. If she's involved with a child, she may let the phone ring so she can give the child her undivided attention without interruptions. "I like scheduling dates with each of my children individually, so I can get to know them one-on-one without distractions," reports an Introverted mother of three.

    0   1   2

- *Limiting extraneous involvements to focus more exclusively on her family.* Because she's not drawn to the external world of activity and doing the way the Extravert is, the Introverted mom may find it easier to say "no" to outside involvements in order to remain centered on her family. Though she may be tempted to overextend, she is more aware that she can't "do it all," and keeps her priorities clear. "I figured out I could be a better mother staying home in the evenings instead of rushing off to PTA meetings."—*Carol*

0   1   2

- *Standing back and watching your children be active and interact on their own.* The Introverted mom is content to stay in the background, without dominating or intruding upon her children. She respects their need to develop at their own pace, in their own way. "My Introverted husband and I built a jungle gym in our backyard for our four children. As soon as the last bolt was tightened, the children ran out to play. We were excited too. We watched them through the family room window as they jumped and hooted for hours. It was perfect bliss!"—*Jean*

0   1   2

Add up your points here: _____

Living at an Introverted Pace

"The most important thing about knowing my type was discovering I am an Introvert and how to best manage my energy. I'm a lawyer. If I have a deposition in the morning, I know not to schedule a trial in the afternoon, because I won't have any people energy left over for the kids by the time I come home."—*Patricia*

"I wanted to be a Cub Scout mom for my son, but all the commotion of little boys is hard for me. I've learned to pace myself. If I have a Cub Scout meeting in the evening, I schedule a quiet day at home. That way I'll have enough energy to manage and enjoy the group."—*Nikki*

"I mark my seminars and presentations on my calendar with a yellow highlighter. It's a visual reminder not to schedule too many in one week. I enjoy leading the groups but I need a day or two in between to recharge."—*Janet*

Struggles of the Introvert

Again, to verify your preference, look at what you struggle with. Continue to rate yourself in terms of how you relate to the following struggles of the Introvert.

If your preference is Introversion, you may struggle with . . .

- *Being focused outward on children and the tasks at hand—beyond your natural limits.* Many times in her busy day, the Introverted mother may find herself in situations that require her to turn her focus outward when she would naturally want to turn inward. The normal hubbub of kids and home may often be too much stimulation for Introverted mothers. Noise, confusion, chaos, children's requests, multiple tasks, and intrusions can make her feel like she's about to explode. Some Extraverted moms may identify with this difficulty; perhaps during the "arsenic hour" right before dinnertime. But Introverted mothers say they can feel this way at 7 o'clock in the morning while packing sandwiches, listening to a child's problem, and answering an unexpected phone call. They need alone time to balance this outward focus. Unfortunately, they often regard "time alone" as a luxury, not a necessity, and they can spend much of the day feeling tense, tired, and ready to snap.

    0   1   2

- *Conflicts between the need to tune out distractions and the family's need to interact.* After a full day of action and interaction with children, or perhaps with people at the office if she works outside the home, an Introverted mom craves solitude and time alone before interacting again with family. But young children crave attention, especially if they haven't seen dad or mom all day. Finding a balance between her needs for reflection and her family's needs for interaction is often a big struggle for the Introverted parent.

    0   1   2

- *Handling a large family or large groups of people.* Because large groups are particularly draining for Introverts, having to deal with lots of children can be particularly challenging. "We stopped having big birthday parties for my son at age eight. Nine bouncing, wrestling boys for two hours were more than my Introverted

One Introverted mom recalls, "Once I had rashly volunteered to chaperone on a field trip to a museum with my daughter's class. The night before, I couldn't sleep. I was so uptight, envisioning a noisy hour-long school bus ride into the city, a day shepherding excited children through a crowded museum and another long trip back. The day of the trip I had to call and say I couldn't do it. I felt terribly guilty, but I learned a lesson about my own limitations. I did chaperone other class trips, but I made sure the groups would be small and there would be plenty of space to spread out."

husband and I wanted to handle. For his next birthday, we took three of his closest friends on a special outing, and even we had a great time."—*Barbara*

0   1   2

- *Finding the energy to maintain the pace of active young children and adolescents.* This can be one of the biggest struggles for an Introvert. Being asked to keep up the pace of a frisky hare when she's a steady tortoise can tax all her energy reserves, leaving her little energy for pursuing her own interests. She must learn to protect and replenish her energy to make it comfortably through the day. "At the end of the day I'm mentally tired, not so much physically tired."—*Ruth*

0   1   2

- *Responding "on the spot" to children's unexpected requests; not having the time you need to think things through.* Introverts need more time than Extraverts to process things. Children have a way of forcing a parent to make a decision *right now*, and that's very difficult. The Introvert may find herself saying no or yes on impulse, and then having to backtrack later or live with a decision she would have made differently had she had more time to think it through.

0   1   2

- *Being as emotionally or cognitively accessible to your children as you think you should be.* An Introverted mom may seem detached and "aloof" to others, because of her need for space. Consequently, she may struggle with the sense that she's not as loving or available to her children as she wants to be. There's this constant push-pull between the desire for connection and the need for personal space.

0   1   2

- *Understanding an Extraverted child's need to be on the go with friends and activities and to think out loud.* It may seem to the Introverted mom that her Extraverted child is overextending, when perhaps that child truly needs that many activities. She may want to place more limits on the child than the child needs. And to the Introvert, an Extravert's need to process by talking may feel irritatingly unnecessary.

0   1   2

Add up your points from this section here: ＿＿＿

Now add up your total points for Introversion from both sections (page 34 and above): ＿＿＿

Who Do You Think You Are?

Write your total points for Extraversion (see p. 31) here: ＿＿＿
Write your total points for Introversion (see above) here: ＿＿＿

Now compare the totals. The greater the disparity, the clearer your preference is for either Extraversion or Introversion. Even if your total points for Extraversion and Introversion are close, it's likely there's still some difference. Again, this is a quick quiz to help you understand your preference, not a well-researched and reliable psychological indicator.

How Mothering Stretches Your E–I Preference

If you feel you're an Extravert but find yourself relating to descriptions of the Introverted mother, there may be several reasons why.

First, mothering—especially in this culture at this time—calls for more Extraversion than even many Extraverted moms can handle comfortably. Having small children constantly underfoot, balancing career and family demands, or trying to keep up with active teens is so demanding, even the Extraverted mothers may feel over-extraverted and close to burnout. For the first time in their lives, they too may crave quiet time toward the end of the day before going out with friends or joining in family fun.

And they like it! Motherhood and family life have stretched them to develop their introspection, getting to know themselves better and discovering more of their inner wisdom.

Similarly, some Introverts say becoming a mother has helped them develop their outward focus. Growing up, Introverts may have been more comfortable as loners. Then along came motherhood, complete with baby-sitting co-ops, play groups, PTA, carpools . . . not to mention the people needs of their children.

Now they enjoy an active family life, but in smaller doses than the Extraverted mothers, remembering to claim the time alone they need every day to manage their energy.

Now that you know your preference, you can use the following tips for making the most of your natural strengths while minimizing the struggles. Remember, the goal is to make sure you have enough of what you need in any given day to keep your "gas tank" full so you will do your best mothering. This means "taking time for me." It's not selfishness, it's just good self-care so that you will be full of the energy you need to take good care of your children.

Tips for the Extraverted Mother

1. "Taking care of me" means having variety, action, and people to recharge. Don't allow yourself to become isolated at home. Some kind of employment or joining a group can be what you need to feel connected with others. If you're stuck inside with babies or sick children, stay in touch with others via email or telephone. "I consider my child's naptime to be my telephone time."—*Pat*

2. But don't overdo it. Learn when you've had enough and how to say "no." Limit your activities to those that are the most meaningful and effective.

3. Consider taking an enforced "stay-at-home" day once a week, to balance being on the go.

4. Don't expect your partner or children to meet all your needs for Extraversion, particularly if any of them is an Introvert. Enjoy a night out with your friends, leaving dad at home with the kids. Likewise, leave your young Introverted child at home with a baby-sitter or older sibling while you run errands.

5. Have faith that your Introverted child will turn out all right. Many Introverts consider themselves "late bloomers." You can encourage your child to have playmates and play dates, but Introverts do best with people when their need for solitude is met first. Be sensitive to your child's need for one-on-one interaction rather than large crowds.

6. Spend time alone getting to know yourself and discovering your needs and opinions separate from your family's and society's.

7. Slow down. Your self-worth is in who you are, not in what you do.

"My older daughter is obviously an Introvert and before I knew type I used to worry about her. As an Extraverted child, I loved running around, being with this friend and that friend, and climbing up on grandma's lap. But my young daughter is turned off by large groups and wants one-on-one contact. At a large family reunion, I could see she was wilting, so I told her she could go for a walk and be by herself for a while.

"'Really?' she asked, thinking it was too good to be true.

"'Yes, I insist,' I told her.

"My mother, also an Extravert, saw her head for the door and asked her where in the world she was going; all her cousins were in the backyard playing.

"'For a walk by myself,' she said proudly, 'My mother *insists* that I have a little time alone.' I took great pleasure knowing she was learning how to meet her need for alone time and giving me credit for supporting her. A half-hour later she was back laughing and playing with her cousins."—*Diane, ENTJ*

Tips for the Introverted Mother

1. "Taking care of me" means getting quiet time for reflection. Take at least half an hour to an hour every day for solitude. Ignore the popular notion that time sitting quietly is nonproductive, a luxury when everything else is done. For you, it's an absolute necessity if you're to be your best.

2. Use naptimes to recharge. When babies are napping, avoid phone calls, household chores, or any other intrusions or distractions.

3. Find ways to meet your young child's need for external stimulation that don't involve you. Consider playgroups, extra classes, and programs where other adults are in charge. Bring in a mother's helper or grandma to play with your child or take them out while you enjoy the quiet at home.

4. If you have a very Extraverted child, set boundaries to protect your needs for Introversion and his or her needs to interact with you. Retreat to solitude before you reach your limit. You'll avoid exploding and feeling guilty afterward.

5. Learn a comfortable way to respond to children's unexpected requests. Share a bit of your unfinished thoughts while also giving yourself the time you need to

think things through. Practice saying, for example, "My initial thoughts are . . . but I need more time to think it over. I'll give you a decision at dinner."

6. Practice ways of saying "no" to events and commitments that require too much Extraversion. Keep a list of responses by the phone: "Rather than chaperone the dance, could I help decorate?" or, "My schedule is busy. Could you put me down for next month?"

7. Claim the strengths of your Introverted preference—the ability to connect with the depth of life. Being in the minority, you may feel inadequate or without energy if you compare yourself to active, on-the-go Extraverted moms.

Extraversion—Introversion Is Only Part of Who You Are

Now you possess a good handle on a key factor in good mothering—are you energized by turning outward (E) or turning inward (I)?

But it's not just the Extravert-Introvert dichotomy that affects what drains or energizes you. The other parts of your personality type represented by the other letters are also big factors. For instance, if you're an Intuitive (N), keeping on top of all the Sensing (S) details of caring for small children can wear you out, even if you're meeting your needs for Introversion or Extraversion. Or a Thinking (T) type will be drained by too much emotion. And if you're a Judging (J) type, dealing with the chaos of small children and family life may drain your battery.

Mothering calls upon such a vast and conflicting set of skills that everyone will struggle with parts of it. The next chapter looks at the next pair of preferences that affect your mothering style—Sensing and Intuition.

chapter 3

. . . .

Information, Please!

Sensing or Intuition

W HEN MY HUSBAND AND I HAD A NEW GARAGE BUILT THERE WAS A TIME WHEN
the rubble from the old one remained in the driveway. The heap sparked my daughter
Jane's imagination. An Intuitive type, Jane thought of a game where she took trinkets
from the house—ceramic animals, wishbones, old jewelry—and buried them in the
old garage's ruins. The neighborhood kids joined her in digging them up as they pre-
tended they were on an archeological dig to unearth an Egyptian crypt.

One day a dad, who has a preference for Sensing, was doing two-year-old duty,
making sure nobody ran out into the alleyway by our yard while the kids played after
dinner. As the summer evening waned into spooky twilight, the children seemed to
become even more engaged in the game. All of a sudden, the father blurted out, "This
is not an Egyptian crypt! This is not an archeological dig! Jane is getting these things
from her own house and burying them."

Jane ran into the house, devastated. "Why couldn't he let us have our fun?" she
sobbed. Indeed, what was the harm in it?

The harm, from this Sensing father's point of view, is that this game was getting
too real, and he didn't want the kids to lose track of reality.

An Intuitive parent probably wouldn't react in the same way. In that situation he or she might well have contributed to the fantasy, fueling the flame of imagination. Intuitive types have lots of practice in going beyond reality and then returning to it, so they aren't as concerned about losing track of what's real and what isn't. In a Sensing person that skill is less developed.

Sensing and Intuition

What kind of information do you trust most about your children—facts or impressions?

The kind of information you attend to as a mother is largely determined by your preference for Sensing or Intuition.

Sensing mothers are most comfortable with information they acquire from the five senses—the facts. The Intuitive mother is more comfortable with what she gleans from her "sixth" sense—impressions. These different approaches to information-gathering manifest themselves in a variety of ways when it comes to mothering styles. For example, Sensing mothers are more likely to stick to what's tried-and-true, while Intuitive mothers like to experiment with the newest theory or a new twist on an old one. Sensing mothers may be at home with notions of "experience," "practicalities," "tradition." Intuitive mothers respond to "possibilities," "theory," and "innovation."

How do these preferences play out in terms of mothering? Let's look at a couple of areas: how each type of mother feels about taking care of the basic needs of children, and how each feels about "being there" for her children.

The Practicalities—Pleasurable or Mundane?

The Sensing mom is probably most comfortable seeing to her children's practical needs—that they are well fed, clean, rested, healthy, and have transportation to their activities. It is not always easy for her to take care of the many practicalities of child-rearing and homemaking, but every day that's where she is apt to direct her best energy. For her, tending to the basics is the foundation of good mothering. She likes to show her love in concrete ways. With this kind of attention, even very young children are apt to get the message that they are loved and well cared for.

Of course, the Intuitive mother also takes care of her children's practical needs. As their mother, she often has no choice—so many of the needs of young children *are* practical. Yet it is unlikely that the Intuitive mother finds much comfort or pleasure in the practical, nitty-gritty side of childcare. In fact, she may find it tedious and end up doing only the minimum to get by. One Intuitive mother said she did many of the tasks typical to Sensing mothers but she did it because she felt she *had* too, not because she was drawn to them. As an Intuitive mom myself, after I've fixed a child's bike lock, gone to the basement to find a shoebox for a child's diorama, and prepared, served, and cleaned up lunch—I'm ready to take a break from practicalities with a nap or a novel.

Sensing, Intuition . . . and Baths

Just for fun, I once asked a group of about one hundred moms to indicate how often they bathed their children. I theorized that, since Sensing mothers naturally gravitate toward taking care of the physical, tangible needs of their children, they probably bathed their children more often. And, since Intuitive types tend to go through the day trying to *minimize* these things, I suspected that they would bathe their children *less* often.

What I found is that most mothers of small children bathe their children every couple of days, Sensing and Intuitive types alike. But when I looked at the daily bathers, they were twice as likely to have the preference for Sensing. And the mothers who bathe their children less often (once a week, when their hair smells, or whenever they can fit it in) were twice as likely to have a preference for Intuition.

I also learned that Sensing and Intuitive mothers often have different objectives for bath time. For the typical Sensing mom, cleanliness is the priority. On the other hand, the Intuitive mother may regard time for imaginative water play equally valuable.

When I shared these anecdotal findings at a seminar, an ENFP mother piped up with her own story. "Talking about baths makes me laugh. My husband is a Sensing type, and we definitely have different approaches to bathing the children. I let them play in the water until their fingertips wrinkle. Then they stand up while I wash their hair. As the shampoo suds drip down their little bodies, I tell them to rub it all around. After a good rinsing dunk, I consider them clean!

> "I taught my kids to pump by swinging with them side-by-side."—*Nancy, ESFP*
>
> "At the park, I don't want to be touching the swings. I'm usually on the sidelines reading a book. Ironically, it might be a book about playing with children."—*Jill, INTJ*

"My husband uses a washcloth and scrubs behind their ears and in the folds under their necks. When he's done bathing them they are as shiny as an apple. On the nights I work as a part-time nurse, he sometimes calls me at the hospital to brag. 'Tonight when you give the children a good-night kiss,' he says, 'be sure to notice how clean they smell.'"

"Being There" for Children

Most mothers want to "be there" for their children. But every type mother defines "being there" a little differently. The Sensing mother needs to "be there" for them, literally, with her physical presence. She's apt to be a "hands-on" mother, either doing things *for* her children or doing things *with* them. If she takes them to the playground, she might offer practical assistance with the swings as she enjoys the fresh air and sunshine. She shows her love by sharing concrete experiences with them.

Of course, Intuitive mothers take their children to the park, too. But given the choice of playing with their children in the "real" playground, or the playground of ideas and imagination, most Intuitive mothers would prefer the latter. Many Intuitive-Thinking mothers, in particular, say they bristle at the "hands on" requirements of the playground. Pushing a swing may seem intolerably mundane.

> "I really encourage imaginary play and that's the most fun for me in parenting. My four-year-old son has taken on an alternate identity. His name is Andy Townsend Chuckles. I show him how to write Andy's name. I leave notes to Andy on the kitchen table. I make costumes for what Andy wears. His creativity stimulates my own ideas."—*Kelly, INTJ*

The Intuitive mother is more apt to "be there" for her children by dreaming and coming up with possibilities. The Intuitive mother values and encourages her children's creative pursuits, whether it be pretending, making up games or inventions, composing songs, writing books, or doing crafts. Always looking for what is unique and original in a child, she gives the world of their imaginations great importance. She's apt to encourage her children's creativity by taking their ideas and building on them.

For example, if two children are playing dress-up, the Intuitive mother may suggest they go further and put on a play: "This can be the stage, this can be the ticket box, and I'll be the audience."

In contrast, the Sensing mother often appreciates a child's creativity, may sometimes marvel at it, but she's apt to be more content leaving the child to his or her own imagination, rather than joining in.

However, both Sensing and Intuitive types can be creative. Sensing types show their creativity through the details. They tend to take an existing idea and make it better and more unique. They may work best from a model. Intuitive types strive to be more original, seeking to do something that's never been done before. Sometimes their ideas prove too grand, and they struggle to implement them with their children.

Practicalities or Possibilities

Sensing and Intuitive mothers might even have different objectives for reading this book. Intuitive types like learning for learning's sake. Discovering a new framework for understanding differences and possibilities for people may energize them. The practical applications are less important.

Sensing types, however, are probably looking for practical suggestions they can apply tomorrow. They evaluate the worth of information by its usefulness and whether it rings true to their own experience.

Sensing types are typically looking for the how-tos and tips. Intuitive types want to understand the why's.

Deciding Your Preference

From the above descriptions, you may already be getting a feel for whether your preference is for Sensing or Intuition. Just as you did in the last chapter, verify your preference by circling the number that describes how you relate to that point:

0—This does not describe me at all.
1—This describes me somewhat.
2—This describes me well.

Strengths of the Sensing Mother

If your preference is Sensing, you may find yourself gravitating toward the following:

- *Taking care of the basics.* "To me, tending to these practical details is the definition of a mother. There are so many ways to be a traditional caretaker and yet make it my own."—*Lucy*

  0   1   2

- *Giving your children a hands-on, practical understanding of how to get along in the world.* It comes quite natural for a Sensing mother to teach her children how to tie a shoe, or balance a checkbook. Quality time for a Sensing dad might be building a birdhouse with his son. It's an opportunity to teach his son how to use a hammer and a saw, and to learn the difference between nails and screws. It will also yield a concrete outcome that will add beauty and interest to their backyard. "I cover what I think they need to know to survive in the world. How to look people in the eye, how to shake hands, how to write a thank-you note. I hit the areas you are supposed to hit and the way you are supposed to do it."—*Jill*

  0   1   2

- *Showing care in concrete ways.* A Sensing mom is likely to demonstrate love by making favorite desserts for family members on special occasions, such as birthdays; filling up the gas tank for a special date; playing a child's board game with him or her. I asked a ten-year-old Intuitive daughter how her Sensing mother made her feel loved. She said, "I know my mother loves me because she spends lots of time fixing my hair and make-up before my dance recital, making sure my costume is clean and I have the right shoes."

  0   1   2

- *Providing children with rich sensory experiences.* She might take them to the gym or a play room, go sight-seeing, spend afternoons in the park, hang out at ball games, or engage them in gardening or redecorating a room. Because she gravitates toward enriching her own senses, she's naturally aware of the importance of providing this for her children as well. "For me, taking a trip to Washington,

D.C., was the ultimate mother/daughter experience. The museums, the government buildings, the history. It was so stimulating."—*Debbie*

0   1   2

- *Valuing and conveying the importance of family traditions.* "I'd rather stay up until 3 a.m. than give up any of our family's holiday traditions—my grandmother's cookie recipes, a handmade ornament for each child, and our family's traditional Christmas Eve dinner," says one mom. Marcy, another Sensing mother, recalls, "Every summer we rent the same cottage on Lake Michigan for a week. Our friends think we should try different vacation places, but we love having a family tradition."

0   1   2

- *Putting importance on the practical side of intelligence: common sense, applied knowledge, and getting the facts straight.* A Sensing mom might be on the lookout for jobs for a young teenager, and place importance on her children gaining skills that will enable them to make a good living. She values "street smarts" at least as much, if not more, than "book smarts."

0   1   2

- *Keeping life simple and grounded in the here-and-now.* So many famous "momisms" come from this common-sense approach to life. ("There's no such thing as monsters." "Don't borrow trouble." "Don't worry, be happy.")

0   1   2

- *Creating comfortable physical surroundings and home environment for her family.* Because she's so tuned in to her senses, the Sensing mom may have a flair for decorating, crafts, gardening . . . the kind of things that make a house a home. She may also find a way to combine practicality with beauty. "I chose a carpet that doesn't show dirt and put a faux finish in the hallway to hide finger marks."
—*Nancy*

0   1   2

Add up your points here: ____

Not All Sensing Types Are the Same

As I hinted at earlier, each preference, when combined with other preferences, begins to create something distinct and unique. Not all Sensing types are alike. Characteristics of the Sensing preference can vary dramatically, depending on whether Sensing is combined with the Judging or Perceiving preference. Both Sensing-Judging (SJ) and Sensing-Perceiving (SP) mothers are down to earth, but they are very different from each other.

The SJ mom is typically adept at providing security, doing "for" her children, and providing what a parent "should." She tends to be traditional in her approach to mothering and strives for daily routines designed to assure stability and consistency in her child's life.

The SP mother prefers to live in the moment, giving her children a spontaneous response to their needs, and probably having more fun. She bristles at routine and would rather enjoy life as it comes. For these reasons, she may find herself identifying with many of the Intuitive mothers' struggles.

Note the different approaches the two types take in the true-life examples on the facing page.

Struggles of the Sensing Mom

Again, to verify your preference it's helpful to also look at your struggles. Circle the number that best describes how you relate to each struggle:

- *Appreciating or joining in with a child's imagination and fantasy.* "I have no imagination," says one Sensing mom. "My kids make up their own stories at school and it blows my mind what they come up with. Sometimes they want to involve me in a pretend play, but I don't get it."

    0   1   2

- *Being overly focused on details and small incidents.* Because it's harder for a Sensing mom to see the big picture, she may get stuck on the "small stuff"—a hair out of place or a dirty dish left in the sink.

    0   1   2

Some Differing SJ and SP Views on . . .

Face Wiping

"My girlfriends tease me about always wiping the noses and cleaning the mouths of my children. If my five-year-old went off to school with a little chocolate in the corner of her mouth, it would bother me all day. It's not only about how it reflects on me as a mother; it's an act of love. I want my very lovely daughter's face to be clean as she goes through her day."—*Mary, ISTJ*

"I used to be a nose-wiper but I never had tissues with me. So I was a shirttail mom. Now I tell the kids to do it themselves. I don't like when they use their sleeves to wipe, but I don't make a big deal of it."—*Nancy, ESFP*

Keeping a Chart

"My husband and I are very committed to our children's health via vitamins, mineral supplements, and protein shakes. I like to keep a chart for each of our three children, what they need, how many times a day and I check off when they've taken it. It makes me feel good to have this system."—*Mary, ISTJ*

"I'd never do a chart. If you're hungry, eat; if you have to go to the bathroom, go. I'd never think to make them go to the bathroom before an outing. Although sometimes I wish I had."
—*Nancy, ESFP*

Family Outings

"Every March, I buy tickets for the family to go to a holiday sing in December. I'm giving my children an experience, a plan, and a tradition."
—*Mary, ISTJ*

"This spring break my husband is going on a golf trip, so I checked last-minute airfares and found a great deal for the kids and me to fly to Iceland. I love an adventure. Everyone's jaw drops when I tell them. 'You're going to another country on your own with three children?' But for me, it would be harder to stay home."—*Nancy, ESFP*

- *Understanding a child who is different from the "norm" or different from you.* Because the majority of the population (75 percent) prefers Sensing, it might be easy to fall into the trap of thinking that way is "normal"—especially to the Sensing mother, who gravitates to the "tried and true." Plus her natural mindset makes it harder to imagine another person's perspective.

0   1   2

- *Seeing possibilities in complicated or difficult situations.* It might be harder for her to deal with a child not getting dressed in the morning, or an adolescent bringing home bad grades. She might feel stuck, and be unable to see any options for dealing with a tough situation.

     0   1   2

- *Feeling overwhelmed or stressed out by all the details and things to do.* Preparing for a large family gathering, getting kids back to school, or cleaning up a huge mess is a challenge for any type mother, but the Sensing mom may struggle to find perspective, prioritize, and distinguish what is essential from what isn't.

     0   1   2

- *Appreciating an Intuitive child's "big picture" orientation.* Because the Intuitive *doesn't* tend to pay much attention to details and facts, a Sensing mom who is tuned into those practicalities might unintentionally make the Intuitive child feel impractical, unobservant, or "flaky."

     0   1   2

Add up your points for this section here: _____
Add up your total for Sensing (from p. 47 and above) and write it here: _____

Strengths of the Intuitive Mother

If your preference is for Intuition, on the other hand, you may gravitate toward the following:

- *Pointing out options and possibilities, and offering children choices.* The Intuitive mother, gifted in seeing beyond what "is," can help her children think up new possibilities and options in a situation. For example, she might sit down with her teenage son and say, "Let's brainstorm ten ways you could make extra money this summer." Perhaps the son can see only the common alternative of cutting grass, but the Intuitive mother may help him see options few people have thought of before. "I have this dream of starting a family business together," says one INFP mom. "At the dinner table, I often initiate brainstorming different ways we can work together to make extra money."

     0   1   2

- *Looking for and encouraging the unique potential in each child.* The Intuitive mom values individuality, and is adept at tuning in to her child's uniqueness and encouraging it. She's unlikely to try to force her child to conform to outside standards; rather, she encourages independent thinking. My daughter was taken aback when she heard her friend's mother remark, "Why can't my kids be like everyone else?" With two Intuitive parents, she'd never been encouraged to be one of the crowd.

  0   1   2

- *Bringing an imaginative and novel approach to the ordinary and routine.* Because she gets bored easily, an Intuitive mother tends to invent ways to make the routine more fun, for herself and her children. One Intuitive mother told me she put slices of banana on round crackers, added a dab of peanut butter and a chocolate chip, and surprised her children with a snack of "monkey eyeballs." Another Intuitive mother says, "We try to invent new traditions for our family. For my children's birthdays, I paint a mural on our big living room window while they are asleep. When they awake, they are greeted by a special Happy Birthday picture made just for them."

  0   1   2

- *Explaining ideas, insights, perspectives, and meanings behind everyday experiences.* For instance, if an Intuitive parent spent time stargazing with her children, she might start out identifying the constellations but end up discussing concepts of the speed of light, the universe, and life on other planets. Here's another example: On the way to the zoo on a class field trip, the children pointed out a police car stopped by a car on the side of the road. A Sensing mother explained, "The driver is getting a ticket." The Intuitive mother seated next to her added, "In our society we have rules to help us live together safely and peacefully. The policeman is enforcing those rules."

  0   1   2

- *Valuing your child's quickness of understanding, insights into complexity, and flashes of originality.* Intuitive moms tend to appreciate the conceptual side of intelligence. "I'm excited by children who have a different perspective. My son once

speculated that dreams might be real and life was really a dream. I thought, *How original, how unique, how beautiful!* That's what turns me on in parenting."
—*Joyce*

　　0　　1　　2

- *Seeking out new techniques and perspectives on parenting.* Open to new ideas and possibilities, the Intuitive mom is always on the lookout for ways to become a better mother. She often follows her inspirations in parenting.

　　0　　1　　2

- *Keeping sight of the "big picture."* The Intuitive mother tends to see different sides of an issue, many possibilities and complications, not just life in black and white.

　　0　　1　　2

- *Valuing mothering as a personal growth experience, a catalyst for developing your own unique potential.* Awareness that there is a personal purpose in mothering can help an Intuitive mom find meaning in the more mundane aspects of what she does. Finding meaning is very important for Intuitive types.

　　0　　1　　2

Add up your points here: _____

Struggles of the Intuitive

Continue to rate yourself in terms of how you relate to the following struggles of the Intuitive:

- *Unrealistic expectations.* Often the Intuitive mom lives with an "ideal" in her mind. She may end up feeling inadequate and discouraged with herself and her family when "real" life falls short of the "ideal." For her, things could always be better. She may be particularly unrealistic about time. Because she can think of ideas and possibilities in a flash, she may incorrectly think anything and everything can be done in a flash, as well. She tends to believe all things are possible and may ignore human limitations. One Intuitive mother of two children with

ADHD and a husband with ADD says, "I have to remind myself on a daily basis that it's okay for them—and for me—to have limitations. Limitations are signs of humanness, not necessarily flaws. There's a difference."

0   1   2

- *Living in the here-and-now, taking pleasure in the moment.* Because of her big-picture and futuristic orientation, the Intuitive mom may have trouble enjoying the moment. She may live with an inner restlessness, giving more energy to the potential of the future moment and ignoring the rewards of the present one.

0   1   2

- *Keeping things simple.* Because of her tendency to see the big picture and many different angles and possibilities in a situation, she may make a situation or problem much more complicated than it needs to be. "I can never give a simple explanation. When I notice I'm getting complicated, I ask my child, 'Are you still with me?'"—*Megan*

0   1   2

- *Knowing how much time and detailed effort a task will take, whether it's getting ready for a trip or mending a shirt.* Usually she underestimates (because of her idealistic nature). But sometimes she overestimates, (in her own mind) making a simple task into something much larger and more difficult than it really is. This may lead her to say yes to things she might be better off saying no to, and vice versa—saying no to things that really would not be too difficult.

0   1   2

- *Giving a child detailed, specific instructions.* I asked my daughter to help me by planting some impatiens in our front yard. When she showed me her finished work, I was critical; she planted them too close together and the holes she dug weren't deep enough. Upon further thought, I realized that although she knows little about gardening, I hadn't provided any specific directions. I expected her to know what to do by osmosis.

0   1   2

- *Appreciating a Sensing child's step-by-step, practical approach to learning.* Unless an Intuitive mom understands the differences between Intuitive learning and Sensing learning, it's easy to get frustrated with the Sensing child's need for concrete models and realistic applications. This could lead to making him or her feel slow or inadequate.

  0   1   2

Add up your points from this section here: _____
Now add up your total points for Intuition from page 52 and above here: _____

Who Do You Think You Are?

Write your total for Intuition (from above) here: _____
Write your total for Sensing from page 50 here: _____

Compare the totals. As with Extraversion–Introversion, the greater the disparity, the clearer your preference is for either Sensing or Intuition. Even if your total points for Sensing and Intuition are close, it's likely there's still some difference.

Understanding your preference in this area also contributes to keeping your gas tank full as a mother. Being overtaxed in your nonpreferred area can drain you just as much as not feeding yourself in the area of your preference. So here are some tips to help you maximize your strengths and minimize your weaknesses.

Tips for the Sensing Mother

1. For the Sensing mom, "taking care of me" means feeding the senses—avoiding sensory deprivation. Too much dullness and sameness in the things around you can make you wilt. Revitalize yourself with rich sensory experiences.

2. If you feel stuck in a rut, use a friend as a "consultant" for seeing things in a new way. Or try a mother support group, books on child rearing, or professional help.

3. Give the Intuitive types in your life the time and space they need to play with ideas and dream without criticism or pressure to be practical. Wait until later to ask about the specifics and practicalities—they'll be more receptive once they've had a chance to fully explore the possibilities.

4. Don't feel compelled to join in your child's fantasy play if you don't feel like it. He or she will find friends, books, and games that can stimulate his or her imagination.

5. Try "brainstorming" as a playful way to consider new possibilities. For example, sit down with your child and try to come up with twenty ideas of "fun" activities to do together. Or make a list of ten ways to solve a problem. The ideas can be impractical or even absurd. Be sure to withhold any evaluations until the list is complete; then go back and consider each one, listening to each person's viewpoint. Usually one or two will make sense.

6. If you're a Sensing-Judging mother, include pleasurable, sensory-rich experiences that keep you fresh in your routine. Set aside a definite time daily or several times a week for needlework, gardening, soaking in a bubble bath, working out, or taking a walk, alone (if you're an Introvert) or with a friend (if you're an Extravert).

7. If you're a Sensing-Perceiving mother, consider an enforced "taking care of business" day once a week—it can vary from week to week—just to get errands done and keep the real world of schedules and routines from overwhelming you. Or consider getting regular help setting the house in order; it may be just the task your Sensing-Judging mate, son, or daughter was looking for.

Tips for the Intuitive Mother

1. For Intuitive types, "taking care of me" means entertaining new ideas, perspectives, and dreams. Give yourself a break from reality every now and then by watching a movie, reading fiction, or pursuing a new interest.

2. Get a better idea of how much time the basics of day-to-day living really take: time yourself with a timer. You might even write them down on a list. Then you'll know how long it takes to drive to school or sew on a button, and you can use this real-life information to plan next time.

3. Use "play" as a way to develop your Sensing function and capacity for concrete information. Developing one's nonpreference is best done just for fun without

pressure to succeed. Children can be great encouragers and "playmates" of such Sensing-type activities as jigsaw puzzles and drawing.

4. The next time you want to change "the way we do things around here," consider making moderate refinements rather than sweeping improvements. Instead of eliminating junk food from the family diet forever, you'll have more success if you downscale to a one-sweet-per-day rule.

5. Have faith in your Sensing child's intelligence and brightness. He or she approaches learning differently than you do and has different interests. Take pleasure in her ability to set the clock on the VCR or his speed in reciting the multiplication tables in 187 seconds.

6. Enjoy living in the moment. Not everything you're doing now needs to be in preparation for tomorrow . . . or the next day . . . or when the kids are getting ready for college. Set aside several minutes each day just to take pleasure in what *is*.

7. Do a little rather than nothing. Many Intuitive mothers say they shy away from doing something that seems small but is really part of a bigger project, whether it's putting one file folder away (because the whole filing system needs to be reorganized) or sweeping the kitchen floor (because the cabinets and walls need scrubbing). Don't let yourself become immobilized by the idea that "there isn't enough time to get into it now and do it right." If it's the first warm, sunny day of spring, taking five minutes to enjoy the sunshine is better than staying indoors because you don't have time to take a picnic to the park.

The next key aspect in personality type and mothering style is how you prefer to make decisions. Whether you instinctively trust your head or your heart most, it makes a big difference in how you relate to your children—and how comfortable you feel as a mother in this culture.

· · · · · · · · · · · ·

chapter 4

Decisions, Decisions

Thinking or Feeling

Every day you make decisions and judgments—dozens of them (some days, it feels like hundreds!). Everything from the weightier issues of childcare and child rearing, to the more mundane choices of which brand of toothpaste to pick. Our world is awash with options, and we must constantly make decisions and judgments.

The doctor says to put the baby down on her back, but she hates that and always flips to her tummy. What do I do?

Is it wise to let my child sleep over at that friend's house tonight?

My teenager broke curfew. What's the best consequence?

How you go about making those decisions and judgments is determined by your preference for Thinking or Feeling. Like the other preferences, this one shapes how you navigate parenting and your world. Given the same situation, Thinking and Feeling moms may come to different conclusions. Or they may end up taking the same action for very different reasons.

Let's say you're at the park with your four-year-old. He runs with glee from the slides to the swings to the monkey bars. Then he loses his grip, falls down, scratches his knees, and bursts into tears. What's your most natural response? Do you rush in to scoop him into your arms and kiss the booboos? Or do you hang back for a moment to give him the space he needs to try to handle it on his own?

Thinking and Feeling

Typically, the Feeling mom will rush in to comfort her child. Feeling moms are natural sympathizers. They bring a warm, nurturing energy to motherhood and want to wipe away their child's hurts and protect them from pain. Thinking moms have a different kind of nurturing style. They are more apt to stand back, give children their space, and let them try to do for themselves. They wouldn't want someone smothering and gushing over themselves, so they are careful to respect their child's independence.

To a Feeling mother, or even a Feeling child, the Thinking mother's approach may seem like "not caring." To a Thinking mother and a Thinking child, the Feeling mother may seem over-protective and intrusive.

My preference is Feeling and my son has a preference for Thinking. When he was little and hurt himself at the park, my instinct was to pick him up and snuggle him on my lap. He would wail and kick. *Wow,* I thought, *he must be really hurting!* Soon, however, I figured out his cries were tears of frustration, not pain. He wanted to be let down to play again. So next time he fell, I learned to back off and see whether he really wanted (or needed) my help.

Likewise, Thinking mothers have told me that knowing personality type has helped them remember to give the hugs, eye contact, and encouraging words that young children need to feel loved.

Different Mindsets

This points to a fundamental difference between Thinking and Feeling mothers. The Thinking mother is more apt to see clear boundaries between people. She naturally sees her children as separate from herself. One Thinking mother told me, "It's as if every person is surrounded by their own picket fence. Inside that fence are each person's individual space, responsibilities, and competencies. You don't tread into someone's yard without first asking. You respect the boundaries the fence represents." When the Thinking mom is doing her best mothering, she is respecting her child's boundaries. As another Thinking mother said, "We don't breathe on our children."

For the Feeling mother, boundaries between people are more blurred. In fact, she tries to penetrate whatever emotional distance exists between her and her children. She puts great importance on giving her children closeness, warmth, attachment, and availability. Ultimately, she wants to be so close with the people she loves that she can feel their pain or joy, and they, in turn, can feel hers.

Because of these differing mindsets, Thinking and Feeling mothers each bring different gifts to mothering. Thinking types are experts at giving their children the physical and psychological space they need to stand on their own two feet and become independent. Feeling types are experts at giving their children the physical and emotional closeness that they need to feel loved, special, and secure.

"Caring for young kids was such a warm and fuzzy time for me. I felt a sense of calling and deep connection. As they've gotten older, I've had to learn to step back and be less intensely, emotionally involved." —Debbie, ESFJ

Says Amy, ISTJ: "I like Ryan the older he gets. I like being able to build things together with him, work on projects, have a rational conversation, and plan stuff together. When he was about five years old I started enjoying being a mom much more than the earlier years."

In my work with mothers, I've learned most of them want their children to be both independent and loving. But when asked to choose which of the two is most important, I've found that Thinking mothers typically give the edge to independence and Feeling mothers tend to emphasize loving.

Many Feeling moms say that they felt like a "natural" mother early on in their mothering. They relish the years when their children want to be physically and emotionally close, and may find it difficult to let go as their children grow up. If their increasingly independent children ask them to back off and "get a life," they may take it personally and feel rejected. Thinking mothers, on the other hand, might feel like they are hitting their stride when their children get older, more rational, and more independent. Although some Thinking mothers enjoy the concreteness of caring for infants, most say they felt out of sync with the irrationality and emotionality of preschoolers.

Different Approaches to Conflict

Another important difference between Thinking and Feeling types is their approach to conflict and confrontation. Here's another playground story: While my son played Little League baseball, I became friendly with another (Thinking) mother on the team. We both had younger daughters and during one game we let the two girls go off together to play at a nearby playground. In a little while, the girls came back, breathless and excited. Some bigger boys weren't letting them use the slide!

I told my daughter to sit on my lap for a while and maybe the boys would leave. As a Feeling type, I tend to avoid confrontation, and resolving this conflict directly seemed more trouble than it was worth. My Introverted need to think things through before acting also probably figured in. However, my Thinking friend (also an E) immediately jumped up and walked over to talk to the boys: "This is a public park; these girls have a right to use the slide; shame on you for being mean to someone younger." I was impressed. The girls returned to the park and were allowed to play in peace, while we mothers kept an eye on them from the bleachers.

The Feeling mother thrives on harmony, and may find it difficult to say anything negative for fear of hurting feelings or causing conflict. Thinking types have the gift of being direct and can tolerate disharmony long enough to deal with the tough issues. They also rely on objective principles for handling conflict and achieving a fair and just resolution.

Cultural Pressures

Motherhood is charged with numerous "shoulds" when it comes to the Thinking-Feeling function. No other function is so loaded. When defining a "good" mother, Thinking and Feeling mothers often misunderstand and devalue one another.

The bottom line is, Thinking and Feeling mothers are equally "good." Their different strengths are equally valuable in mothering.

Cultural influences are part of the reason this function is so loaded. Our culture overvalues Thinking and has traditionally associated Thinking with men and Feeling with women.

Many of today's mothers grew up when it was expected that girls would prefer Feeling—be relationship-oriented, personal, and warm. Girls with a preference for Thinking—logic, analysis, and objectivity—often felt out of the mainstream. With gender-based cultural pressures, many learned how and when to function in traditionally feminine and Feeling ways. As a result, many Thinking women embody Feeling characteristics that Thinking men are not necessarily encouraged to develop. There is a very real difference between a Thinking woman and a Thinking man. Likewise, many Feeling women have developed their Thinking side to succeed in business, science, law, and other traditionally male-dominated professions.

The Best of Both Worlds

Women today deal with different societal expectations than women of previous generations. We are now expected to be equally comfortable and competent in both the Thinking and Feeling modes, which can lead to confusion.

As I've said before, one of the tasks of motherhood is to allow it to stretch you so that you grow. It is an opportunity to sort out your natural way and use enhanced self-knowledge to your best advantage. This life-changing experience may also help you tune out societal pressures to be someone you're not.

Just as important, motherhood may stretch you to cultivate some of the strengths of your opposite type to meet the changing needs of your growing children. Typically, a Thinking mother may make a conscious effort to meet a young child's needs for closeness and affection. One Thinking mother says, "If my kids act unusually upset when I am meting out some correction, I ask myself what am I missing here? I'll make a point of listening, giving a hug, and telling them that I still love them."

A Feeling mother may decide to take on a more objective viewpoint to meet a maturing child's need for independence. "If I'm taking on too much of my children's emotional pain," says one Feeling mother, "I know it's time to draw on the objectivity and problem solving of Thinking types."

Knowing your preference on the Thinking-Feeling dichotomy lets you realize where you stand in the context of cultural pressures. Knowing what comes natural to you can inform your decisions and help you eliminate some of the guilt, stress, and conflict inherent in mothering on a day-to-day basis. It will let you honor your strengths (knowing they're but one piece of the truth) and help you relax, observe, appreciate, and learn a piece of the truth from your neighbor with the opposite preference.

Let's explore further what Thinking and Feeling look like in the context of mothering so that you can confirm your preference. By now you know the routine. Verify your preference by circling the number that describes how you relate to that point:

0—This does not describe me at all.
1—This describes me somewhat.
2—This describes me well.

Strengths of the Thinking Mother

If your preference is Thinking, you may find yourself gravitating toward . . .

- *Giving your children the physical and psychological space they need to stand on their own two feet and become independent.* The Thinking mom values independence, in herself and others, and one way she expresses her love is by fostering this in her children. She encourages her children to do for themselves, promoting self-reliance and self-sufficiency. One Thinking mother says, "At the first sign of readiness, I moved my children out of their cribs and put away their strollers."

    0   1   2

- *Helping your children analyze situations and problem solve.* For example, if two siblings are involved in a squabble over sharing a toy, the Thinking mother may use the situation as an opportunity to demonstrate objective analysis and logical problem solving. She will point out opposing viewpoints, suggest some options for resolution (take turns, replace it with an equally attractive toy, play with it together), and perhaps help develop a rule for handling similar situations fairly in the future.

    Note that, although she might be temped to jump into a difficult situation to dispense the justice herself, the Thinking mother is more likely to provide the guidelines and principles and let her children ultimately resolve the matter at hand.

    0   1   2

- *Paying attention to how your children think things through, encouraging them to think for themselves . . . to think independently.* Whereas the Feeling mom is particularly tuned in to her children's feelings, the Thinking mom is tuned in to her children's developing rationality. She may initiate and fuel their thinking by sharing her own thoughts, playing devil's advocate, and pointing up inconsistencies. The Thinking mother may relish frank and meaty discussions with her older children. Even if they express different points of view, she will respect a child for a well-reasoned argument and standing up for what he thinks.

    0   1   2

- *Fostering ongoing intellectual development—curiosity, love of learning, mental challenges—by talking, teaching, discussing issues on a mature level, answering your children's "whys."* Thinking moms make their children's education a high priority, and enjoy getting involved, whether they run for the school board, home school, or just do it informally. They seek out experiences that will foster intellectual development, such as taking children on educational field trips or looking up words together in the dictionary. One son told his Thinking mother, with obvious love and pride, "Do you think other people have deep conversations like we do?" The Thinking mother may enjoy teaching her child how to play bridge, chess, or board games, and believe a healthy dose of competition sharpens a child's acumen.

    0   1   2

- *Encouraging competence and a can-do attitude, helping them excel in school, do their best, and work up to standards.* Sports, music, extracurricular activities—Thinking moms know these things teach children how to succeed in life, and they strongly encourage their children to participate in them. Although every mother takes pride in her child's accomplishments, achievements, and successes, the Thinking mother probably puts greater stock in them. One Thinking mother says, "When I am having a difficult time with my teenage daughter, worrying about where her life is headed, I soothe myself by remembering that she was voted captain of tennis team, got an A on her statistics exam, and earned a college scholarship." The Thinking mother is apt to view mistakes objectively, and teach her children how to use them as learning experiences.

    0   1   2

- *Encouraging children to seek justice and fairness in all situations.* When her children are young, the Thinking mother strives to provide an even playing field for her children, at home and at school. "If my children say 'that's not fair,' I stop to consider their point. I either explain to them why it is fair or do what I can to make it fair," says one Thinking mother. As her children get older, the Thinking mother expands the concept of fairness to the larger world. "Life isn't always fair," says a Thinking mom, "but I think we should do what we can to make it fairer for everyone. Even if it means self-sacrifice."

    0   1   2

- *Relying on logical consequences and cause-and-effect as a method of teaching and modifying behavior.* The Thinking mom's logical, fair, consistent approach to discipline fosters security and strong boundaries in her children. She tends to deal with issues in a straightforward manner as they arise, maintaining perspective and rationality. She isn't wishy-washy about consequences; if you break the rules, here's what happens—always. Two favorite Thinking momisms are, "You broke the rule, now pay the price," and "If you can't do the time, don't do the crime." She may rely on a system of rewards and punishments, or use contracts with children, wherein everyone agrees together upon the standards, rewards, and consequences, and signs off. One Thinking mother I know had her five children sign a behavior contract as a prerequisite to their long-awaited family vacation to Disney World.

  0   1   2

- *Providing your children with a role model for a competent, independent woman.* Because she naturally counters the cultural stereotype for what a woman should be, the Thinking mom offers another model of womanhood for both daughters and sons. Her very example shows that women need not be confined to rigid roles in terms of what women can do or be. "My children have watched me follow my own career and make my own contribution," says a Thinking mother. "I've taken a stand for the equality of women and demonstrated through the way I've gone through life how to be your own person."

  0   1   2

Add up your points here: _____

Struggles of the Thinking Mother

If your preference is for Thinking, you may struggle with . . .

- *Tuning in to and being patient with feelings.* Although the Thinking mother is caring and concerned, she may struggle with tuning in to feelings and being patient or sympathetic with emotions. Dealing with feelings that seem irrational (as most feelings are), unrealistic, and are "going nowhere" can be particularly draining. She may throw up her hands in desperation, saying, "But there's no *reason* to feel that way!" A Thinking mom may resist plunging into her child's feelings because they seem like a bottomless well. One Thinking mother said, "I can do feelings. But if the emotions continue for too long, I become uncomfortable 'wallowing' in them."

0   1   2

- *Maintaining energy for lengthy, emotionally charged discussions pertaining to personal issues or relationships within the family.* Although the Thinking mother may push herself to hear out a loved one's concerns, such as, "You're bossy" or, "You're overly strict," there's a point where she may think the conversation is going nowhere and decide to call a halt and get some distance. "Sometimes there's just nothing left to talk about. If we keep going, I'm either going to get defensive or start feeling bad about myself," one Thinking mother says. "I need to take a break to think about it some more. I ask myself are they just being mean or is this a legitimate issue?" When my Thinking friend was going through a difficult divorce, I marveled at how she never missed a day of work. She explained, "What I do on the job is logical and rational. It gives me a break from having to deal with everyone's emotions."

> "Before I knew type, when my daughter would come home from school saying her teacher hated her and so did her friends, I would try to logically argue her out of her feelings. Now, I just say, 'It sounds like you've had a really discouraging day. Do you want some milk and cookies?' It's amazing how fast she cheers up."—*Fran, INTJ*

0   1   2

- *Accepting a child as he or she is, not being critical or expecting greater success.* Finding the flaws in a situation comes naturally to Thinking types. In mothering, the Thinking mom may have to curb this natural tendency and focus on acceptance and the positive instead. "When my child asks me to read his report, I immediately see ten ways to make it better. I've learned to bite my tongue and start with what I really loved about the paper before trying to improve it."
—*Meagan*

0   1   2

- *Feeling comfortable and confident with a clingy, needy, or overly sensitive child.* Clingy, dependent children are a challenge for many type mothers, but the Thinking mom, who so values independence, may have a particularly uncomfortable reaction and become impatient quicker. She may interpret the child's clinginess as a sign she or he will never be independent. Her child's "excessive" neediness may threaten her own sense of autonomy. She may worry about how an emotional child will be able to survive in the world.

  0   1   2

- *Picking up on cues in delicate situations, and not being "heavy handed" in your response.* Sometimes a Thinking mother will speak her mind or say what she thinks needs to be said, and have no idea that it might upset someone. When family members ask what she thinks, she may be direct and blunt when a more indirect or tactful response would have been more effective or appropriate.

  0   1   2

- *Hanging in there with situations where there's no clear-cut answer or solution.* Not everything has a logical solution, especially when we're talking about emotions and relationships. The Thinking mom will want to fix the situation and move on, even when it's not necessarily wise to do so yet.

  0   1   2

- *Not sounding harsh.* The Thinking mom's logical approach enables her to cut through many ambiguous situations, but it may give her words an unintended edge, unless she consciously tries to soften the impact. She can sometimes sound harsh, or even angry, especially to Feeling types.

  0   1   2

Add up your points for Thinking from this section and from page 65 here: _____

Strengths of the Feeling Mother

If your preference is for Feeling, you may gravitate toward . . .

- *Giving children physical and emotional closeness that they need to feel loved, special, and secure.* Focused on relationships and harmony, the Feeling mother puts great importance on giving her children closeness, warmth, attachment, and availability. When her babies are infants, she may use a sling to keep them close to her at all times. As they get older, she'll find ways to continue the closeness through, for instance, an "I love you" note in the lunchbox to remind her child she's thinking of him or her.

  0   1   2

- *Paying close attention to how children feel.* The Feeling mother is naturally tuned in to children's feelings and tends to be sensitive, sympathetic, and comforting. She seems to have her antennae constantly up and turned on, picking up even subtle cues about what children are feeling. She tends to get actively involved with her children's hurt feelings, trying to smooth out the pain with a comforting word or hug. With her close and personal approach, the Feeling mom may find her children's feelings automatically invoke a personal response that can weigh heavily in her actions. For example, a Feeling mother may find herself not liking a child who has caused her child to cry. Or she may ease up on a rule to avoid hard feelings.

  0   1   2

- *Tuning in and being responsive to your children's needs.* The Feeling mother expresses love by giving to her children and doing things for them and with them. She goes to great lengths to make her children happy, aiming to please, even if it means self-sacrifice.

  0   1   2

- *Fostering family harmony by encouraging and expecting cooperation, accommodation, and give-and-take.* The Feeling mom models these things and expects her children to do likewise. She teaches her children good relational skills, promoting consideration of others, sympathy, and consensus, so they can get along well with others.

0   1   2

- *Seeing mothering as the "grandest intimacy."* For many Feeling mothers, mothering is an opportunity to experience a special connectedness that is not possible in any other relationship. She warmly expresses her love and because she aims to raise a loving child, she takes special delight when her child reciprocates with expressions of appreciation and acceptance. For her, mother/child togetherness is a necessary foundation for life.

0   1   2

- *Looking for what's good in a child.* The Feeling mother tends to see and express the positive, so she's likely to be accepting and affirming of her children. Because she enjoys compliments and praise, she is apt to give them freely. One Feeling mother I know refers to herself as her children's biggest cheerleader.

0   1   2

- *Sharing and confiding.* The Feeling mom seeks to initiate "heart to heart" talks— frequently. "How did that make you feel?" may be the Feeling mother's signature question. She relishes discussing feelings and often asks probing questions or reveals personal information to establish intimacy. She often has a very well developed feeling language to verbally communicate emotional nuances. Instead of just feeling happy, she may ask her child if he feels thrilled, fulfilled, or flattered.

0   1   2

- *Protecting your children from life's "hard knocks."* Sensitive to the fact that children are like tender plants, the Feeling mom does all she can to protect them. She tends to anticipate problems and head them off before they materialize or rescue children from a bad situation. If a child is feeling bad, it's natural for her to jump in with help, encouragement, and understanding. Letting children learn from the consequences of their actions may seem mean or harsh to her. A Feeling mom explains, "I heard a parenting expert say that if your child forgets his lunch, don't bring it to them if they call. They're more likely to remember it next time.

> ## Heather and the Alarm Clocks
>
> Diane's friend, Heather, is a single mom. She told Diane one day how stressed she felt every morning because her kids, ages thirteen and eleven, were not getting up on time. She had to be at work at a certain time, and the kids needed to dress and eat and be on their way to school. In keeping with her personal style (ESTJ), Heather was able to step back and analyze exactly what the problems were and what steps she could take to alleviate them. She bought each child an alarm clock and showed them how to set it. She expected them to set their clothes out and set the table for breakfast the night before. And if they dawdled when getting dressed, they might just miss their breakfast. "They'll be hungry, but then they'll learn," she told Diane matter-of-factly.
>
> Diane (INFP) marveled at how easily Heather could use "reality discipline," letting children experience the consequences of their own choices, unpleasant though they may be at times. Diane, a Feeling mother, does not like to see her children suffer—even if it's a necessary step in developing age-appropriate independence and responsibility. "When I find myself wanting to curtail discipline because I don't want to see my child hurt, I consciously switch into Thinking mode and remind myself that this is good for the child," she says. When she struggles with an issue she can't see clearly, Diane often calls one of her Thinking mom friends to gain perspective.

That may be true, but if I forgot my lunch, I'd certainly expect a family member to help me out if they could. If they didn't, it would feel like they didn't care."

0   1   2

Add up your points here: _____

Struggles of the Feeling Mother

Continue to verify your preference by looking at the struggles of a Feeling mother:

- *Keeping your own emotions separate from children's issues.* The flipside of the Feeling mother's natural strength—being tuned in to feelings—is the difficulty she has getting some distance and objectivity at times when it's appropriate. She struggles in those situations where it would be best to keep her emotions separate from her children's personal issues. She may become devastated by a child's hurts or manipulated by her children's anger—or lovingness. And when things go wrong, her first response may be to take things personally. She is prone to feeling guilty and overly responsible.

For instance, say her son brings home a report card with a C- in math. The Feeling mother's first response might be to feel guilty. She remembers one time when her son asked for help with his math homework and she, late for a meeting, didn't stop to help. Her first thought might be, *It's all my fault*. In the grip of her own emotions, she may not be able to see the situation objectively.

0   1   2

- *Confrontation—saying "no," being direct and firm, especially when it may cause disharmony and friction.* Feeling moms may understand the need for setting appropriate limits and correcting behavior, but feel uneasy doing it. Most of them find it hard to be calm, cool, and confident as disciplinarians. Some Feeling types may shy away from being direct and confronting because of the disharmony and friction it may cause. Others may go "overboard"—being overly zealous and even "mean"—because they feel so uneasy and out of their comfort zone.

> "Before I learned about type, I didn't understand why their little hurts were my big hurts. Knowing my type has helped put it all into perspective. If I feel my heart breaking because my child didn't get invited to a friend's birthday party, I step back and say, hey, this is what my personality type does, it doesn't mean it's the end of the world, let's put it into perspective."—*Pam, ISFJ*

0   1   2

- *Getting your own needs identified and met.* The Feeling mom may be prone to giving too much and then feeling taken for granted when she doesn't always receive the appreciation she deserves. She may give in before she gets what she needs when family members' needs conflict with hers, in order to maintain harmony.

0   1   2

- *Dealing with multiple wants and constant demands.* Because she strives to meet others' needs, a Feeling mom can feel overwhelmed when everyone in the family needs something from her at the same time.

0   1   2

- *Separating from your children too frequently or when you feel your children are too young.* This conflict is especially felt keenly by the Feeling mom who is employed outside the home. But even if she's not, putting the child in the nursery during a church service or a "mom's night out" can feel very unsettling. "I went to the opera with my father the other night. I couldn't enjoy the show because I felt so guilty about leaving my children for five hours with a baby-sitter. I worried that they might be missing me, needing me."—*Pat*

    0   1   2

- *Holding your children too close.* A Feeling mother is much more likely than a Thinking mother to overprotect or "smother" her children. She can find it very difficult to let go and back off as the children get older. She may be devastated at the empty nest stage.

    0   1   2

- *Feeling guilty whenever your attention has not been 100 percent on your children's needs.* Because she believes a good mother connects with her children and meets their needs, any time she's *not* doing these things, she may feel guilty.

    0   1   2

Add up your points from this section here: _____
Add up your total points for Feeling here (from page 70 and above): _____
Write the total points for Thinking (from page 67): _____

By now, you should have verified your preference for Thinking or Feeling. Again, it's likely you came out with a higher score on one or the other, but if it's evenly split, think back to how you were as a child. Did you tend to care more about whether other kids played by the rules (T), or about how they felt (F)? Did you have trouble saying no to people for fear of hurting their feelings (F), or did people accuse you of being "too honest" (as in frank—a T tendency)?

Now that you know your preference, here are some tips for making the most of your strengths and lessening the struggles.

Tips for the Thinking Mother

1. If your preference is Thinking, "taking care of me" means getting validation of your competence. Competence resonates with Thinking types the way harmony resonates with Feeling types. Therefore, consider putting your skills and talents to use on behalf of a volunteer organization or in an employment setting. Being recognized for your competency will give you the boost you need to keep doing your best in the more subjective and personal realm of family relationships and home.

2. Remember to validate the competence of your children. Neither you nor they can take it for granted. Since one of your strengths is honest, truthful feedback, you may be perceived as "critical." When your ten-year-old asks you to review her book report, be sure to balance criticisms and suggestions for improvement with a healthy dose of appreciation and praise for what she has accomplished on her own.

3. Keep in mind the power of smiley faces, hearts, and flowers when writing notes to Feeling children.

4. Have confidence that even the most "dependent" children become independent. Don't worry about your "clinging" three-year-old or kindergartner who has trouble separating. Feel free to relax and enjoy how much they want you. Children need to have their needs for attachment met and feel secure in your love before they can begin to disengage and become truly independent.

5. When you're problem-solving, remember that feelings have as much validity as do facts and logic. Think of feelings as another criterion to be factored into the equation.

6. Don't rush the healing process. Hurt feelings need time to hurt for a while. So do painful issues—like career changes or letting your twenty-four-year-old move back home. Just like you can't instantly heal a scraped knee, you can't fix everything. In fact, solving a problem too quickly can cut off both the natural healing process and the best solution.

7. Know that you are loved for who you are—not for your accomplishments or competence. You don't have to prove yourself to be loved by your children. That is your birthright as a mother.

Tips for the Feeling Mother

1. For Feeling mothers, "taking care of me" means time off from constantly being needed. One mother with six children takes off every Monday night to survive. She goes up to her room at 5 p.m. and doesn't show her face until the next morning. Good self-care means sometimes putting your own needs first.

2. Find out what your own needs really are. Mothers, especially Feeling mothers, often forget what they need because they're so focused on others' needs. Perhaps you like pepperoni on your pizza, or maybe you long for a day to curl up with a stack of magazines. Remembering what used to nourish you before you had so many responsibilities is a good place to start.

3. Remind yourself that focusing on your needs can be *good* for your children. When not totally tuned in to their children, many Feeling mothers say they believe their children will suffer. Or they question whether they're being selfish. Actually, taking the focus off your children every so often and putting it on you teaches your children respect for you. It gives a clear message of *your* self-worth. It also encourages children's self-sufficiency.

4. If you find yourself muddled in an emotionally laden situation and you can't see your way out, use your frustration as a signal to get some help. Imagine yourself an outsider looking in or get a Thinking friend to consult with you.

5. Instead of expecting family harmony all the time, set the goal at 80 percent . . . for the sake of intimacy. Sibling bickering may be a sign of a truly loving relationship. No two people (much less three or four or more) can be perfectly in sync all the time. Showing love means honoring how you feel and sometimes saying what you think, even if it results in conflict.

Thinking–Feeling Communication

Feeling mothers often express concern that their Thinking children and/or Thinking spouses seem "insensitive" and "uncaring." And Thinking mothers are often uncomfortable initiating or participating in conversation about feelings. Some Feeling and Thinking mothers have had success "quantifying" feelings to ease their situations. One Thinking mother told her Thinking son, "I'm only 25 percent mad that you forgot to make your bed." A Feeling mother asked her Thinking daughter, "On a scale of one to ten, how upset are you about not making the soccer team?" A Thinking mother asked her Feeling preschooler, "How many hugs would it take to make you feel better?"

6. Rather than asking, "How do you feel about that?" ask the Thinking types, "What do you think about that?"

7. Don't expect your Thinking child to be as comfortable with feelings as you are. You can't look for the same signals of caring as you would with a Feeling child. Rather than offering hugs and kisses or sharing feelings, your Thinking child may show her love through responsibility, respect, persistent questioning, and honest feedback.

Making Better Decisions

When you have to make a tough call about a situation, you'll do better if you consciously incorporate into your decision-making all four perspectives: Sensing, Intuition, Thinking, and Feeling. Depending on your type, you may enter this four-step process at your preferred point, but be sure to cover all four bases.

For example, my twelve-year-old son and his friends wanted to play on a hill of dirt at a construction site by the harbor. I was uncomfortable with the idea. What if they rolled down the hill, into the water, and drowned? Every year several teenagers die in the lake. Instead of saying no right away, however, I used my knowledge of type to make a better decision.

Step #1: Focus on the facts and the actual situation (Sensing). I visited the site to see firsthand how big the hill was, how close it was to the water, and if there were sharp objects or glass lying around. I discovered it wasn't as close to the water as I first thought, but still it was in an isolated area away from the lifeguards.

Step #2: Generate options and possibilities (Intuition). I could: say no; supervise them; call a Thinking mother for her perspective; tell them they can't play there alone or after dark; make sure one of them has a cell phone; limit the time they can play there; find out whether the nearby boating office is open in case of an emergency.

Step #3: Weigh the consequences of each alternative (Thinking). In our area, twelve-year-olds are allowed to go to a public beach by themselves. The other parents allow it. Even if I said no, chances are my son would go to the hill with his friends without my knowing. If I say no, he may consider me unreasonable. I may be encouraging him to disobey me. I know as a Feeling parent I tend to be overprotective. If I say yes, I am practicing letting go and honoring my son's need for independence. But he might get hurt.

Step #4: Consider the impact on people (Feeling).   I want to be responsible as a parent and comfortable with my decision. I want my son to know I love, respect, and support him.

Decision.   I involved my son in my decision-making process, discussing my concerns, and together we set some limits that increased my comfort level and allowed him to play on the hill.

The final dichotomy of personality type is the one that will probably stretch you the most as a mother. It all has to do with lifestyle . . . how you like your outer world structured. No matter what your preference is in this area, you'll find there's nothing like children to change your outer world and turn it upside down!

chapter 5

· · · · · · · · · · ·

Lifestyles of the Planned and Flexible

Judging or Perceiving

CAN YOU GUESS WHICH IS THE JUDGING MOTHER AND WHICH IS THE PERCEIVING mother in these quotations?

"Before children, I prided myself on how well organized I was. I finished what was on my things-to-do list no matter what. I kept my home well ordered. Most aspects of my life were under control.

"After having children, I'm finding that my carefully thought-out plans frequently go up in smoke, and I have very little control over my day. In order to survive, I've *had* to become more flexible."—*Joyce*

"Before children, I relished living life on the spur of the moment. My husband and I often packed up for last-minute trips. We were casual about certain commitments. If we felt like doing it, we would; if not, we wouldn't. We preferred spontaneity rather than planning.

"After children, however, it's been a completely different ballgame. The school bus leaves *on time* and I and my children have to be ready. If my husband and I want to go out, we have to plan ahead and get a babysitter. Making it to a meeting requires the same kind of foresight and planning. I've *had* to become more structured, or I would lose my mind."—*Peggy*

Judging-Perceiving seems to be the dichotomy that is most changed by becoming a mother. Apparently, the more people you feel responsible for in your family, the more structured *and* more flexible you need to be. No matter what your natural preference, the day-to-day demands of motherhood force you to develop your opposite preference.

Judging-Perceiving is about lifestyle—how you like your outer world structured. It's all about "way." Which way are we going to approach the day, the project, even the living of a life? The J way (Joyce): planned and orderly, with schedules, deadlines, getting things done, and doing things the "right" way? Or the P way (Peggy): going with the flow, enjoying the process, trying things out, following whims, and letting life happen without forcing or controlling?

Personality versus Choice

Picture yourself in the kitchen cooking dinner. Your son bursts through the door shouting, "Mom, there's a frog outside. Come look!"

Which is your *first impulse?*

- You say, "I'll come as soon as I finish preparing dinner."

- You turn off the stove and go out and take a look.

The first response is a Judging response. The J mom's gift is coming up with a plan and then sticking to it. Until she comes to closure on making dinner, she isn't likely to be open to other opportunities that come up.

The Perceiving mother's first response would likely be the second choice. The Perceiving mom tends to be spontaneous. It's easy for her to give up the plan of making dinner by a certain time to respond to the child's needs of the moment. She's probably even interested herself in seeing the frog.

However, even though the Perceiving mom's first impulse is to go look at the frog, she may feel guilty. *If I go look, then I won't have dinner done on time. Good mothers have dinner on time. So I'd better stick to the preparation, even though it's more boring.*

The Judging mother's first impulse is to finish dinner first. But then she, too, might feel guilty, thinking, *They're only young once. He's excited about the frog. Good mothers should take an interest in their children's interests. So I guess I'll go take a look.*

Although the Perceiving mom may have stuck with continuing her dinner preparations, and the Judging mom may have stopped herself to take a look, each was acting against her natural preference because of her idea of what a "good mother" is and does.

Both the Judging and Perceiving mothers bring wonderful gifts to the mothering experience. Yet many mothers say that knowing their preference on this dichotomy has also helped them recognize and use the strengths of their opposite. Sometimes you'll make a choice that better fits your values or idea of what a good mother is and does. Sometimes your choice will be a matter of necessity.

Ultimately, you want to be Judging enough to keep your children safe and Perceiving enough to be open to who your children are. And, I believe, knowing when to take control and when to let go is the cutting edge of maturity and wisdom.

But before you can develop a healthy balance, you must, of course, know your preference. With this dichotomy of preferences, it may not be so easy or clear-cut for the reasons I just mentioned. So, as you think about verifying your type, please note what your *first impulse* would be, or what you naturally gravitate toward, rather than what you may actually end up doing now that you're a mom.

As we've been doing, circle the number that best describes how you relate to each characteristic:

0—This does not describe me at all.
1—This describes me somewhat.
2—This describes me well.

It's about Time

Time is an issue for both Judging and Perceiving mothers, but they approach it differently. Responding to an internal clock as well as external pressures, Judging mothers are at home with notions of "promptness," "deadlines," and "schedules." They are often natural time managers. They know how to make the most of time.

Perceiving mothers are less driven by an internal schedule and the need to quantify what can be done in a certain time frame. They view time less literally and are more comfortable just living in the process. They know how to make the most of the moment.

A Judging mother and a Perceiving mother may both like to have dinner on the table "on time." However, the Perceiving mom might call "on time" any time between 5 and 8 p.m. If dinner took place during this three-hour period, she considers it "on time." However, for a Judging mother a meal that is even 15 minutes past the set mealtime may feel late.

Strengths of the Judging Mother

If your preference is for Judging, you may gravitate toward the following:

- *Planning and organizing day-to-day living.* The Judging mother prefers order, structure, and schedules. She's apt to start the day with a things-to-do list and a plan. If she can cross things off her list and stick to the plan, she feels like it's been a good day.

  She organizes the details of day-to-day living so her children don't miss out—school carpools, snack for snack day, permissions slips, and lunch money.

  One Judging mother says, "I love writing things in my calendar." And Jill, an ENTJ, says, "I love it when I have everything planned for the day and I know what I'm going to do when."

  0   1   2

- *Keeping your children on an even keel with set mealtimes, bedtimes, and family routines.* The language of the Judging mother will likely include a lot of "time" words—dinnertime, bath time, story time, bedtime. For her, there is a right time for this and a wrong time for that. Her day naturally breaks down into time slots to organize and schedule. This tends to make the children feel secure because they know what to expect when.

  0   1   2

- *Approaching motherhood as a serious responsibility.* The Judging mother is no slacker when it comes to mothering, or any other commitment she cares about. She tries her hardest, aiming to do the "right" thing. She is conscientious and may seem intense at times.

  0   1   2

Ugh! "Judging"

Unfortunately, the word "judging" has negative connotations. Many people resist claiming their Judging preference because they don't want to label themselves as judgmental. Be assured—Judging in this context means preferring a structured, orderly, planned lifestyle. It does not mean being judgmental. Perceiving types can be just as judgmental as Judging types. Yet, if you prefer, it is perfectly acceptable to use the J abbreviation instead.

- *Guiding and shaping your children and who they become.* The Judging mother is an intentional and purposeful mother. She often has clear goals about what she wants to accomplish in parenting and works toward those goals on a day-to-day basis. She wants to make sure her children are well raised and become the best they can be.

  0   1   2

- *Setting limits and being directive.* The Judging mother is generally willing to call the shots when she thinks being directive and setting limits are in the best interests of her child. She may have a "no cookies after 4 p.m." rule, for instance, because she thinks that's what will ensure her child gets a good dinner. The Judging mother, comfortable and secure with limits when she was a child, knows that setting limits is one way children know they're cared about.

  However, other functions play into the dynamics as well. A Feeling-Judging mother may not like enforcing the limits if it means anger and tears. And an Intuitive-Judging mother may set the limits and then not be as consistent in following through as she thinks she "should."

  0   1   2

- *Making a smooth-running, orderly household a high priority.* The Judging mom knows how—or learns how—to make sure her household runs smoothly. She often has high standards for neatness and cleanliness and knows how to factor in housework as part of the weekly schedule. She may not always be able to meet her standards, but she consistently works to stay on top of household disorder.

  0   1   2

- *Showing children how to get a lot done.* The Judging mom both teaches and shows by example how to organize, plan, focus, discipline oneself, and follow through. "I consider myself a to-do junkie. I love working hard and am addicted to getting things done."—*Joyce*

  0   1   2

> "I'm good at strategizing and planning. Sometimes I see people who are much more laid back than me, and I envy them. But I think if I try to be too much like them I will give up my own gifts." —*Sue, ENTJ*
>
> "As a P, I don't plan unless I absolutely have to."—*Joan, ESFP*

- *Encouraging your children to respect and use their time wisely.* Since she doesn't want to waste time, the Judging mom feels it's important to teach her children time management—making lists, deadlines, punctuality, respect for others' schedules.

  0   1   2

Add up your points here: _____

Struggles of the Judging Mom

If your preference is Judging, you may struggle with the following:

- *Living with the never-completed aspects of housekeeping and childcare.* The Judging mother is naturally focused on getting things done, finishing projects, getting matters settled, and coming to closure. But many parts of keeping house and raising children are never really done once and for all. No sooner does she mop the kitchen floor, feeling a sense of accomplishment and completion, than her young son walks in tracking mud over the clean floor in his enthusiasm to show her the frog he just caught. In a flash, her momentary pleasure in "getting things done" is gone, replaced by frustration. One Judging mother confessed that after she'd emptied all the wastebaskets in the house, she found herself getting angry when someone had the nerve to toss a tissue in. Another Judging mother says, "The hardest part of mothering is living with constant 'undoneness.'"

  0   1   2

- *Adapting to the unexpected and coping with last-minute changes that "blow the plan."* A Judging mom has trouble switching gears and may struggle to respond to spontaneous events, even if they are "opportunities." Helen, INFJ, describes an experience she had: "I was making dinner one night and some friends of ours came by, tooted the horn, and very spontaneously asked us to go out to dinner with them. My children were jumping up and down saying, 'Let's go, let's go.' But I couldn't. I had dinner planned. My table was set, I was stirring a pot. I told them, 'I can't go; I have dinner on the table.' One said, 'Oh come on, let's just go, it will be so much fun. Just put a lid on dinner and put it into the refrigerator for tomorrow.'

But I couldn't switch gears that fast. So what we ended up doing was eating our dinner at home and then joining them at the restaurant for dessert."

0   1   2

- *Letting go of "shoulds" and needing to have things done the "right" way.* The "shoulds" can come from her own high internal standards or from accepting what others impose upon her. Judging types spend a lot of time trying to figure out the "right" way to do something. So, if a child or spouse does something a different way, she's apt to think of it as the "wrong" way. She tends to be inflexible to different approaches. For example, the Judging mother might think the "right" way to do homework is sitting quietly at a desk with good lighting. Therefore, she may find it difficult to tolerate her son doing his homework lying on the bed with the television or radio on.

0   1   2

- *Giving up control so your children can take increasing control of their own lives.* It's not easy for a Judging mom to back off and let kids do it "their way." She may find it especially hard to let a Perceiving child have flexibility. Partly because the J way is so affirmed in our culture, and partly because of the Judging mentality itself most Js don't understand or value the strengths of a P's mindset and motivation. It feels foreign and undependable to the Judging mom as a way to get through life, so it's difficult to honor or trust the P way for her children.

0   1   2

- *Relaxing and having fun when things still need to get done.* The Judging mom's maxim is "work before play." But as I already noted, a mother's work is never done. There is always

> ### Shoulds
>
> "As a Judging mother, I start the day focused on what I should do rather than just doing what I want or what comes up."—*Irene, ESFJ*
>
> "I rarely think about shoulds. Nothing really has to be done."—*Linda, ESFP*
>
> "I enjoy having kids over to play and don't mind the disorder. But my husband is a Judging type, so he expects the house to be neat and tidy. In his mind, that's what being a good mother is all about. I spend my whole day criticizing myself and telling myself, I should, I should, I should."
>
> —*A mother in a seminar that wasn't sure on her J-P preference*

some unfinished task waiting, and the J mom is apt to feel frustrated about not accomplishing as much as she wants and expects to. She might even find herself thinking, *If it weren't for the kids, I could be so much more productive*.

0   1   2

- *Hearing children out before making judgments*. Because of the J mom's desire for closure, she may jump to conclusions and not take enough time to understand a child or a matter thoroughly. This may be especially difficult if feelings need to be worked through, and she's a Thinking-Judging type.

0   1   2

- *Functioning in the midst of children's clutter, disorder, commotion, and messes*. Judging moms need order to function. If she lives with Perceiving types, the problem is compounded, because Ps typically are not bothered by messes and therefore don't have much motivation to keep things in order.

0   1   2

Add up your score here: _____
Add up your total points for Judging (from page 82 and above) and write it here: _____

Strengths of the Perceiving Mother

If your preference is for Perceiving, you may gravitate toward . . .

- *Being tolerant and accepting*. The Perceiving mother tends to let her children be themselves without pushing or shaping. For example, a Judging mother may grapple with what is the "right" age to take away a child's pacifier. The Perceiving mother is more likely to be tolerant and accepting of her child's own developmental timetable. Her attitude: "Who's it hurting? She'll give it up when she's ready. She won't take it to college with her." Whereas the Judging mother tends to make her child fit her plan of what "should be," the Perceiving mother tends to fit her plan to the child. Adult children of Perceiving mothers often feel grateful for their mothers' gifts of acceptance.

0   1   2

- *Being spontaneous.* The Perceiving mom is often considered a lot of fun by her children (and their friends) because she can be in the moment. She often likes to just "hang out" with her children, enjoying simply being with them.

  0   1   2

- *Being responsive to a child's interruptions.* The Perceiving mom, remember, was the one whose first instinct was to stop dinner preparations to go look at the frog. She is more flexible when her own plans are interrupted and can turn her attention to the needs of the moment.

  0   1   2

- *Staying open-minded while listening to your children.* Because she doesn't have a strong need for closure, the Perceiving mom is more willing to hear out her children on a matter.

  0   1   2

- *Exposing your children to a variety of experiences and people.* Because the Perceiving mother is more process- and experience-oriented, she emphasizes exploration, discovery, and curiosity. She's adept at getting her children to experience everything they can (especially if she's also Extraverted).

  0   1   2

- *Letting your children make many of their own choices.* The Perceiving mom is willing to follow her children's lead, encouraging them to move at their own pace and follow their own interests.

  0   1   2

- *Being relaxed about children's clutter, disorder, chaos—as long as they're having fun.* The Perceiving mom relishes "letting kids be kids," and doesn't mind the mess. Life is to be enjoyed! Her house often looks "lived in." One Perceiving mother says, "A messy table top holds more interest to me than an orderly one." Another put this sign on her front door: "Child development in process. Pardon our mess."

  0   1   2

Judging at Work, Perceiving at Home

In the business world, there's no doubt "the J way" predominates. You're expected to be at work or meetings on time and to be as efficient as possible as you do your work. Often you're asked to set goals and make specific plans as to how you will reach those goals. Judging types thrive on such approaches.

Home life, however, often requires more flexibility. Children's needs continually upset plans. You thought you were going out to dinner, but your child (or the baby-sitter) gets sick and your plans are ruined. Your normally reclusive teenager decides to open up, finally—just as you were going to bed (planning to be well-rested for the big presentation you have to give at work the next day).

Some mothers say they are Js at work and Ps at home. This raises the question: Can you be one type at work and a different type at home? The answer is no. Although it is natural to stretch and flex to the needs and expectations of different environments, your innate type remains the same. A Perceiving mom may consciously be more Judging at work, but compared to a Judging type in the same environment, she will likely still seem like a Perceiving type. Likewise, a Judging mother may work to be more Perceiving at home, but compared to a Perceiving type at home, she's still Judging.

Similarly, some mothers say they are Thinking types at work and Feeling types at home. Once again, Thinking seems to be the preferred language and culture of many work environments. You may find that compared to the work world, mothering youngsters seems to require a more Feeling approach. Although you can consciously learn to use your nonpreferences in one sphere or another, and even develop proficiency with them, your innate type doesn't change.

There are great variations in how we express our type from situation to situation, or even from moment to moment. For example, a mom may be tolerant and flexible to the first interruption, but snap at the third. Yet, according to Jung's theory, our true type is constant through it all.

- *Being easy-going and relaxed when milk spills, plans get upset, or children misbehave.* Maxims such as "don't cry over spilled milk," "go with the flow," or "when life gives you lemons, make lemonade!" probably originated with Perceiving types. They don't have set ideas about the way things "should" be and, instead, adapt to whatever life hands them.

    0   1   2

Add up your points here: _____

Struggles of the Perceiving Mother

Continue to verify your preference by noting how much you struggle with . . .

- *Keeping your household organized and in order; doing chores on a regular basis.* While the Perceiving mother is exercising her very strengths—responding to her child's interruptions and needs of the moment, being flexible, adaptable, and tolerant—she is also diverting her energy and attention from laundry, cooking, and cleaning up after the children. At the end of the day, she may look around at her house full of clutter and dirty dishes and ask herself, "What have I done all day?" (Or her partner may ask her the same question when he gets home from work.) The fact that she doesn't have anything concrete to show for her efforts (five loads of folded laundry and a tidy house) can make her feel inadequate and worthless. Our societal standard for productivity is tangible outcomes, not pleasure in the process, so the Perceiving mother may feel out of step at times.

    0   1   2

- *Keeping yourself and your children on task and on time.* Getting out the door in the morning for school, getting the kids to bed on time, ensuring homework is done—these can be daily challenges for the Perceiving mother. It is difficult for her to stay focused on finishing a task, so it is doubly hard to keep her children on task. Especially if the task is routine or boring, a Perceiving mom is apt to abandon it if something more interesting comes up.

    0   1   2

- *Not leaving things until the last minute or letting things go too far.* Because she tends to resist the planned and scheduled and go with whatever comes up, procrastination can become an issue for the Perceiving mom. She may leave things to the end and then not have enough time. She may shy away from tackling the tough stuff and let a situation get out of hand.

    0   1   2

- *Not taking on way too much.* The Perceiving mother's experience of time can also lead her to accept too many commitments. She may say yes to something she thinks she can handle at that moment, but later find out she's taken on more than she can follow through on. This problem may be compounded for an Intuitive-Perceiving mother, whose idealistic attraction to possibilities may lead her to believe she can do more than she actually can.

0 1 2

- *Living with daily routines and everyday sameness.* Being tied down to family schedules and routines is more difficult for the Perceiving mother, who gravitates toward new experiences. Perceiving types often feel that routines and schedules box them in and cut off their enjoyment.

  0 1 2

- *Juggling everyone else's schedule, even though your children's exposure to experiences is a priority.* The Perceiving mom feels this built-in tension of conflicting values: she wants her children to experience many things, yet that often means living with a tighter than comfortable schedule. Getting one child to gymnastics and the other to soccer practice on time means arranging car pools ahead of time and, perhaps, getting dinner on the table at a certain time, and all that juggling wears on a Perceiving mother.

  0 1 2

"Normally it doesn't matter, but one Sunday, for some reason it was very important for me to clean up the house and get it in order. I revved up my J side and turned into a terror. I was snapping at my children, yelling at my husband; I even stormed up the stairs in tears. I don't know how the other mothers do it. It's beyond my capabilities. If someone unexpectedly comes to the door, I'd rather run and hide than let them see what my house looks like on a regular day. Luckily, my husband says he'd rather have a happy wife than a clean house."

–Susan, INFP

- *Setting limits for your children, being consistent, and following through.* The Perceiving mother tends not to make a lot of rules, but rather takes each situation as it arises. This can make it difficult to be consistent and follow through with discipline. She may also struggle to provide the structured environment a Judging child may need to feel secure. Unless she understands this type difference, a Perceiving mother may not even be aware of this need in her child.

0 1 2

Add up your points here: ____

Add up your total score for Perceiving (from page 86 and above) and write it here: ____

Write your total for Judging from page 84: ____

As before, compare the totals. The greater the disparity, the clearer your preference is for either Judging or Perceiving. Yet motherhood demands proficiency in both these functions. The more you can capitalize on your strengths, and the more adept you can become in your nonpreferred areas of functioning, the easier your days will be.

> "My husband and I are both Perceiving types, but my husband's preference is much stronger than mine. Before I go out for an evening, I go over the children's schedules with him: homework, TV program they can watch, when to start reading, when to turn the lights out and say goodnight. Then when I come home—after their bedtime—I find the children still up watching TV, or playing with their dad. Everyone got so caught up in the moment that the schedule was totally forgotten. This really irks me, especially on school nights."
>
> —Diane, INFP. Note: I've heard many Judging mothers with Perceiving spouses express the same complaint.

Tips for the Judging Mother

1. "Taking care of me" means having a place or project of your own to control, organize, and complete. Claim one room or area of the house as your own—a place where you can keep things exactly as you want them. When life seems chaotic and out of control, you can regain your sense of order by retreating to this place. One Judging mother told me about how good she felt after volunteering at her children's school. Her job was to punch lunch tickets, tally lunches sold, and count up the cash box. Being able to organize and finish a concrete, specific job renewed her patience for going with the flow of small children.

2. When you're frustrated at not being able to control what your children do, focus on organizing and coming to closure on projects that are under your control—balancing your checkbook, finishing PTA phone calls, sorting the mail.

3. Make "having fun" a top priority on your things-to-do list. Judging mothers tend to think, *I'll relax as soon as my work is finished,* but when it comes to mothering, the work is never done. Be sure to build in to your schedule some time

off—at least thirty minutes a day—to talk to a favorite friend, take a walk, or read the newspaper or a magazine.

4. Find new ways to have fun with your children. Many Judging mothers worry that they don't enjoy time with their children as much as they think they "should" or as much as they'd like to. Try taking your children out of the house—so you're not distracted by what needs to be done at home. Or introduce your child to what was fun for you when you were your child's age. Particularly with young children, it's easier for them to "play" at what's fun for you than for you to "play" at what's fun for them. And remember, real fun won't happen on schedule, regularly, day after day.

5. Try to balance your need for order with other family members' (perhaps lower) needs for order. Find ways to contain their disorder so you can function without forcing loved ones to continually meet your standards. Try a closed-door, clear-path rule: "Your room can be as messy as you'd like as long as the common areas are neat and there's a clear path between the bed and door."

6. Adopt a weekend-off policy: "Monday though Friday we'll stick to my plan, Saturday and Sunday we'll keep open."

7. Allow yourself to take pleasure in straightening up the house. Think of it as therapeutic, not a job. As "un-fun" as that sounds, Judging mothers often say they enjoy setting the house in order. If you have young children, consider hiring a sitter so you can clean your house uninterrupted, or send them to Grandma's so you can straighten up.

Tips for the Perceiving Mother

1. "Taking care of me" means freedom from a tight schedule. Allow yourself at least one slow, unscheduled morning or afternoon on the weekend to "hang out" and recover from the busy week. Consider taking a summer off from schedules, if you can. When taking a vacation, don't over-plan; you'll do best if you allow some time for spontaneous activities and discoveries.

2. On days that will be busy and scheduled already, try not to add anything else. Or, you might try the converse: schedule several things for one day, to give yourself a bigger block of unscheduled time on another day. If you have a doctor appointment, try also to do some necessary shopping in the same vicinity. But be careful not to schedule too tightly; remember, as a Perceiving type you have more difficulty judging how much time things actually take.

3. Start your day with a crisis list rather than a things-to-do list. Write down one to three things you must do or everything will fall apart—"get bread and milk, call the plumber, take Sue for her check-up"—and post it on the refrigerator. Keeping this list of "essentials" may help you stay focused and flexible to handle what the day brings.

4. Don't back yourself into a corner with a lot of rules you'll ultimately find too restrictive. Perceiving mothers usually function better with a few basic intents or ideals.

5. Time some of the tasks you do routinely, and keep the information handy. If you know it takes twenty minutes to fold a load of laundry, when you have twenty minutes free you can tackle that task. Otherwise, "fold the laundry" floats around in the back of your mind, you don't really know how long it takes, and you keep putting it off until it's a monumental task.

6. Give yourself some breathing room when making plans, particularly when you're dealing with Judging types. They hear Perceiving types coming to "firm" decisions even when Ps are still keeping their options open. If plans change, Judging types feel let down, that they can't count on Ps to follow through. Say, "I'll be home for dinner between 5:00 and 6:30," instead of "I'll be home at 6." Then when you show up at 6:15, you'll be considered on time.

7. Remember that although you're drawn to many experiences for your children, each organized activity involves structure, scheduling, planning, and focus on your part. Limit your children to one structured activity a week that you're responsible for. Let the rest of your child's experiences be spontaneous and unstructured. Yes, your child can participate in swimming, dance, basketball, choir . . . but consecutively, not concurrently.

Putting It All Together

It's time to combine your results for the four dichotomies: Extraversion or Introversion, Sensing or Intuition, Thinking or Feeling, and Judging or Perceiving, based on your rating of your strengths and struggles in mothering.

——	——	——	——
E or I	S or N	T or F	J or P

How does this understanding of the four letters of your own particular type compare to your initial guess from Chapter 1? Do they match or do you have a discrepancy on one or two aspects? In the next two chapters, you'll have another chance to find the type that fits you best.

Some women say that it helps to guess the types of several other people in their lives while the information is still fresh. It gives them a personal framework to remember what the preferences are all about. Before you go on, I recommend making a list of five mothers you know, including your own. Then make your best guess of their personality type. You might want to consider your spouse, as well.

Now that you have a sense of your strengths and struggles and are armed with some practical tips, let's fine-tune this information by looking at the mothering profile for your unique type. As you determine which mothering style typifies you, you'll discover exactly why your children are lucky to have you as their mother!

chapter 6

Mothers of Many Styles—Part I

In the last four chapters we explored how the eight preferences—Extraversion and Introversion, Sensing and Intuition, Thinking and Feeling, and Judging and Perceiving—affect your strengths and struggles as a mother. By now you should have a pretty good handle on your own four preferences and their one-letter abbreviations (E or I, S or N, T or F, J or P)—the basic building blocks of your personality in parenting.

Now let's focus on your particular mothering profile. There are sixteen distinct, unique personality types, and therefore sixteen different mothering styles, each with its own dynamics. If you are pretty sure of your personality type, this more specific description of you as a mother should ring true as well as offer new insights that will improve your satisfaction with mothering.

However, it's not uncommon for people in the early stages of learning about personality type to be considering one, two, or even three possibilities. If you are still searching for the "real me," use the following profiles to try to figure out who you are by reading several descriptions of personality types. Chances are one of these profiles will leap out and say, "That's me, all right!"

In this chapter I will describe the eight Sensing mothering styles: ISTJ, ESTP, ISTP, ESTJ, and ESFJ, ESFP, ISFP, ESFJ. In the next chapter, I focus on the eight Intuitive mothering styles: INFJ, ENFP, INFP, ENFJ, and INTJ, ENTP, INTP, ENTJ. After you've found the profile that seems to fit you best, you may want to search for your mother's, your sister's, or your best friend's. Think back to your list of five other mothers from the end of the previous chapter and read their descriptions. Do these mothering profiles seem to fit them? Most important, think about your own mother and her type, since she, no doubt, is one of the biggest influences on your own mothering. You may find that you have internalized some of her values or ways, even though it may not fit your own type.

Shopping for the Perfect Mother

When I went about interviewing women who represented the sixteen different personality types, I realized I was in a unique position. I could pretend I was "shopping" for a mother. If I had been able to choose my ideal mother, which type would have been the best one for me? I interviewed groups of five to eight moms of each type, asking each group, "What do you think you do better than other mothers?" As they began to list their strengths, I would listen and think, *Wouldn't it be great to have a mother like that?* A mother who was accepting, or helped you learn how to navigate successfully through the world of organizations and institutions, or someone who would take charge and make you feel protected.

When I asked, "What do you think the other mothers do better than you?" they would begin to discuss their perceived shortcomings. As I listened I would think, *Yuck, who would like to have a mother like* that? A mother who could be intrusive or overly structured, or someone who might push me to be more popular than I needed to be.

After going through each of the sixteen types, I realized no mother would have had all the strengths I yearned for and none of the weaknesses. Any one would have pluses and minuses. I came to appreciate that my own mother, despite her shortcomings, had given me many gifts and perhaps had been the perfect mother for me, after all.

The truth is, *every mother is a mixed bag.* No matter how much you try, you are never going the erase the fact that you are a human being. Each of us has wonderful gifts and abilities and goodness, but we also have limitations, frailties, gaps, vulnerabilities, inadequacies, struggles, and needs. I coveted other mothers' strengths but not the downside that inevitably goes with them.

This is why for each mothering profile I list both the strengths and the struggles. As you read and relate to your own profile, keep in mind that children don't need perfect mothers. Children need *human* mothers who can model for them how to make the most of their strengths, come to grips with their limitations, and manage their humanness to be the best they can be.

My research revealed that each type mother had a special gift for her children—something she does effortlessly and better than any other type mother—indeed, something that makes her children lucky to have her as a mother. Each profile tries to capture that essence and provide additional strengths, struggles, and personalized mother-to-mother tips. As much as possible, the profiles make use of the women's own words to describe themselves, as gleaned from my in-depth interviews. Yes, each type mother has a language all her own!

Mothers of the Sensing Style

The eight mothering style profiles below are organized by the middle two letters of each type because these mothers tend to share many characteristics and values. For example, SF (Sensing-Feeling) mothers are typically sympathetic, helpful, and traditionally feminine. ST (Sensing-Thinking) mothers are matter-of-fact, analytical, and no-nonsense. Then, adding the first and last letters into the mix produces a distinctive personality for each type.

ISTJ—The "Responsibility" Mother

(Introverted, Sensing, Thinking, Judging)

"I have a serious love affair with to-do lists. I could sit for hours reading, organizing, and rearranging my weekly calendar."

The ISTJ mother has a highly developed sense of responsibility: for work, home, family . . . particularly her children. Whether she's overseeing daily baths or insisting on a 10 p.m. curfew, her efforts are largely focused on providing her children with order and routine. She wants them, regardless of age, to be able to count on her and the structure she provides.

In carrying out her commitment to her responsibilities, the ISTJ mother is organized, industrious, and detail-oriented. Because her focus is the day-to-day realities of life, her children are likely to feel secure and well provided for.

The ISTJ mother also sets a good example and provides her children with practical guidance on being a productive, responsible individual. Still, with all her seriousness, she may delight family members with her quick wit and observations about the details of life.

Strengths

- *Providing for her children's practical needs.* The ISTJ mother tends to her children's basic needs on a day-to-day routine, seeing to it they're healthy, well fed, clean, warm, and well rested.

- *Providing security.* For the ISTJ mother, children thrive in a family structure where roles and boundaries are well defined. She makes it clear: Parents are parents, children are children.

- *Preparing her children for life in the real world.* The ISTJ mother believes children must ultimately be independent and on their own. Her goal is to instill good study habits and show them "how to be organized" and make effective use of time. She also views it as her responsibility to discuss the pros and cons of different ways people earn a living.

- *Teaching her children how to work hard.* The ISTJ mother encourages her children to do for themselves. Not only does she set the standard for hard work, she gives them responsibility for specific "jobs" around the house, expects them to do their best at school, and insists they clean up after themselves.

TIPS

- The best gift an ISTJ mother can give herself is uninterrupted quiet time each day. She may need to have someone take her children to the park each afternoon or turn off the phone to savor the stillness during the hours they're at school or at a friend's. She may choose to spend her private time setting things in order or getting caught up.

- Because she needs structure to relax fully, the ISTJ mother may need to plan regular times that are okay to let down, knowing it won't disrupt the entire day. If her family can help finish what she needs to complete before relaxing, everyone may benefit.

Struggles

- *Flexibility.* If structure is her byword, the ISTJ mother may struggle most with being adaptable. Little children are spontaneous and unpredictable, older children have minds of their own, and letting children invite friends into the home can leave her feeling there's no order in her life.

- *Being hard on herself.* Aware of all that needs to be done, the ISTJ mother may be a perfectionist who wants things done right and on time. Proceeding at an intense pace, she may find it difficult to relax until all her work is done.

- *Exhaustion.* Private and inwardly focused, the ISTJ mother may find herself constantly drained by disorder and children's commotion. She may feel overwhelmed, unable to maintain order or struggling to find any time alone to recharge.

ESTP—The "Action Adventure" Mother

(Extraverted, Sensing, Thinking, Perceiving)

"I can't do anything the same way more than one or two times. Today can't be like yesterday. Let's do something different!"

Active and spontaneous, the ESTP mother can turn ordinary life into a fun-filled adventure. She makes dull routines exciting and chores a "let's do it again" kind of game. Her best times are those spent with her children actively doing, particularly if it's spur of the moment, innovative, and unconventional.

Full of energy and enthusiasm for living in the moment, the ESTP mother gives her children every opportunity to experience all that life has to offer—touching, seeing, moving, doing . . . and meeting people. She's interested in stimulating their senses so they can take life in and live it.

The ESTP mother is matter-of-fact—"what you see is what you get." She mothers without hidden agendas and takes life and people as they are. Her children know where they stand. She is able to develop a close relationship with them based on honesty and a strong family orientation as well as sharing a wide variety of experiences.

Strengths

- *Making the ordinary exciting.* The ESTP mother is a whiz at creating fun, turning "boring" aspects of day-to-day living into interesting things to do. She may detest making dinner at a scheduled time each day but thoroughly enjoy spending a Saturday with all family members up to their elbows in flour and laughter making homemade ravioli.

- *Encouraging her children to explore the world.* Classes, outings, travel, sports teams, mud puddles, friends—all are to be experienced and enjoyed . . . and used as opportunities for a child to discover and develop his or her strengths and special interests.

- *Doing and going with her children . . . on their level.* Action-oriented and constantly on the go, the ESTP mother gets actively involved in what her children are doing. She doesn't just sign them up for football, she goes out and tosses the football with them. She doesn't just listen to their newest CD, she joins in and imitates the rock star.

- *Flexibility.* Easy going and straightforward, the ESTP mother is content to go with the flow and rarely loses her cool. In fact, she thrives on "chaos" and lives a no-strings-attached lifestyle.

TIPS

- The ESTP mom needs a repertoire of activities that balance her need for action and spontaneity with a child's need for downtime. Having intimate talks while walking in the woods or driving around in the car may meet her need for "going" while responding to a child's need for quiet togetherness.

- The greatest gift the ESTP mom can give herself is acceptance of her mothering gifts. She needs to stop comparing herself to the "other" mothers—the ones who seem to keep a smooth-running household, have dinner on the table at 6 p.m. every night, and do laundry on Mondays. The ESTP mother may feel out of step with this more domestic mother, but her love of action and spontaneity make her very much in tune with children everywhere.

Struggles

- *Routine.* The ESTP mother struggles with household routines: organizing children every morning for school, keeping shopping lists, straightening the house on a regular basis, and cooking dinner every night. Doing the same things the same way day after day may be what some children need to feel secure, but it requires intense effort for the ESTP mom.

- *Being still.* The ESTP mother struggles with the quiet and slow times of family life—sitting down to talk or read with a child one-on-one.

- *Maintaining focus.* The ESTP mother may struggle to see a household task or other routine project through from start to finish. Easily distracted, she will likely drop everything when something else captures her attention.

ISTP—The "Give 'Em Their Space" Mother

(Introverted, Sensing, Thinking, Perceiving)

"My feelings are my own business. Not theirs. So I honor their privacy too."

Nonintrusive and respectful of differences, the ISTP mother gives her children the personal space they need to develop as separate, self-sufficient individuals. As children grow and mature, she enjoys observing how each one becomes his or her own person. She seeks to accept and honor each child's interests, opinions, and choices.

The ISTP mother does not believe in authority or control for its own sake. Instead, she favors a nondirective approach. Yet she has high expectations for each child's self-discipline as a key to self sufficiency.

To these ends, the ISTP mother wants to "be there" for her children—to meet their basic needs and keep them safe. Her goal is to help her children think for themselves and take responsibility for their own actions.

Strengths

- *Honoring differences.* While she may not always agree with them, the ISTP mother fundamentally believes her children have the right to their own points of view. She tends to follow their lead in what interests them, rather than trying to shape or control what or how they think.

- *Respecting a child's privacy.* The ISTP mother provides her children with the physical and emotional privacy she values for herself. She is careful to knock before entering a child's room, doesn't ask who called on the phone, and backs off from asking personal questions that to her seem intrusive.

- *Fostering self-sufficiency.* The ISTP mother believes in self-discipline. Not liking to be confined by rules or authority herself, she may be intentionally "lenient" with her children so they can think situations through on their own, choose their actions, and then assess their own behavior.

- *Engaging children in intellectual discussions.* As she helps her children think for themselves, the ISTP mother enjoys intellectual discussions with them at any age. Her best times as a mother may be those moments when she and her children discuss what they are studying at school—grammar, geography, world events—or what they want to do in life.

TIPS

- The ISTP needs to find a comfortable way to connect with her children's feelings and concerns on a regular basis. She can develop systems or techniques the family can use to initiate more personal conversations. For example, a child might place a baseball cap on his door handle by 7 p.m. as a signal to his mother that he would appreciate a bedtime chat that night. Or she might keep an open mother-daughter journal that allows for each one to communicate personal thoughts through written conversation.

- The greatest gift the ISTP mother can give herself is a break from day-to-day household routines. She may enjoy going out by herself to visit a bookstore or see a movie. Or she may prefer to hire a housekeeper (if she can afford it), or delegate those chores she finds intolerable to other family members.

Struggles

- *Providing emotional support.* The ISTP mother may feel out of her element when it comes to giving a child the emotional closeness he or she needs. She may struggle with showing warmth and affection, coaxing a scared child, or figuring out the emotional aspects of a child's behavior.

- *Asking personal questions.* When her child needs help handling an emotional issue, the ISTP mother may be reluctant to probe his or her feelings—she doesn't want to put the child on the spot or set off an emotional outburst. But her children may confuse her nonintrusive behavior with not caring.

- *Traditional domestic tasks.* Handling the domestic side of child-raising does not appeal to the ISTP mother. She tends to be uncomfortable if called on to fix home-cooked meals regularly, insist children sit down to eat, dress them in matching outfits, or provide little touches that make their rooms homey.

ESTJ—The "How To" Mother

(Extraverted, Sensing, Thinking, Judging)

"We're the mothers you like to carpool with. Not only are we on time,
we organize the driving schedule for everyone."

Organized and comfortable being in charge, the ESTJ mother knows "how to" get things done, make things happen, and accomplish much on behalf of her children. Whether she is encouraging them to get involved in organized activities or talking with them about their personal concerns, children of the ESTJ mother learn "how to" succeed in life.

Upbeat and matter-of-fact, the ESTJ mother is intent on her children having the best. She puts her skills and talents to work to this end, from planning trips that supplement their studies to raising funds for new playground equipment. She is happiest when her efforts produce concrete results—children who try out for teams, participate in academic competitions, or are leaders among their peers.

The ESTJ mother runs a tight household. She is apt to have predictable expectations, consistent routines, standard procedures, and well-defined boundaries, all of which help her children feel protected and secure.

Strengths

- *Organization and planning.* The ESTJ mother is naturally suited to managing a busy, active family. She can juggle many tasks and get a lot done. Her children know they can depend on her to follow through and take care of their basic needs.

- *Teaching children practical skills for success.* The ESTJ mother knows what it takes to succeed—do your work before you play, don't burn bridges, look adults in the eye when you shake hands, make new friends but keep the old, plan ahead for deadlines, organize your time.

- *Teaching children how to problem-solve.* The ESTJ mother loves talking to her children about what's on their minds. She uses their issues and concerns as "teaching moments" to help them with their problem-solving, whether it's handling a school assignment or managing trouble with friends.

- *Social adeptness and people orientation.* By word and example, the ESTJ mother teaches her children the joys and skills of moving comfortably among people and groups. She does what she can to create a network of friends, extended family, and community organizations for her children.

Struggles

- *Sense of self.* The ESTJ mother often feels overly responsible for her children's successes and failures. She may find herself living through their successes or using their behavior to measure her competence as a mother.

- *Letting go.* The ESTJ mother struggles to let children of all ages do things their own way. When her children are young, she may be frustrated that she can't make them eat vegetables or fall asleep on schedule. As they get older, she may stay involved, at the risk of "trying to run their lives."

- *Acceptance.* The ESTJ mother may struggle to accept each child just the way he or she is. Because she has a picture of what would be best for each one, her children may feel that anything short of her idea of perfection isn't good enough.

> **TIPS**
>
> - The ESTJ mother needs opportunities to feel competent separate from the job of mothering. Getting feedback for her ability to manage projects—both paid and volunteer—can provide objective measures of her competence.
>
> - The ESTJ mother needs a place where she can exercise her need for structure or a project that is "totally under control." If she can claim such a place or project, she may find it easier to be more flexible and spontaneous when it's called for.

ISFJ—The "Tender Loving Care" Mother

(Introverted, Sensing, Feeling, Judging)

*"I want my children to feel they have an ally,
someone who knows them completely. I want to be a haven for them."*

Gentle and kind, the ISFJ mother provides her children with generous amounts of tenderness, affection, and the comfort of daily routine. Her aim is to "be there" for her children, physically and emotionally. She is sensitive to their feelings, offering closeness, understanding, and quiet support.

Loyal and devoted, the ISFJ mother has a strong sense of duty and consistently puts her children's needs first. She delights in taking care of the little things that matter to a child, making each one feel loved and special.

To provide her family with security and warmth, the ISFJ mother tends to the practical and domestic, aiming for a smooth-running household and an attractive home. She also observes and conveys the value and importance of family traditions.

Strengths

- *Showing love in practical ways.* The ISFJ mother shows her love with home-cooked meals, an orderly house, neatly folded laundry, hand-made holiday decorations . . . and time with each child in quiet togetherness.

- *Tending to the little things.* The ISFJ mother goes the extra mile to take care of what's important in a child's life—from the child's point of view. Whether it's searching for hours for a lost toy, reading a favorite bedtime story for the fifty-first time, or volunteering as a teacher's helper in her child's classroom, the ISFJ knows what matters to her child and comes through.

- *Establishing boundaries.* The ISFJ mother provides a secure environment for her family by defining clear roles for parent and child, steady and consistent rules, and predictable routines. Her children know what they can count on.

- *Sensitivity.* Loving and kind, the ISFJ mother is a patient listener, valuing and respecting each child's feelings and concerns.

Struggles

- *Appreciation.* Because she serves behind the scenes and makes household and mothering tasks look effortless, the ISFJ mom may struggle with feeling taken for granted. She may feel hurt if loved ones fail to notice or appreciate her efforts.

- *Guilt.* With a fierce sense of being duty-bound to family, home, and other commitments she has made, the ISFJ is vulnerable to both internal and external "shoulds" and feelings of guilt.

- *Fear of being a "wet blanket."* The ISFJ, knowing she pours herself into her family and has a high need for order and structure, wonders about the impact she has on her loved ones. She may worry that her children find her too serious, overly sensible, or stifling.

ESFP—The "Totally There" Mother

(Extraverted, Sensing, Feeling, Perceiving)

"I like to give my children an immediate response.
It's not like there's one time for hugs and another to make sandwiches."

Energetic and people-oriented, the ESFP mother lives in the moment, "totally there" for her children—totally focused on them when she is with them. She enjoys being with her children and can respond to their needs "on the spot," ensuring that they feel loved and cared for.

Fun-loving, friendly, and outgoing, the ESFP mother actively engages her children in a wide variety of experiences. They can count on her to strike up a conversation with a fellow shopper at the market or with the bus driver, introducing them to the joys of people everywhere.

Devoted and practical, the ESFP mother also enjoys doing for her children. She is attentive to their feelings and is deeply touched by every joy or hurt they experience.

Strengths

- *Being there*. The ESFP mother may consider herself 100 percent devoted to her children. As such, her first priority is "being there" for them whenever they need her—being on call twenty-four hours a day, showering them with unconditional love, comforting them when they hurt.

- *Playfulness*. Child-oriented and filled with joy for living, the ESFP mother knows how to have fun and laugh with her children, perhaps acting like a kid again herself. She delights in having children around, and that includes other people's children. Her house may be the neighborhood hang-out.

- *Family focus*. A proponent of family closeness and unity, the ESFP mother seeks to instill a strong sense of family in her children. She encourages everyone to spend time together and wants her children to know that family comes first . . . that family members support each other through thick and thin.

- *Flexibility*. Unstructured and nonrestrictive, the ESFP mother is spontaneous. She enjoys going with the flow of children of all ages.

> **TIPS**
>
> - The ESFP mother can benefit from joining a group of mothers who have children the same age as hers. Together these women can point out different perspectives, options, and ways of doing things, as well as affirm that "she's not the only one." Supporting one another in their mothering can help provide the objectivity and reassurance she needs.
>
> - The ESFP mother needs to remember to tune in to her needs and put them first once in a while. Always giving and being "totally there" for her children, she may burn out and have nothing left for herself, which can leave her feeling resentful and angry. The added benefit of putting the focus on herself: she gives her children space and time to develop their independence.

Struggles

- *Discipline*. Although well-behaved children are a high priority for her, the ESFP mother may not feel confident as a disciplinarian. Struggling to gain an objective point of view, she may wonder, "Should I make an issue of this or let it go this one time?" If she is confronted with a situation where her actions could make a child unhappy, she may think setting limits is "mean." And sticking to limits over the long run may be harder for her than for her child.

- *Letting go*. Encouraging independence in her children can be difficult for the ESFP mother. Backing off goes against her natural inclination to get involved, be close, and do things for them.

- *When her children are hurt*. The ESFP mother may become overly upset when her children's feelings are hurt or when they're facing life's hard knocks. She may need steady reassurance that they'll be okay.

ISFP—The "Giving" Mother

(Introverted, Sensing, Feeling, Perceiving)

"A people pleaser from Day One, it took me 30 years to figure out I could say 'no.'"

Quiet and unassuming in her devotion, the ISFP mother is responsive to her children's needs, offering behind-the-scenes love and support. She is gentle and nonintrusive, flexible, and adaptable.

A "be there" mother, the ISFP takes pleasure in physically caring for her children and doing for them. Her best times might be "doing little things" with each child one-on-one.

More than anything, the ISFP mother wants her children to know they are loved. And she enjoys being needed in return.

Dedicated to raising children who are responsible and care for others, she favors a nondirective approach: instilling values by setting a good example. She may be a strong role model for community service.

Strengths

- *Accessibility and flexibility.* The ISFP mother is available to her children. Because she can readily "go with the flow," the ISFP is well suited to meeting the unpredictable needs of small children. Adult children of ISFPs say they always knew they were loved and accepted growing up—mom was never too busy to spend time together, give a hug, work a puzzle, or help with homework.

- *Her personal touch.* The ISFP mother is responsive to each child, tending to the needs of the moment. When one is sick, she makes Jell-O, and when he wants to learn to ride his bike, she runs along holding the seat. She'll work with another child on a puzzle or bake favorite cookies. The ISFP likes doing the little things that matter most to her children.

- *Providing gentle support.* Sympathetic and comforting, the ISFP mother soothes a child's upset feelings with physical closeness and quiet talk. She is reassuring and encouraging, helping her children believe they can do anything they want.

- *Teaching by example.* To impart the values she holds most dear, the ISFP mother does not preach, force, or push her children. She believes children learn best by the example set for them; if her children see her do a good deed, they will learn to do it as well. She strives to set a good example of a life of service to family, friends, and community, and to care for all living creatures.

TIPS

- The greatest gift the ISFP mother can give herself is a break from constantly giving to her children—and give to herself instead. Long blocks of time alone to read, watch a movie, or putter around the house are well deserved. And outside interests can give her perspective. By putting the focus on herself once in a while, the ISFP mother is actually giving to her children as well: they have time and space for their own needs, and she's setting a good example of how one takes care of oneself.

- The ISFP mother may benefit from outside support in learning how to say "no" and assert herself. A supportive partner, good friend, or professional coach or counselor may be able to model new approaches, offer insight, and encourage her to stand up for herself more often.

Struggles

- *Selflessness.* Because she is generous and a "people pleaser," the ISFP mother may struggle with giving too much of herself. As a result, she may not know her own interests and needs. She may also become burned-out and angry with loved ones asking so much of her.

- *Assertiveness.* As she naturally adapts to the needs and wants of others, the ISFP mother may find it extremely hard to stand up for herself and say "no." She may also have difficulty asking for help . . . even when it's in everyone's best interest. She may struggle most to assert herself with traditional authority figures, such as teachers and medical professionals.

- *Routine and productivity.* Organizing and keeping daily family routines can seem overwhelming to the ISFP mother, whether her task is overseeing homework, getting children to school on time, or preparing meals. Sporadic in her focus, she tends to procrastinate; she often feels unproductive, wondering at times how other mothers accomplish so much.

ESFJ—The "Happy Together" Mother

(Extraverted, Sensing, Feeling, Judging)

"I like it when my children are happy on their own,
but I love it when the whole family is happy together."

The ESFJ mother has a highly developed sense of family and what it takes to be happy in life. Capable and personally invested, she strives to create a happy family where togetherness and harmony flourish. Whether it's taking her children to the park or putting on a holiday feast, her efforts are directed toward having everyone be "happy together."

To many, the ESFJ personifies motherhood. She promotes traditional values, tends to the practical and domestic, provides the family with order and structure, and is directly involved with her children's day-to-day living. The ESFJ mother is a "doer," and she's never happier than when she's "doing" for her family.

Believing the home is central to family life, the ESFJ mother excels at creating an atmosphere that is attractive and offers security.

Energetic and people-oriented, she is drawn to community and the social scene. She helps her children discover the joys of people and groups.

Strengths

- *Cultivating close relationships with her children.* The ESFJ mother is devoted to taking care of her children's needs, physical and emotional. She is especially sensitive to their feelings, offering personal warmth, comfort, and plenty of "I love yous."

- *Making people connections with the larger world.* Sociable and friendly, the ESFJ mother provides her children with opportunities and activities to connect with community and friends as well as family, often serving as the family's "social director."

- *Sharing practical wisdom.* The ESFJ mother wants her children to know how to get along in the world. She values what is "appropriate" and teaches her children the right things to do and say in a wide variety of situations.

- *Providing a home base.* The ESFJ mother creates a home atmosphere that can serve as an anchor in the storm for her children. Home to her is also the place for informal gatherings and special events, such as family birthdays and holidays. A gracious hostess, she extends the warmth and hospitality of her home to family and friends.

TIPS

- When her children are squabbling, the ESFJ mother needs to remind herself that healthy relationships require a certain amount of conflict and "clearing the air" to grow and flourish. Allowing family members to work out differences on their own can sometimes be the best way to promote the close, harmonious relationships she wants for her family over the long run.

- Driven by a lot of "shoulds," the ESFJ mother is susceptible to others' judgments and the desire to please, not to mention her own perfectionism. She may have a hard time relaxing. The greatest gift the ESFJ mother can give herself is enforced regular breaks from the intensity of family life and constantly giving and doing for others. A little relaxation and fun need to be put at the top of her to-do list every day.

Struggles

- *Family disharmony.* The ESFJ mother gladly puts forth effort to orchestrate good times for the whole family together. She can feel frustrated, annoyed, and hurt, however, when family members are fighting, someone is hurt, or some don't want to participate.

- *Judgment and control.* The ESFJ mother has a good idea of what she wants for her child, and she worries when her child chooses a path different from the one she has envisioned. She may struggle to understand and accept a child who is different, finding it difficult to back off and let go.

- *Perfectionism.* In an effort to get everything done right and on time, the ESFJ mother is prone to over-functioning. The stress may lead her to nit-pick or over-focus on details to make everything perfect.

These are the eight Sensing mothering styles. Although each style is unique, all Sensing mothers tend to be down-to-earth and practical. SJ mothers are the caretaker mothers, providing security with their daily routines; whereas SP mothers are typically more fun and spontaneous.

If you think you are more a mother of possibility than practicality, go on to the next chapter. It's likely one of the eight Intuitive mothering style profiles will fit you better.

· · · · · · · · · · ·

chapter 7

Mothers of Many Styles—Part 2

IN THE LAST CHAPTER WE DESCRIBED THE EIGHT MOTHER TYPES OF THE SENSING style. Now let's take a closer look at the eight mother types of the Intuitive style, the NF mothers (INFJ, INFP, ENFP, ENFJ) and the NT mothers (INTJ, INTP, ENTP, ENTJ). Both NF and NT mothers are "big picture" and gravitate toward new possibilities, but NFs are idealistic and seek to understand people and NTs are more rational, theoretical, and knowledge-seeking.

In addition, NF mothers are adept at "tuning in" to a child at his or her own level, often playfully, and encourage a close connection based on communication, authenticity, and emotional support. NT mothers, on the other hand, tend to relate to their children on an intellectual, adult level, even when they are quite young. They are less apt to talk baby talk or perpetuate the myth of Santa Claus. The NT mother strives to instill a "can-do" attitude in her child and takes great joy in her child's growing independence, rationality, and academic achievements.

As with each of the Sensing types, each Intuitive type of mother brings her own special strengths and struggles to the mothering experience, and contributes her own unique gifts to her children.

Mothers of the Intuitive Style

INFJ—The "Know Thyself" Mother

(Introverted, Intuitive, Feeling, Judging)

"I believe the joy of motherhood is self-discovery—
for them and for me."

Sensitive and family-focused, the INFJ mother looks for and encourages the unique potential of each child. Self-knowledge may be her byword. Her aim is to help each child develop a sense of identity and cultivate personal growth. In fact, she may value the mothering experience as a catalyst to her own personal growth and self-knowledge.

The INFJ mother spends time observing and understanding each child. She is drawn to intimate conversations and seeks a free exchange of feelings and thoughts.

Sympathetic and accommodating, the INFJ mother strives to meet the important yet sometimes conflicting needs of each family member in harmonious and creative ways.

She is conscientious and intense as well. Probably no one takes life and child-raising more seriously than the INFJ. She approaches mothering as a profession requiring her best self.

Strengths

- *Connecting one-on-one with each child.* The INFJ mother listens, observes, and reflects to develop an understanding of who each child really is. She "knows" her child and desires a close relationship. She connects and keeps in touch with each child as a unique individual.

- *Providing her children with emotional support.* The INFJ mother is sensitive to her children's feelings, not shying away from helping them deal with even their heaviest emotions. She seeks to smooth out the rough edges of their experiences with a comforting presence and her broader perspectives.

- *Profundity*. Focused on understanding values, spirituality, culture, and society, the INFJ mother provides awareness and insights into the subtleties and lessons of life beyond a child's immediate experience and questions.

- *Creativity*. The INFJ mother can dream up unusual, fun projects her children can do to occupy their time and enrich their day-to-day experience, such as fantasy games to play, theme parties, or special snacks to make from healthy foods.

Struggles

- *Details*. The INFJ mother may gravitate toward the idea of getting the family and household organized and in order, only to exhaust herself with nitty-gritty follow-through. Regular baths for small children, weekly laundry, daily meals, picking up clutter, and ongoing repairs can be overwhelming.

- *Real life versus the ideal*. Because she lives with an ideal in her mind, the INFJ mother often has unrealistic expectations of herself and others. She may feel inadequate and critical of herself when reality falls short of her ideal.

- *Giving too much*. The INFJ mother may be prone to over-accommodation and self-sacrifice as a way to maintain family harmony. She struggles with the ramifications: a child who is too dependent and a mother who is depleted and resentful.

TIPS

- Although she is drawn to people, the INFJ mother must remember that she needs time alone on a regular basis. Since her children are greatly affected by her mood swings, she is also giving to her children when she accommodates her Introversion. Time alone to meditate, journal, listen to music, and enjoy nature as well as intimate discussions with close friends can do wonders to bring peace to herself. For the INFJ especially, "If Mom ain't okay, ain't nobody okay."

- The INFJ mother needs to try to take life less seriously . . . to lighten up and take time to look at what life "is" rather than try to make it what it "should be." By living in the moment rather than the future, she can also help curb her tendency to take an isolated fact and extrapolate a catastrophic outcome.

ENFP—The "Kids R Fun" Mother

(Extraverted, Intuitive, Feeling, Perceiving)

"Whatever I enjoy—playing tag or singing in the car—
I can do it with kids around. And it's totally legitimate!"

Playful and energetic, the ENFP mother finds her children to be good company and enjoys being with them. In fact, she says being with children justifies her own "being a kid again." And children say she's fun to be with because she is spontaneous, hearty, and imaginative.

Naturally drawn to introducing her children to the joys of life, the ENFP is something of a free spirit. She is less concerned with rules, routines, and schedules, and more inclined to give her children plenty of free time to play, explore on their own or with her, and have fun together.

Tuned in to her children, the ENFP mother enthusiastically encourages each one's individuality and unique potential through a great variety of experiences. She is also quick to identify with others' feelings and thoughts, making her an empathetic supporter of her children, not to mention of her mate and her many, many friends.

Strengths

- *Playfulness.* The ENFP mother provides her children with delightful companionship. Comfortable playing at their level, she may enjoy dancing on the table, jumping rope in the house, or doing somersaults in the swimming pool. She is equally happy "hanging out," watching a movie, or window shopping, as long as everyone is having fun together.

- *Helping a child identify and cultivate his or her gifts.* Perceptive and people-smart, the ENFP mother helps her children recognize their talents. Enthusiastically, she helps each one develop his or her unique potential—she provides experiences and opportunities that expand a child's interests and offers her ongoing encouragement and support.

- *Sensitivity and empathy.* The ENFP mother is aware of her children—what they're feeling and what's going on in their lives. Drawn to the pleasures of conversation and adept at heart-to-heart talks, she listens to them empathetically without judging.

- *Flexibility.* Despite the confusion of a busy, fast-paced lifestyle and concurrent family activities, the ENFP mother can usually stay calm and go with the flow. She is rarely flustered by a change of plans, a spilled glass of milk, or last-minute requests.

Struggles

- *Maintaining emotional boundaries.* When one of her children is having a difficult time, the ENFP mother may struggle to maintain a helpful emotional distance. She may over-identify with a child's concerns, aching with his or her every hurt, exaggerating its importance, and ultimately needing reassurance from the child that he or she will be okay.

- *Details.* The ENFP mother struggles with the details, organization, and routines of day-to-day living. Being on time, remembering permission slips, regular mealtimes, and laundry can drive her to distraction. She may let mundane chores turn into mini-crises, because she enjoys the "rush."

- *Firmness.* Worried about making a bad decision or taking a wrong course of action, the ENFP mother may find it difficult to be objective, decisive, and firm-minded, when appropriate. Teenagers especially may find her indulgent and inconsistent.

TIPS

- When dealing with her children's personal concerns, the ENFP mother needs to step back and ask herself, "Whose problem is this anyway?" and "Is this really that terrible?" To keep from over-functioning, she might enlist the help and support of a Thinking-Judging spouse or friend who can give her a more objective perspective.

- Because she is naturally drawn to a variety of activities and tending to family members' emotional well-being, the ENFP mother can easily burn out. She may find it hard to relax; however, fifteen-minute catnaps, physical exercise, and long walks can keep her energized. Four-handkerchief movies, sad books, and pouring out her heart to a close friend can help her release her emotional stress.

INFP—The "Tuned In" Mother

(Introverted, Intuitive, Feeling, Perceiving)

"Inside our children, I believe, is a truth that tells them what's best
for them. I am always listening for that truth."

Aware, astute, and understanding, the INFP mother is sensitive to her child's needs, feelings, and perceptions. By observing and listening to the cues of the whole child, she is "tuned in" and naturally develops an intuitive feel for what he or she needs. Responsive and helpful as well, she tends patiently to those needs as they arise.

The INFP mother is comfortable letting her children follow their own course of development and make their own choices. She offers encouragement and uses her insights to head off trouble and difficult issues.

The INFP mother takes vicarious pleasure giving her children good experiences and watching them enjoy childhood. She's happiest creating pleasant, memorable times for the whole family.

Strengths

- *Cultivating a one-on-one relationship with each child.* Accepting and gentle, the INFP mother places a high value on having a close relationship with each child. In cultivating that relationship, she readily makes time available for each child one-on-one.

- *Interacting with her children.* The INFP mother spends time playing with her children side by side when they are young—making yarn dolls or clay figures, playing catch, or reading books together. As they get older, she finds other ways to engage them and interact with them.

- *"Tuning in" to feelings.* The INFP mother pays especially close attention to her children's feelings, really listening, trying to understand, and finding appropriate ways to respond. She is also comfortable sharing her own feelings with her children, inviting them to listen and understand her feelings as well as their own.

- *Building happy childhood memories.* The INFP mother is dedicated to creating good times for her children, making sure they experience a wide variety of fun activities traditionally associated with a happy childhood: picnics, pets, Winnie the Pooh, Girl Scouts, a day at the beach, fireflies, ice cream cones . . . opportunities that will soon pass and never come again.

Struggles

- *Focus.* "Tuned in" to feelings and responsive to everyone's viewpoint, the INFP mother may feel overwhelmed if everyone is needing something from her at the same time or when different points of view are being expressed. To whom should she listen? And whom should she "tune out"?

- *Decision making.* The INFP mother works hard at sorting through various options to decide what's right for her children, and she tends to deal with each situation as it arises. At the time, she may feel disadvantaged by her ability to see all sides and may wonder if she is doing the right thing. Her reluctance to formulate black-and-white "rules" and policy statements for her children can leave her feeling permissive and guilty.

- *Societal expectations.* The INFP mother struggles to balance society's expectations for order, organization, and schedules with her need (and desire) to turn to a child's need of the moment. Keeping a household running may seem at odds with the job of raising children. Her motto may be, "Pardon our mess, child development in process."

TIPS

- Rather than constantly doing, the INFP mother may function at her best when she has large blocks of unstructured time—time to deal with the unexpected, time to pursue creative projects, and time to think things through. Always giving to others, she can benefit from giving to herself as well—time to take an afternoon nap, read, walk, bike, or watch a movie or a play.

- Naturally tuned in to what others think and feel, the INFP mother needs to practice tuning in to her own wisdom (and trusting it!) when making decisions on behalf of her children. Because the INFP often represents a minority point of view, she may have learned to discount her own intuition about her child when facing a teacher, physician, or administrator. The INFP mother can empower herself as a parent by confidently acting on her tuned-in understanding of her child, even when others don't see it her way . . . and by giving herself room to make mistakes and learn from them.

ENFJ—The "Heart-to-Heart" Mother

(Extraverted, Intuitive, Feeling, Judging)

"We have so many good talks, I think I understand
my children better than they understand themselves."

Expressive and warm, the ENFJ mother is adept at talking about personal concerns, both her children's and her own. She is likely to initiate heart-to-heart talks frequently and provide her children with an open forum for articulating their feelings and perspectives.

Tuned in to each child as a unique person, the ENFJ mother nurtures her children through affirmation, praise, and encouragement. She takes great pleasure when they reciprocate, offering admiration and encouragement of her, a sibling, or a friend.

Organized and energetic, the ENFJ mother is a competent, efficient family manager. She is involved in her children's lives, providing structure, direction, and guidance.

The ENFJ mother is also socially adept, relating well to people wherever she goes. She strives to keep her children connected to family, neighborhood, and the larger community.

Strengths

- *Communication skills.* The ENFJ mother provides understanding, closeness, and emotional support through open communication. She has a keen interest in her children's feelings and wants them to feel free to express themselves. She may also express her own feelings clearly and work at being understood by her children.

- *Organization.* The ENFJ mother keeps day-to-day living and special projects organized and moving along. Methodical and energetic, she gets a lot done and may seem like "supermom" to other mothers.

- *Resourcefulness.* Enthusiastic and imaginative, the ENFJ mother brings a creative flair to everything she does. Her children are sure to delight in her theme birthday parties, dress-up ideas, and involvement in the class play. She in turn takes pleasure in their creativity, imagination, and fantasy play.

- *People orientation.* The ENFJ mother places a high value on her own relationships and her children's relationships with friends, family, and community. She encourages her children to extend themselves through service as well as friendship. She may, for example, organize a neighborhood play group to help a shy child make friends.

Struggles

- *People or order?* Committed to cultivating close relationships and getting things done, the ENFJ mother may feel guilty or conflicted when she must choose one or the other. She finds it stressful to focus on her children and have fun knowing there are schedules and deadlines to meet . . . and much to be accomplished before the day is over.

- *Backing off.* Intense and personally involved with each child, the ENFJ mother may worry about being "overbearing" and "bossy." She tries to listen without jumping to conclusions and be less directive with a child's decision-making.

- *Objectivity.* Sensitive to her children's anger, pain, bickering, and compliments, the ENFJ mother struggles to handle family situations objectively and avoid responding to children's attempted manipulations. Emotionally expressive, she may "fly off the handle," or she may attempt to use affection to diffuse or control difficult situations.

TIPS

- Humor is a wonderful way to temper the down side of the ENFJ's natural intensity. Insightful about human nature, she is quick to laugh at herself and the situation if someone helps her see it from a comic perspective. Harmony can be quickly restored when irritations are turned into mutual family jokes.

- Although she is people-oriented, the ENFJ needs some peace and quiet each day. A walk or lunch by herself can help her re-energize. She can also benefit from opportunities to engage in lively, heart-to-heart discussions with a close friend or group of friends beyond her immediate family.

INTJ—The "Individual Integrity" Mother

(Introverted, Intuitive, Thinking, Judging)

"My kids are better off arguing their own point of view than telling me, 'But everyone else is doing it.'"

Individualistic and independent, the INTJ mother is both a role model and teacher of how to be an individual and live life with integrity. She is introspective, defining her own success from within, and generally confident in her decisions. She is unlikely to be persuaded by her children saying, "But all the other mothers are doing it."

The INTJ is competent in providing for her children's basic needs, but she is likely more focused on developing their self-esteem and confidence. Observant and insightful, she puts great importance on independent thinking and self-sufficiency, yet she is comfortable providing protection and boundaries.

Self-motivated and intense, the INTJ works hard and takes life seriously. As a mother, she lives for those moments when she can impart knowledge and offer her children perspectives on life and important issues.

Strengths

- *Nonconformity.* The INTJ mother follows the beat of her own drum and is able to support a child who is different from the crowd. She respects each one's individuality, encouraging him or her to "think for yourself" and "act on your own beliefs." Because of her nonconformity and inner drive, she may break stereotypes and provide her children with a role model of what a nontraditional woman can be.

- *Thoughtfulness.* A natural teacher, the INTJ mother is intellectually concerned with addressing the complexities inherent in a child's everyday life. She accepts very few situations at face value, lifting the day-to-day to a higher level of importance and meaning. In discussing the broad lessons of life, she is respectful of a child's questions and reasoning.

- *Expecting those around her to do their best.* The INTJ mother lives with high standards, encouraging self-motivation and improvement . . . from herself and others. She expects her children to stretch themselves, accept the challenges of life, and do their best despite obstacles along the way.

- *Commitment.* Because she takes life seriously, the INTJ mother often chooses an issue, job, or project to which she fully and tirelessly commits herself. Her children may catch the spirit and learn the meaning of persistence as they watch her persevere.

Struggles

- *Noise and confusion of family life.* The INTJ mother is drained by much of the hubbub of raising children: intrusions, noise, bickering, chatter, messes, and disorder. She may find it difficult to relate to several children at once, preferring instead some one-on-one time with each child.

TIPS
• It is essential for the INTJ mother to have some work or project to call her own. Volunteer responsibilities and paid employment (full- or part-time) can meet her need for mental stimulation, adult conversation, time to concentrate, and a worthy goal to achieve.
• The INTJ mother may need more time alone away from her children than many other mothers. To be her best self, the INTJ must nurture her introspection and analysis—both of which require time and space. Being physically and emotionally available to her children needs to be balanced with time for her to think, read, or listen to the silence. A walk alone, a visit to the library, or a self-improvement class are ways to renew her energy for mothering.

- *Mothering confidence.* Despite her commitment to doing the job of mothering right, the INTJ mother may struggle with not feeling like a "natural" mother. Believing she is different from other mothers, she may feel inadequate if she compares herself to more domestic mothers who have a house full of homey knickknacks and daughters with bows and braids.

- *Leading a balanced life.* The INTJ mother may find it difficult to strike the right balance between her "accomplishment self" and "mother self." Wanting to tackle any responsibility with 100 percent effort, she may wonder where to put her focus and energy—sometimes she ignores her own competency needs for the sake of the family and sometimes she feels alienated from her children because she's so involved in a project.

ENTP—The "Independence" Mother

(Extraverted, Intuitive, Thinking, Perceiving)

"When I held my babies, I always faced them
outward so they could take in the world."

Full of energy and confident in her own self-sufficiency and competence, the ENTP mother encourages her children—as a role model and as a teacher—to be independent and confident on their own in the world.

A "big picture" person, she points out options and possibilities along the way. Objective and logical as well, the ENTP wants her children to evaluate their choices and learn from the consequences of their own decisions.

The ENTP mother is resourceful and action-oriented. She likes going places and doing things with her children, exploring all that life has to offer. She is less concerned with rules, routines, and schedules. Introducing her children to new concepts and activities, challenging them, and stimulating their intellectual development are top priorities.

Strengths

- *Energetic spontaneity.* The ENTP mother is "always" ready to drop what she's doing for an outing or new experience, from accepting a last-minute invitation to a museum to assisting young entrepreneurs with the start-up of a lawn care business. Seldom bogged down with day-to-day "drudgery," she can bring a breath of fresh air and a new perspective to any situation.

- *Encouraging independence.* The ENTP mother gives her children the space they need to develop self-sufficiency and confidence. Early on, she creates and supports opportunities for them to be out on their own, mastering their independence.

- *Teaching.* From grocery shopping to standing in line at the post office, the ENTP mother brings her children along to experience the world. A wonderful teacher of "life," she sees every activity and moment in the day as an opportunity for children to learn about life and expand their minds.

- *Tolerance and acceptance.* The ENTP mother takes pleasure in the variety each child brings to the family. She lets children do their own thing and refrains from pigeonholing them. In action and words, she demonstrates respect for self and others.

Struggles

- *Inactivity.* With her need for action, variety, and independence, the ENTP mother finds it draining to be homebound with a newborn or sick child. She may also find it difficult to adjust to children who are slower paced than she.

- *Clingy children.* If she has a child who is physically clingy or emo-
tionally needy, the ENTP mother may worry that he or she will never be independent or self-sufficient. She also finds she's uncomfortable in the "tender loving care" role.

- *Household routines.* Impatient with the details and schedules of day-to-day living, the ENTP mother may struggle to carry out daily routines. She may let mundane chores turn into mini-crises . . . and end up doing laundry at 2 a.m. when there's no clean underwear.

TIPS

- The ENTP mother needs to provide herself with intellectual stimulation, variety, and situations that allow her to function independently. Whether paid or volunteer positions, work outside the home may be ideal if she can be her own boss and follow a flexible schedule. She is also likely to be energized by time spent with interesting friends or engaging in solitary, physically active pursuits such as jogging.

- The greatest gift an ENTP mother can give herself may be help in those areas where she is least comfortable. A child-care provider who enjoys spending time with children at home, a reliable housekeeper, or a spouse who is a homebody may provide balance for children who thrive on tradition and routine.

INTP—The "Love of Learning" Mother

(Introverted, Intuitive, Thinking, Perceiving)

"I keep the encyclopedia in the kitchen so we can
look up things together while we eat."

Intellectually curious and patient, the INTP mother relishes those times with a child when they are learning something interesting together. Whether they are at the zoo or computer terminal, she sparks to answering his or her "whys" with in-depth responses or new knowledge.

The INTP mother is also objective and introspective. She listens to and discusses children's ideas and questions as she would those of a peer, fostering self-esteem and confidence. Open and nondirective, she allows children the freedom to do for themselves and quietly encourages them to believe they can do it.

Independence, autonomy, intellectual development, and self-reliance are probably the INTP's highest priorities for her children. An avid reader, she naturally imparts an appreciation and love of reading as well.

Drawn to all types of learning, the INTP may also value her mothering experience for all the new insights about life it provides her.

Strengths

- *Fostering her child's intellectual development.* The INTP mother has respect for her child's mind, thinking, and reasoning, regardless of his or her age. Her goal is to shape her children's intellectual development, taking seriously their thoughts, ideas, and questions. She enjoys watching how they absorb and use new information.

- *Teaching.* Desiring to meet her children's need to learn and know, the INTP mother is born to teach. She instills a love of learning by finding ways to build on a child's natural curiosity. Beyond tirelessly answering a multitude of questions, she enjoys leading him or her to new books, real-life experiences, or hands-on activities.

- *Encouraging independence*. The INTP mother gives her children the space they need to develop independence. Although it might be easier for her to carry out a particular task herself, she can back off and let them try to do things for themselves so they will begin to master the task. She lets her children test themselves and has high aspirations for their competency, but she seldom pushes.

- *Calmness*. The INTP mother is usually tolerant and calm, not highly critical of children's mistakes—she may see them as learning experiences! She seldom gets upset if they do something that displeases her. Her children may find her a model of patience, kindness, and fairness.

> **TIPS**
>
> - The INTP mother can benefit from setting aside regular times when she can turn inward and lose herself in reading, thought, or work. Energized by time alone to think, her "mind time" is a necessity, not a luxury. To do her best mothering, the INTP may need to get up early, stay up late, or use children's nap time to read, daydream, or gaze out the window in thought.
>
> - Believing she is different from other mothers, the INTP may feel uncomfortable if she compares herself to more traditional mothers. If she can learn to trust in her own unique strengths and enjoy her relationship with her children (rather than compare hers to other mothers'), she can boost her mothering confidence and take greater pleasure in day-to-day living.

Struggles

- *Noise and confusion of family life*. The INTP can become easily exhausted by children's nonstop chatter, constant activity, lack of self-control, and their never-ending demands for her to look, listen, and respond. She may retreat, physically and emotionally.

- *Routines*. The INTP mother is likely to struggle when a family member needs to meet a schedule. Getting young children dressed, fed, and out the door for school on time or keeping them on task for bathing, teeth brushing, and bedtimes can seem like overwhelming tasks.

- *Singular focus.* When she is focused on reading, thinking, or work, the INTP's children may feel as though they can't break through her concentration. She may worry that she seems distant and detached.

ENTJ—The "Executive" Mother

(Extraverted, Intuitive, Thinking, Judging)

"My mind is always going. How can I fine-tune the system to everyone's advantage?"

Competent and confident in a management role, the ENTJ mother organizes the needs and schedules of family members into a workable family system. Within the system, she provides her children with care-taking, direction, and limits, but she also gives them space to develop their own self-sufficiency and judgment.

Analytical and adept at problem-solving, the ENTJ mother listens to her children's concerns empathetically and then strategizes with them how to improve the situation—either by intervening on their behalf or backing off to let them solve problems on their own. She particularly enjoys watching them take responsibility and accomplish something they find important on their own.

Intense and insightful, the ENTJ mother is cued in to her children's intellectual and emotional development. She uses her quickness and communication skills to talk things through and help her children connect with people and better understand life.

Strengths

- *Commitment to a family system.* Energetic and hard working, the ENTJ mother organizes a family system designed to bring out the best in each family member. Her children feel secure that someone competent is in charge, things are in order, and their needs are being addressed fairly.

- *Fostering independence.* The ENTJ mother is focused on building her children's competence and self-sufficiency by allowing choices and autonomy within a structured family environment. She is constantly seeking the optimum balance between being directive and increasingly giving a child the freedom to make his or her own decisions.

- *Problem-solving.* The ENTJ mother is a natural strategist and teacher. She helps children of any age think through solutions to a variety of situations, pointing out options, offering her analysis and perceptions, and instilling a "can do" attitude. When appropriate, she advocates for children at school or in any system where their best interests are not being addressed.

- *In-depth conversations.* The ENTJ mother stimulates her children's intellectual development by engaging them in thought-provoking conversations. Interested in what they're thinking, she listens with respect, perception, and empathy. She uses ordinary life events to explain connections and broad meanings as well as to challenge children to think logically and analytically.

Struggles

- *Busyness.* Fast paced and tightly scheduled, the ENTJ mother finds it difficult to slow down to a "normal" pace and be flexible to changes in plans. More often than she'd like, she finds herself rushing and telling her children to "hurry up." Frequently over-scheduled and over-committed, she may worry she's not as available to her children as she'd like to be on a regular basis.

TIPS

- The ENTJ could benefit from some unstructured time for herself and her family. She needs to factor "unrushed time" into the family system. Scheduling a slow morning after a major push on a project or building in an hour of downtime midday can help her recharge with the time she needs to regroup and relax.

- The ENTJ mother needs to examine realistically—and ultimately reject for herself—the myth of the "supermom." If she can accept her human vulnerabilities and limitations, she will not only enjoy life and her children more fully, she will also avoid passing on her legacy of "perfection" to the next generation.

- *Self-criticism.* Intensely committed and wanting to be equally competent at work and family, the ENTJ mother struggles to live up to her "superhuman" expectations for herself. She may find herself constantly assessing her performance, confident about what she did well but even more self-critical when she thinks she should have done more.

- *Letting feelings "be."* The ENTJ struggles to be patient with children's feelings. She is more comfortable trying to solve the problem and getting on with things than letting children experience unpleasant feelings for a while.

Together with the eight Sensing types described in Chapter 6, these are the sixteen types of mothers and their mothering style profiles. If you've found you fit one of these profiles, no doubt your head is buzzing with thoughts of what types your husband and children might be. How can this information help you with conflicts you may have experienced with other family members? What happens, for instance, when your need for solitude clashes with your child's seemingly endless need for stimulation? Part 2 takes a look at the many dynamics of family interaction.

Dynamics of Family Interaction

"The great gift of family life is to be intimately acquainted
with people you might never even introduce yourself to,
had life not done it for you."

—Anonymous

chapter 8

· · · · · · · · · · ·

Getting Started
Using Type Day-to-Day

Congratulations! You have identified your true personality type (or made your best guess) and followed the suggested steps to verify it. You understand how your individual preferences and your personality type shape your mothering style.

You may have already experienced many "Aha!" moments. On the other hand, at this point you may be thinking, *Okay, now that I know my mothering style, what am I supposed to do with this information?*

That is what the rest of this book is all about.

Personality type is a very rich concept, once you fully grasp it. Many Extraverted mothers say they are most interested in using personality type to understand others, whereas most Introverted mothers say understanding themselves is the biggest benefit of using type. This chapter contains a potpourri of topics that will deepen your knowledge and prepare you to apply the wisdom of personality type to children, parent-child interactions, spousal relationships, and whole family dynamics.

Your Personality Core

So far we have described type differences by single preferences and four-letter types. But some two-letter type combinations display distinctive characteristics. Understanding these distinctions will help you know yourself and interact with others better.

For instance, many experts refer to the middle two letters of your type as your "personality core." Those who share the same middle letters (ST, SF, NT, or NF) will likely feel like "kindred spirits" and "on the same wavelength" even if they are different in other key aspects. They probably "see" things the same way and share many values.

My daughter Jane, for instance, is an ENFP and I am an INFJ. So we are both NFs or Intuitive-Feeling types. We both enjoy tuning in to and understanding the people around us. We readily share our feelings; we value creativity, personal expression, and open-mindedness; and we have a similar sense of humor. When we are verbally interacting we feel like two peas in a pod.

My mother, on the other hand, is an ISTJ. She and I have opposite personality cores: ST for her and NF for me. When I ask her about her feelings she thinks I'm probing and being too "psychological." She'd prefer to talk about the increase in her house taxes, what she uses to wash her bathroom walls, and how to use her new TV. In fact, she'd rather do something practical and productive than sit around talking about feelings at all. People with opposite personality cores often misunderstand each other and have difficulty finding common ground.

The Living Differences

The first and last letters of your type also present unique shared characteristics. Elizabeth Murphy, co-author of the *Murphy-Meisgeier Type Indicator for Children (MMTIC)*,[1] refs to them as the "living differences"—how you like to live with others on a day-to-day basis. For example, these preferences determine the amount of verbal interaction you prefer and how orderly you like your common living space. If you share E-I or J-P with someone, you are likely to understand each other's lifestyle and be compatible roommates.

Despite being opposite in personality core, my mother and I are both IJ types, so we enjoy this "roommate" compatibility. We both thrive in a quiet, orderly living space and need to balance time together with time alone. If our plans for the day change unexpectedly, we are thrown for a loop. We like to think about things before doing them. She and I like interacting on a predictable schedule, talking by telephone every Sunday afternoon. If something noteworthy happens during the week, we're more apt to write ourselves a reminder to bring it up on Sunday than pick up the phone and call right away.

Even though my daughter and I are both NFs, we are opposites in living differences. As an EP she loves being on the go, interacting with people, making new friends. Heaven for her is being with friends every night, but for me, several consecutive evenings of socializing leave me feeling out of balance. She, on the other hand, worries that I'm alone too much and often asks if she should stay home to keep me company. She eats and sleeps at irregular hours and doesn't mind a bedroom that to me looks messy. She sometimes wishes I would lighten up; I sometimes wish she would tighten up.

Here's another example of how our living differences factor between us. Once I was complaining to my ENFP friend how my ten-year-old daughter continued to take my scissors and tape from my desk without returning them, even after I bought her scissors and tape of her own. "It's so annoying," I told my friend, "and it feels inconsiderate and disrespectful."

"Oh, I kind of like it when my children use my things," my ENFP friend replied. "It makes me feel like we're connected." Hearing this, I realized I had to alter my IJ interpretation of my EP daughter's behavior. Her borrowing was less a sign of disrespect and more like a mother-daughter hug.

My son Dan is an ESTP and I am an INFJ; we are opposites in both living differences and personality core. One evening we were together in the kitchen when I heard my upstairs home office phone ring. As an INFJ, my reaction was, "Why is someone bothering me after work hours? Don't they know this is my family time?" My son, about ten at the time, responded like an ESTP: "If someone were calling me it wouldn't matter when; I'd be happy they were thinking of me and curious to know what they wanted."

The living differences have implications for mothering style, too. In my research, I asked mothers to rate their overall ease and fit with motherhood. Results suggested that EP mothers find mothering the easiest and IJ mothers struggle the most. EPs thrive on the process, the more the merrier, go by the seat of their pants, and feel comfortable "winging it." Introverted-Judging mothers thrive on order, quiet, and predictability. They spend most of their energy trying to have a smooth-running, organized, and calm household. Extraverted-Perceiving moms may seem overly laid-back as parents, as if "anything goes," and IJs may seem overly careful.

When I interviewed EP mothers, many told me that what they loved about being a mother was the chaos. As an IJ mother, I could hardly believe my ears!

> "I thrive on chaos. The crazier my house, the better I feel. After getting a college degree and then getting pregnant right away, I often think I should be out there working. But if it's crazy and wild then I feel worthy, like something is being accomplished at my house. Friends tell me they love coming to my house, but they love leaving, too."—*Jeannie, ESFP*
>
> "It's difficult for me as a mother. I need structure and when I impose it on the entire family, it doesn't work. I'm constantly pushing the river, instead of letting it flow by itself. I want my son to do X, and he wants to do Y."—*Molly, ISTJ*

Mothers with EJ and IP preferences tend to rate the ease of motherhood somewhere in between. Extraverted-Judging mothers may be the ultimate family managers. They structure the household, like IJ moms, but they typically have enough oomph to enforce and maintain it. One ENFJ mother held weekly meetings with her family to look at the week ahead and make a master schedule of everyone's sports practices, rehearsals, meetings, doctor's appointments, and parties. Introverted-Perceiving types are typically "live and let live" mothers. They are receptive instead of initiating, accepting instead of directing, and can seem unassertive at times. One ISTP mother says, "I don't like being controlled so I'm uncomfortable controlling others, what they do or when they do it." EJ mothers may come on too strong for IP children, and IP mothers may struggle to stand up to their EJ children.

Lessons from Other Mothers

Although helping you appreciate yourself as a mother is my first goal, many mothers say learning about mothering styles has helped them value the gifts of other mothers, too. In fact, Sue Scanlon, a mother and editor of *The Type Reporter*, tells how she has gone beyond appreciating others' styles to *imitating* them.

"I was impressed by the SJs' ability to help their children find comfort and security in traditional ways of relating to people. So I volunteered to collect dues for our civic association and brought the kids with me to meet all their neighbors. . . .

"I was impressed by the NTs' ability to help their children become competent and independent. So I stopped myself from zipping up my four-year-old daughter's jacket and let her do it herself. . . .

"I was impressed by the NFs' ability to help their children understand their feelings. I'm an NF, but I think I could stand some improvement there, especially when respecting their feelings means I have to change my plans. . . .

Living Differences in Mothering Style

EJ mom: Structures and directs her child's life to keep it on a steady course; typically the family manager, she is effective with rules and limits. She may be intrusive and put the "family plan" above her child's individual needs.

IP mom: Responds to rather than directs her child; quiet receptivity makes her a good listener. She may seem to be detached and is apt to say nothing rather than no. She may abdicate authority.

IJ mom: Provides a balance of direction and letting her child be. She is conscientious and focused. She may be inflexible and stressed-out in mothering and find it hard to balance her needs with her child's.

EP mom: Provides energy and action, and lives in the moment; she wants her child to experience the world and enjoy life. She may neglect the meat and potatoes of parenting in favor of dessert, or seem irresponsible due to a lack of follow-through.

"I was impressed by the SPs' ability to be immediately attentive and responsive to their children. The other day I put down my chopping knife and went to the window *the first time* my son called, 'C'mere mom,' to admire a leaf-vacuuming truck. . . .

"I've gone from comparing myself in a defensive way with other mothers, to using them as role models for how to incorporate their gifts into my own style. I've always felt that the best thing about psychological type is that it makes human goodness easier to understand, which makes it easier to imitate."

Other Type Shortcuts

In addition to the four temperament groups, the TJ and FP two-letter combinations describe a distinctive mothering style. Thinking-Judging mothers are firm, direct, and decisive, and tend to "take charge." Feeling-Perceiving mothers are perhaps the most responsive and accepting. FPs may view TJs' parenting style as rule-bound and insensitive. TJs may consider FPs' style permissive or wishy-washy.

I often asked mothers how much and how often they felt guilty. Some TJ moms claimed to never feel guilty. This is probably because they naturally analyze situations objectively, come to a logical conclusion, and move on. FP moms were most likely to say they often feel guilty. Perhaps this is because they make their decisions based on personal, subjective, and situational criteria. These factors are ever changing, so the FP may be constantly revisiting her decisions and second-guessing herself. For her, nothing is ever settled once and for all.

The combinations of EF and IT also have distinctive characteristics. The Extraverted-Feeling mom seems to be the most vulnerable to outside expectations and has the highest need to connect with others. The Introverted-Thinking mom seems to be the most individualistic of all types and to need the most personal space.

When Your Mother-in-Law Isn't Your Type

Now that you understand your personality core and the living differences, as well as a few other two-letter type shortcuts, you can begin to use this information to solve everyday problems. Katie, an ESTJ, explains how she used type knowledge to improve her relationship with her mother-in-law, an ENFP. Note she and her mother-in-law differ in personality core (ST versus NF), living differences (EJ versus EP), and TJ versus FP. See if you can identify how those differences play out in this situation:

"I consider my mother-in-law goofy; she thinks I'm rigid. For example, she invites us over for Sunday dinner. I tell her ahead of time the baby goes to bed at 8 p.m. To me that means the dinner needs to be served no later than 6 to give us time to eat and get back home on time. But at 7, we're still waiting for the food. I think, *How inconsiderate!* If I complain, she and my husband (also an ENFP) roll their eyes at me and ask, 'Can't the baby go to bed a little later just for tonight?' But why should the baby be inconvenienced because of her poor planning?

"She offered to baby-sit the children a few hours a week. I told her I'd like it if she came every Tuesday morning at 9:30 a.m. But at 9:45, I'd be looking at my clock wondering where she was. By the time she came, I'd be so angry, I couldn't enjoy my time away. So I told her not to come anymore. That probably hurt her feelings. Then she started calling me at unexpected times to say her next two hours were free, should she come over and give me a break? I'd be in the middle of something and couldn't just up and leave. Unless I can plan for it, baby-sitting is no help at all.

"Then I learned about personality type and mothering style. Immediately, I understood she meant well, but our differences were getting in the way of our relationship. I asked her to read both her profile (she's a teacher and already knew her type from work) and mine; then we discussed our different styles. I stopped expecting her to be like me and vice versa. Now if something comes up and I need help at the last minute, I know to call her. When I had to take my older child for stitches, she came right away to watch the baby. She now knows how important my rules are to me and makes a point of following them with the children—no candy before dinner and only an hour of TV. I really appreciate it. When we go to her house for dinner, we take two cars. That way, if dinner ends up being too late, I can politely leave with the baby and ask my husband to bring home the leftovers. We've also rescheduled our Sunday family dinners to Friday. It's easier for me to be flexible with the children's bedtimes knowing they don't have to get off to school the next morning."

Two Kinds of Balance

Within each type's dynamics there are two kinds of balance. One is a balance between taking in information and being decisive, and the other is a balance between the external and internal worlds. Good judgment begins with taking in an adequate amount of information and making a decision about that information. If you only took in information, you'd have no grounding, like a sailboat without a rudder. If you make decisions without information, you'd be a know-it-all, jumping to inaccurate conclusions. Making sure to use both of your middle two letters can improve your judgment in every situation. For example, as an INFJ I have learned to temper my inspirations (N) by evaluating them against my personal values and the effect they might have on people (F). My ESTJ friend has learned to moderate her strong opinions (T) by opening her mind to a few more facts (S). As my ESTP son has matured, he has learned to draw on his principles and priorities (T) to regulate his experiences (S).

In addition, each of us uses one of our middle two letters in the outer world and the other in the inner world. Therefore, being too active and involved with external matters can cause imbalance and poorer judgment in all types. When a difficult or important decision has to be made, "sleeping on it" for a while is a good strategy for Extraverted and Introverted types alike. This is particularly true for Introverted types, who do most of their processing internally.

Most of us can recall a time when we were in inner turmoil and reacted by frantically picking up the house or overreacting to a child's minor misbehavior. When our inner world seems out of control, we try to compensate by making order in the outer world. At times like these, it is probably wiser to stop for a moment to deal with what's going on inside rather than flail around mindlessly. In general, J types, and Introverted-Judging types especially, can increase their flexibility by giving themselves some think-time before acting. For example, if I'm busy getting dinner ready and my child asks to have a friend sleep over, my first instinct may be to say no because at that moment things seem out of control. Later, while lingering over a cup of tea, more facts or options may come to mind, and I may realize that a sleepover is fine after all.

Your Nonpreferences Add Spice

Even though they don't show up in your four-letter type, your nonpreferences are still part of your type dynamics. We call on our nonpreferences to fill in when our middle two letters can't handle a situation on their own. As an INFJ, when I have to negotiate a contract, I need help from my T side to be direct and objective, and my S side to check for thoroughness and accuracy. But using my T and S sides is so difficult and draining, it would be a strain for me to use them full-time as a lawyer would.

Some say that at mid-life, we are sure enough about who we are that we can begin to experiment with who we are not. In type language, that means you may be drawn to experimenting with and developing your nonpreferences. For many, this happens through recreation and play. For example, an absent-minded INTP professor may suddenly decide to buy a flashy red convertible (Sensing and Feeling). I've had great fun as a middle-aged INFJ using my ST side playing video and computer games. Beforehand, I'd considered them a waste of time. But after giving them a try, I became hooked for a while just like my ESTP son. It was exhilarating to experience something I'd previously considered so "not me." For each of us, there's a side that's just waiting to finally get some attention and add spice to our life.

Rare Types

Personality type is a wonderful way to understand your own individuality, but it also provides an excellent framework for understanding your identity within the larger community. If all of the sixteen types were distributed equally, each would be approximately 6 percent of the general population. However, some types are much more common than others. Six rare types for women are INTJ, ENTJ, INFJ, INTP, ISTP, and ENTP—each roughly 1–4 percent of the population.[2]

Being a mother is difficult for almost everyone, but it's even harder if you don't see things the same way as most mothers do and your point of view is not validated by mainstream culture. If you are one of these less common types, you may feel like a stranger in a strange land and lose confidence in yourself. Many women have told me that knowing that their type was just 1–4 percent of the population helped affirm their uniqueness and explain why they've often felt like "oddballs."

What's It Like Being a Rare Type?

I asked women of some of the least common personality types when they feel most different, and here's what they said:

"At parties. I'm very uncomfortable walking into a situation where I have to mingle and make small talk. Other people think a party is going to be great. I go in with visions of disaster. I worry whether I can read a situation and how I'm doing," says Julie, an INTJ.

"When I'm with a group of women who are all dressed appropriately, look alike, and are making pleasant conversation, I wonder how they all know what to wear and how to act. Conformity is such a mystery to me. I couldn't do it even if I tried," says Karen, an INTP.

Rare types often feel separate from the group, but they also have a unique ability to be okay with being different and taking a minority point of view. An ENTP admits, "I don't mind being different. I feel above people who would compromise themselves for friendship."

"Growing up, I had no need to mix with others. I needed lots of quiet time, so I learned to do things by myself. In many ways, I find being part of a group is a drawback to reaching your goals," says Julie, INTJ.

Still, some talk about having "type envy." Karen, INTP, says, "All my life I've wanted to be a different type—more organized and more popular. I often feel like I don't measure up. Women don't get positive feedback for being INTPs."

The most frequent types for American adult women are ISFJ, ESFJ, ESFP, and ISFP, all together accounting for about 55 percent of the female population.[3] These type women are most likely to feel in sync with mainstream culture. By joining the right groups, working in conventional jobs, and participating in popular pastimes, they can spend most of their time with women of similar types who share their values, communication style, and approach to life.

But what happens when a baby "oddball," with a completely different type, arrives in their lives? Often it's their love for their new unique child that motivates these women to learn about personality type differences. They often need help understanding and appreciating a child who seems so different from themselves.

Type differences can be instrumental in shaping family relationships, and the next chapters will show you how to make practical use of type in co-parenting and in parent-child interactions.

Notes

1. The Murphy-Meisgeier Type Indicator for Children is published by Consulting Psychologists Press, Inc.

2. Charles R. Martin, Ph.D. and revised by Allen L. Hammer, Ph.D. *Estimated Frequencies of the Types in the United States Population.* Center for Applications of Psychological Type, Inc., Gainesville, FL, 1996, 2003.

3. Ibid.

chapter 9

· · · · · · · · · · ·

What about Dads?

No MATTER WHAT YOUR MARITAL STATUS OR LIFESTYLE, FATHERS ARE A SIGNIFICANT part of the parenting equation. But how does personality type apply to fathers, if at all?

If you haven't already done so, talk to your partner about what you've learned about type and your own mothering style. He may even want to guess his own type. Chances are, he'll recognize himself somewhere, whether in the strengths and struggles sections of the four personality dichotomies or in the profiles outlined in chapters 6 and 7.

The reason I think he will recognize himself is because my research indicates that at least 80 percent of the MotherStyles content applies to dads. When dads read the mothering profile and preference descriptions for their own type, most said they related to the strengths and unique characteristics. Some even said, "This fits me to a 'T.'"

It's very helpful to know the personality type of your co-parent and vice versa. Not only do you each possess strengths and weaknesses as individuals, but as a parenting team you each also give your children unique advantages and experience particular struggles. Pinpointing areas of both harmony and imbalance goes a long way toward creating a stronger, happier family.

What Dads Say

To further help you and your partner understand his type, here are some comments about the fathering experience from dads with different preferences.

EXTRAVERSION

- "I'm happiest with kids who talk openly. Sitting with silence is difficult."

- "I love active, energetic games with the kids—wrestling, chasing, tickling, getting everyone riled up."

- "I should listen, but that's hard. I tend to talk first."

- "I always seem to be over-extended, unable to unhook myself from work, friends, and other commitments that take energy from family."

INTROVERSION

- "My greatest pleasure is just watching my children."

- "When their mother is around, I usually hang back and let her interact with the kids. When she's away, it's easier to develop my own relationship."

- "All I do is work and family. I have no time or energy for friends or outside interests."

- "I keep a lot inside. I wish I could interact more."

SENSING

- "I enjoy taking care of my kids—baths, washing hair, rocking them before bed."

- "I'm not the primary caregiver. I'm more involved in ball games or agreeing to buy a special toy."

- "For me, quality time is doing something together, like bowling, or apple-picking. I also like to give them some unexpected money once in a while."

- "I tend to see things as good or bad. It's hard to accept differences or shades of gray."

INTUITION

- "I love discovering what's going on in their little minds and being there when they 'get it.'"

- "I think I do a good job helping them see their life issues within a larger context."

- "My favorite times are road trips when we can spend hours making up stories and talking about our ideas and dreams."

- "It's sometimes hard for me to have realistic expectations for their age. I have to remind myself that they are little children, not adults."

THINKING

- "My favorite times are when they fight back, argue their point of view, and let me know there is a real thinking person inside."

- "The best part of being a father is watching my children become independent, strive toward goals, and do well academically."

- "I like to teach. Every outing is an opportunity."

- "Sometimes hard decisions have to be made, like discipline. I hate it when that's not interpreted as caring—because it is."

FEELING

- "I try to be open with my feelings, hoping they'll be open in return."

- "We have an intimate relationship. My daughter can talk to me, just like she does with her mom."

- "While a lot of fathers would like to devote more time to their kids—I do."

- "It's hard being the disciplinarian. Either I'm too permissive trying to be a buddy. Or I go overboard, and I'm volatile and overly punitive. I feel like a wimp or an ogre."

JUDGING

- "I'm the anchor: strong, steady, and always there. When my kids find themselves in a tough situation, they've always got me."

- "My wife sets the house rules Monday through Friday. I try to honor her authority when I'm home on the weekends, but I have other ideas on how to raise the children."

- "It's hard to switch gears from work to family at the end of the day. I do best if I give myself extra time to make the transition from 'work me' to 'family me.'"

- "I'm still learning to accept the limits of my control. It's not like work. I can't make a child do what he doesn't want to do, especially an older child."

PERCEIVING

- "I won't feel guilty that I didn't spend enough time with my kids. I might regret not spending enough on the hard stuff—like succeeding in school."

- "I'm good at getting kids to try new and different things, whether it's jumping off the diving board or trying an exotic food."

- "I don't have many rules. But when the kids don't respect the few I do have—like 'be honest'—it bugs me. And I'm not sure how firm to be."

- "Sometimes I think I'm too flexible. If I'm not careful, I find myself renegotiating curfew every night."

How Dads Differ

While you may recognize similarities between dads and moms in terms of strengths and struggles, there are, of course, also differences.

Fathers most often note different struggles compared to those experienced by mothers of their same type. A variety of cultural, gender, and role expectations may explain these differences. Mothers and fathers who are actively parenting today likely grew up with a societal and perhaps family model of mother as the primary caregiver and father as the head of household. This traditional mother role can be described by Sensing-Feeling-Judging characteristics, while the traditional father role calls for Sensing-Thinking-Judging attributes.

In trying to live up to their ideal, therefore, Thinking mothers have different struggles than Thinking fathers. Thinking mothers talk about lack of mothering confidence and work/family conflicts, whereas Thinking fathers say they can't relate to these concerns.

Similarly, Feeling fathers have different struggles than Feeling mothers. Feeling dads are not as likely as Feeling moms to wrestle with issues of over-protecting, over-giving, or over-sacrificing.

In addition, most Thinking women and Feeling men have had to develop their opposite preferences to fit in with cultural expectations of gender ("women are Feeling types and men are Thinking types"). As a result, Thinking moms often have a well-developed Feeling side that helps them be more emotionally supportive of children than Thinking dads. Similarly, Feeling fathers frequently have a well-developed Thinking side and therefore may be more able to provide objectivity and firmness than Feeling mothers.

Introverted dads also differ from Introverted mothers. Both struggle to balance their need for solitude with the family's need to interact. But because mothers are supposed to give, give, give, they tend to ignore their own need for downtime and explode later. Introverted fathers tend to meet their needs for solitude, even at the expense of having the family feel ignored.

What about the Judging function? The cultural ideal for both moms and dads favors Judging. But a Judging dad might be more J than a J mom if he spends all day in a business environment and has less hands-on experience with children. Tending children all day is apt to temper a parent's natural style of structure and control, whereas the workplace is likely to reinforce it. On the other hand, it could work the other way. If a dad doesn't consider home life his responsibility or domain of control, he may be more relaxed at home than at work and act like the "fun dad"—that is, more like a Perceiving-type dad.

A Perceiving dad may be the easy-going one, who allows mom to be responsible for home life, but then bristles when it comes to following her rules and schedules.

Mothers and fathers typically divide responsibilities within a family. Despite recent trends, mothers are usually expected to assume primary responsibility for family and home, whether they work outside the home or not. Their struggles are typically the result of trying to meet these responsibilities.

Fathers, on the other hand, are still generally expected to be the primary wage earners. Their struggles are focused on meeting that responsibility. Those dads who are stay-at-home fathers or single parents with primary responsibility for children and the home relate most closely to the complete mothering profile for their type.

Moms and dads also tend to use different models for comparison when measuring their successes. Mothers, for instance, most often compare themselves to other mothers, neighbors, co-workers, and social peers. Thinking they must match every other mother's strengths, they often feel deficient and vulnerable.

Fathers tend to compare themselves to their own dads. Given family trends over the last generation, they frequently consider themselves to be more personal and involved with their children, which enhances their sense of doing a good job.

When Mothers and Fathers Interact

Ideally, children have both a mother and father who are active parents and can co-parent effectively, regardless of whether they are married or live in the same house. Some children are also blessed to have grandparents, stepparents, siblings, aunts, or uncles who serve as co-parents.

What can type knowledge teach us about co-parenting? When parents have different preferences, children experience a home environment that is rich with a variety of personality styles. Children may be freer to explore who they are and feel the validation that comes from knowing at least one parent shares a particular preference.

For the mother and father, differences in personality type can provide perspective and balance in co-parenting. But differences can also cause misunderstandings, friction, and lack of consensus.

When parents' preferences are similar, it's easier to create a well-defined home environment. Children with similar personality types are likely to feel in sync, but children with opposite personality preferences may feel like misfits. Similarities among parents can create a harmonious, unified parenting style. But they can also reinforce weaknesses and a sense of being stuck when facing shared struggles. Sometimes we can end up resenting our like-type partners when they fail to rescue us from our own shortcomings.

Knowing your own personality type and your partner's can help you make the most of differences and be aware of common blind spots. You can learn to fill in as best you can for the other, and work together as a team . . . so you can be effective with your children. Here are some common examples of how couples of various type combinations use their differences and similarities to bring balance and strength to the co-parenting relationship.

Extraversion–Introversion: Energy, Initiative, Focus, Connection

Extraverted mother, Introverted father

Sarah and Jim are the parents of four. Sarah says, "As two NTs, we share a vision of raising the children, but we express it differently.

"For example, we both want our kids exposed to cultural events. As the Extravert I'm the one who initiates the plans and takes them to the events. Jim doesn't always participate. I'm more engaged and actively involved with the children. But Jim will bring home an unexpected gift that's just right, and I know we've been in his thoughts.

"Knowing type has helped me understand Jim's Introversion and not interpret it as rejection or not caring. I know we are present and important in his inner world, even though he may not show his caring like I would."

Introverted mother, Extraverted father

Mike says, "Sue is more of a homebody. She may share more intimate moments with our two boys, but I get them out and about.

"In addition to my job as a salesman, I coach both softball teams and have season tickets to basketball games at the local university. I also initiate father-son camping weekends with my friends. Sue's happy when we go—she gets the house to herself."

Extraverted mother, Extraverted father

Meg struggled over Extraversion-Introversion differences with her first husband, an INTP, and the father of her two daughters. "Curt was good at understanding our kids' needs for privacy and silence. But I felt there weren't enough people in our lives. Curt found all-family outings, birthdays, and holidays overstimulating."

Now Meg is married to John. "We are both busy and on the go. We both understand everyone's need for friendships, and we want all four of our kids to enjoy an active social life. We're willing to ask the family to sacrifice on behalf of friends.

"Sometimes all the busyness gets out of hand. It's hard to say no to friends, work, volunteer commitments, and other external demands. Usually one of us starts to feel resentful because we haven't had enough time together as a couple or as a family."

Extraversion–Introversion Differences and Marital Satisfaction

Extraverts need adult interaction and activity to recharge and unwind at the end of a day. Introverts crave solitude. These opposite needs may be accentuated if the E is isolated at home with small children and the I interacts with lots of people at work. Conflicts may arise if the Extraverted spouse expects more conversation and socializing than their Introverted partners are able to give. Extraverts might do well to get out with friends and leave their spouses at home every once in a while to better balance each other's needs. Or here's how one couple arrived at a compromise: "I'm an Introvert and an artist; my husband is an Extravert and a salesman. On weekends he wants to go out and I like to stay home. Art shows helped us find middle ground. He's happy being with the people, I'm content browsing the artwork."

Introverted mother, Introverted father

Julie and Scott have two teenagers. Julie says, "As Introverts, we provide a quiet, calm haven where any of us can retreat after a busy day at school or on the job. We give each person plenty of space to do his or her own thing. But it's easy to begin to feel out of touch with each other. When we do, we purposefully schedule a family outing just to do something all together."

Sensing–Intuition: Expectations, Context, Anticipation, Specifics

Sensing mother, Intuitive father

Christine co-parents with Peter. "As a big picture person, Peter keeps me from being overly focused on details. But I'm more realistic, and we need that realism to temper Peter's expectations of the children. He's not always clear about what's appropriate be-havior for a child of a particular age."

Intuitive mother, Sensing father

Bess says, "As an Intuitive, I'm better at anticipating needs and planning ahead. Harry is quick to point out what's likely to be too much. Before learning type, I resented his negativity. But now I seek his perspective as a way of making my expectations more workable."

Sensing mother, Sensing father

"As a family, we've enjoyed so many rich experiences, from fishing trips and football games to holiday celebrations with our extended family," says Frank. "But when we face a complex problem, it's hard to see a way out."

"Our son was struggling academically in high school," explains Leslie. "Both of us had been good students. So we couldn't imagine what was wrong or come up with ideas for fixing it. We felt stuck until we consulted with the school counselor."

Intuitive mother, Intuitive father

"As two Intuitive parents, Meg and I both take the long view, looking for overall trends in our children's personalities and needs," says John. "We try to react to the situation at hand within that larger context. Neither of us wants to win the battle but lose the war."

"Still, some household details don't get our attention until there's a crisis—like no food in the refrigerator and company's coming," laughs Meg. "More than once we've argued as we push ourselves to get everything done, including mowing the lawn, planting flowers, and buying a grill for a barbecue."

Thinking–Feeling: Directness, Compassion, Emotionality, Independence

Feeling mother, Thinking father

Raquel compares herself to Lou: "I'm emotional and can overreact. He's rational, cool, self-controlled, and even-tempered. Lou teaches our daughter money management and computers. I teach her how to handle sticky people problems."

"When I'm worried about our sons," explains Mary, "Charles comforts me with a rational perspective.

"We have a different approach with teachers. He's direct, and I'll do anything to avoid confrontation. If something at school is unfair, Charles is quick to call and set the situation right. We all feel protected with him."

Still, Feeling mothers say they need to smooth over what Thinking fathers say and do.

"Although he doesn't mean it," says Mary, "Charles's bluntness feels like an attack. It gives me a knot in my stomach. I try to smooth things over for the boys with softer words.

Thinking mother, Feeling father

"In our house," says Meg, "John takes the compassionate approach, and I take the just approach. I tell him he's gone too far giving the children the benefit of the doubt. He lets me know I need to back off when I'm expecting too much. We're a good sounding board for each other.

"Sometimes I think he invites dependency. He jumps in to drive our daughter to school when she's late. I'd rather encourage self-sufficiency by letting her face the logical consequences—embarrassment with teachers and a detention."

Feeling mother, Feeling father

Bess says, "Harry and I share 50/50 in everything. We make a good team. If someone cooks dinner, the other cleans up. We're equally nurturing and affectionate—lots of I love yous, hugs, kisses. We both make the kids' special events a top priority, even if it means sacrificing work.

"If I go out of town, I don't make casseroles or leave notes about after-school activities. Harry can care for the children as well as I can."

Sam has a similar point of view: "I don't see a big difference between the role of the mother and that of the father. Sure, Debbie did the breastfeeding. But I've painted my daughter's fingernails and taken my son clothes shopping for his first dance.

"I believe a natural division of labor evolves between mother and father based on tradition, individual interests, and circumstances—not gender."

Mike sees a difference, however. "Sue is the primary caretaker and homemaker. I do the fun stuff and play the 'heavy' when the kids need to be disciplined."

Thinking mother, Thinking father

"As two Thinking parents, Max and I have a lot in common," says Kate. "Neither is ashamed of being strict, putting limits on kids or encouraging self-sufficiency.

"But there are differences. Max is more direct and less inclined to consider the impact of his words. He might offend a coach with an off-handed remark. I'm more likely to tone down my critical comments or keep them to myself. Sometimes Max will see that one of the kids is hurting, but he'll ask me to deal with it."

Judging–Perceiving: Rules, Routines, Fun, Flexibility

Perceiving mother, Judging father

"Lou wants things done, and he wants them done a certain way," says Raquel. "I prefer to start projects and keep them open, following my inspirations. To compromise, we've come to this motto: 'Done is better than perfect.'"

Judging mother, Perceiving father

Kate says, "Max does fun really well, whether it's bike rides, ball games, or outings. He takes care of all the gear needed and has fun interacting with the kids. While they're playing, I'm free to get a lot done.

"We've all come to accept the fact that Max starts a lot of projects and doesn't finish them according to our timetable. At first the kids felt let down. Now they factor his style into their requests. In fact, I'm beginning to admire his way of doing things for as long as he feels like it, and no more."

Judging mother, Judging father

"With two Js for parents, our kids know how things work in our house—the rules, consequences, routines," says Bess. "Harry and I like order, and we're consistent in setting limits and providing structure. Our way of doing bedtimes, getting ready for school, or celebrating birthdays and holidays is almost ritualized. We're especially sensitive to the stress transitions cause and work hard to keep the children in a familiar routine even when we travel."

"On the downside," adds Christine, "neither Peter nor I is good at making spontaneous fun. Sometimes I realize the weekend is over and we've taken care of all our chores, but we haven't had one ounce of fun together as a family."

Perceiving mother, Perceiving father

"A household run by two Ps is different," says Jack. "Sue, the kids, and I have lots of freedom. People have said our spontaneous lifestyle seems out of control and stressful, but we love it.

"On the other hand, sometimes we lose track of time and forget things like soccer practice or getting the recycling out in time for pick-up."

"My Husband Is My Opposite Type!"

This is one of the most frequent comments I hear from women learning about personality type. However, the body of type and marriage research suggests that we are more likely to marry someone who is similar to us on at least two or three of our preferences than to marry our opposite type.[1] So why do so many women tend to view their husbands as "opposite"?

Again, gender differences play a big role. We expect men to be different than women and may look for and exaggerate our differences rather than similarities. When I first learned about type, I was surprised to discover my husband (INFP) and I (INFJ) were different on only one letter. I'd always considered us to be opposites! But then again, marriage is so intimate and demanding, perhaps even one letter type difference can become so significant over time that you end up feeling like "opposites."

Two Kinds of Compatibility

You may recall that the middle two letters of your type are sometimes referred to as your "personality core." If you are married to someone who matches you on ST, SF, NF, or NT, you are likely to think your spouse is "on your same wavelength." You probably will "see" things the same way and share many values.

Pat, married to Jim, says, "As two NTs, we share similar outlooks in raising children. Both of us take great joy in our kids' growing independence, their academic achievements, and their striving in school. But because we differ in EI and JP, I can see how our common vision gets expressed in different ways. I serve on the School Board's curriculum committee and he spends evenings on children's homework questions."

Compatibility, while it can make for marital harmony, can also cause a blind spot. Meg, ENTJ, recalls what it was like to be married to her first husband, an INTP: "Both being NTs, we were in sync. We reinforced each other's points of view and were confident in our logic and analysis. We began to believe our way was the right way. The problem was we had no NT children, and ultimately had conflicts with each child. We couldn't use each other to tap into a different point of view."

The first and last letters of your type describe "living differences"—how you like to live with others on a day-to-day basis. If you share E-I or J-P with your spouse you might feel comfort and compatibility, like good roommates do.

Christine and Peter are both Introverted–Judging, but they have different "personality cores"—Christine, Sensing–Feeling, and Peter, Intuitive–Thinking. She says, "We both emphasize responsibility, getting things done, and total commitment to the children's well-being, even it means sacrificing our own immediate needs. We both strive for a calm, orderly household, and need time alone to recharge. But I'm more sensitive to the children's feelings and tend to see things from their perspective. He is equally involved, but sticks to their physical care and household jobs."

However, sometimes the IJ similarity can be a problem. Christine says, "The burden to create fun falls to me and I'm not good at it."

Making Use of Differences

Many couples we talked to said type helps most in increasing their understanding of differences and enables them not to take things so personally. One ISTJ/ENFP couple, Lou and Raquel, learned that they were exact opposites before marrying. How do they make it work? "We give each other space to do our own thing. We seek out each other's perspectives and gifts when needed. Sometimes you feel like you've married an alien invader. But when that happens, we try to be respectful, verbalize what we're thinking, and be on the look-out for areas of commonality."

How Type Knowledge Has Improved My Marriage

- "My Introverted husband has started spending four hours alone in his little meditation room every Saturday," says Sally, ENFJ. "He says he really needs that time to rejuvenate. After thirteen years, I no longer take it personally! And he's always in such a good mood when he finishes his time alone."

- "My husband and I are the same on all dimensions but one. I'm an ISTP and he is an INTP. I like corporate jobs and he's drawn to start-ups. Understanding that this is part of his personality has made me less nervous about his entrepreneurial endeavors."

- "Knowing my husband and I are both Thinking types, I have tried to find ways to put more Feeling in our relationship. Whenever we greet each other we kiss for six seconds. (Our kids do the counting!) As frequently as I remember, I ask my husband to name one thing I could do for him that day that would make him happy. I try to remember to give my spouse at least one compliment or statement of appreciation a day. These activities may come naturally to Feeling types, but we have to work at them. They've really enhanced our relationship."

- "My husband and I have a lot in common," says Sue, ESFJ, "but he's a P and I'm a J. We have a different way of organizing our worlds and managing our belongings and schedules. Without type knowledge, I'd be prone to think he just wasn't raised right, or he's doing it just to spite me. Knowing that's just the way he is helped me accept it more. Without understanding, J and P differences can wreak havoc in a relationship."

- "My husband and I are both Ps. Now I understand why our house is a mess, and why it is always going to be a mess. Neither one of our personalities is drawn to orderliness."

- "It's really helpful for both parents to know type because then we have a common language. We now discuss issues that arise in an impersonal and more positive way."

Lou says, "When an issue comes up with our daughter, Raquel gives a hands-on, immediate response. I'm more delayed and thoughtful."

Raquel says, "Recently, my daughter was crying over her two-timing boyfriend. I got so upset over the boy being such a jerk. Lou saw the situation more simply: a young man confused about which girl he likes best. Suddenly the situation wasn't so earth shaking. His more objective perspective has a calming influence on me."

Pat, ENTP, married to Jim, INTJ, says, "When we get into an angry argument, I might threaten, 'I'm not going to talk to you anymore,' and he may say, 'If you keep arguing, I'm going to start yelling!' To me, silence is the worst-case scenario; for him, it's when things get out-of-control and overly emotional. Oddly enough, he'd probably prefer me to shut up and I'd be okay with him yelling. Our differences sometimes make me chuckle."

But they've also capitalized on their Judging–Perceiving differences. "When I'm struggling day after day to get kids to brush their teeth, use the bathroom, and put their pajamas on for bed, I'll tell Jim. He turns it into a house rule and a daily ritual—'do your three bedtime things and I'll read you a story.' What's hard for me can be easy for him, and vice versa."

Christine, ISFJ, married to Peter, INTJ, talks about how they constructively use their SF versus NT difference. "Together we make a good team dealing with the school staff. I tell him my concerns beforehand, what responses I think we'll get, and what I know about the personal histories of those involved. He'll take in all my specifics and come up with a strategy for presenting our thoughts that accounts for everyone's agenda and uses their language of budgets, administration, policy, and fairness."

Notes

1. Isabel Briggs Myers, Mary H. McCaulley, Naomi L. Quenk, Allen L. Hammer, *MBTI Manual—A Guide to the Development and Use of the Myers-Briggs Type Indicator,* Third Edition. Palo Alto: Consulting Psychologists Press, 1998. p. 240–244.

chapter 10

· · · · · · · · · · · ·

Playing to Your Child's Strengths

"Once we've accepted ourselves in the role of mother, how do we raise the kids?"—*Katy*

LIKE THIS MOTHER, YOU ARE PROBABLY EAGER TO USE PERSONALITY TYPE AS A TOOL for understanding your children, as well as your spouse and yourself. Many mothers say that as they grew in self-appreciation and confidence, they became more open and appreciative of their children's uniqueness.

Personality type gives you permission to be yourself, and therefore, it becomes easier for you to let your child become him or herself. You can play to your children's strengths and give them a break when they fall short of expectations.

Some parents believe fairness means treating every child the same. If Sue gets new shoes, then so should Aaron, even if his are still good. But to be truly fair, you need to treat children as individuals. An active Extraverted child may need to be in more classes and activities than her Introverted brother. A structured home life might make a Judging child feel secure and a Perceiving child feel restricted. Type knowledge helps you tune in to your children's individual differences and act/react to their needs accordingly.

If you've put stock in "one-size-fits-all" parenting techniques that assume all children should be treated alike, it may sound like I've just made parenting harder. But actually, the wisdom of type makes parenting easier. It's easier because ultimately it is more effective. I've heard mothers joke about how they wished their baby had come with childrearing directions, just like a new TV set. Knowing your child's personality type is the next best thing: It's like being able to see your child with X-ray vision. Type-based parenting also helps build a stronger parent-child relationship. Nothing feels more loving to children than to be understood and appreciated for who they are. A lot of teenage misbehavior is based on a child's need for a parent to see who they really are. Older children act in ways that call attention to the differences between who the parent wants the child to be and who he really is. If as parents we ignore these expressions of identity, the child will need to say it louder and stronger. We can pre-empt a lot of behavior issues simply by being open to our children as separate individuals from the start.

This chapter introduces the basics of guessing your child's type as well as several tips for raising children of different personality types.

Guessing Your Child's Type

A common question parents ask is, "How early can my child be 'typed?'" I find that many 8- to 10-year-olds are able to grasp the concepts of personality type, identify most of their own preferences, and even guess their parents' types. For younger children, parents can make useful guesses about preferences, remembering that they are hypotheses only and that some preferences become apparent before others. In fact, in the early years, you might be able to identify only one or two of your child's preferences. Often it's the areas of difference between you and your child that are the easiest to spot.

Some type experts believe signs of Extraversion-Introversion and Judging-Perceiving emerge first and are easier to guess in young children than Sensing-Intuition and Thinking-Feeling. Still, some parents say they know early on that their child has a preference for Thinking or Feeling. As more research on type and children is completed, we will start to better understand how children's preferences are expressed in the early years and how they develop over time.

Before children can express themselves well verbally, your hypotheses will be based on your observations of their behavior and your understanding of type theory. Keep in mind, however, that behaviors can spring from different motivations. For example, a preschooler may refuse to participate in one of the teacher's innovative group activities. Is that because he's a Thinking child and doesn't see the point? Or an Introvert who needs to observe others before trying it himself? Or something else entirely?

Type is great for understanding behavior but less effective at predicting it. As children mature, they can help you understand their differences by telling you how they see things and giving you the thoughts behind their actions. Take time to listen.

As you try to guess your child's type, remember that it is still developing and regardless of type he or she needs all kinds of opportunities and experiences. Be open to new information and be willing to change your hypothesis as you learn more about your child. Labeling a child, whether it's accurate or not, may limit who he or she can be. A child, or anyone, wants to be understood as a person, not merely as a type. Don't be lulled into thinking that type explains everything about a child and provides a foolproof recipe for how to raise him or her. Personality type used well enhances your understanding of your child and increases intimacy. Childrearing can go awry if a parent begins to relate to a child as an ISFJ or an ENTP, instead of as Julie or James.

Birth order, family configuration, gender, physical differences, ethnic and family culture, socioeconomic influences, intelligence, and other aptitudes all combine to create great variations among children of the same type. Keep in mind, as well, that personality type is intended for use with healthy children. It won't explain psychological disorders, learning disabilities, or pathology.

I have found the best use of type knowledge is in providing a new and more positive perspective of your child, and in helping generate new parenting approaches, particularly when the usual ones aren't working.

What Are Your Child's Preferences?

If your child is eight years or older, I encourage you to explain the concepts of personality type as presented in this chapter and ask for his or her input. Approach type as an opportunity to get to know your child better, and you will likely gain his or her interest and cooperation. If your child is younger, use the basic personality descriptions to help you guess your child's personality type. As you read through the descriptions of each dichotomy, keep a tally of your thoughts by writing your best guess of your child's type in the chart below.

Best Guess of Your Child's Type

Names	E or I	S or N	T or F	J or P
1._____	_____	_____	_____	_____
2._____	_____	_____	_____	_____
3._____	_____	_____	_____	_____

Extraversion–Introversion

Does your child burst in the door after school full of news? Or does she enter quietly, respond to questions with a simple yes or no, and head for her room?

Many Extaverted children say that until they've told someone about the events of the day, those events haven't really happened. One mother described her Extraverted child as a chatterbox with never an unspoken thought. Introverted children say they need to be alone for a while after school to recharge. After being with peers, teachers, and other caregivers all day, they don't want another conversation with mom. They might not feel like talking again until dinner or bedtime.

Extraverted children prefer to be with others rather than be alone. They may enjoy group projects and doing homework with friends. A special birthday party might involve hosting the whole class for games, music, balloons, and clowns.

Introverted children are apt to spend their time playing alone or reading by themselves, even at an early age. Their idea of a special birthday party might be to invite just one friend for pizza, a movie, and a sleepover.

When I volunteered in my children's classroom, I found some children wildly waved their hands to be called on before I'd finished asking my question and others averted their eyes hoping to be overlooked. Extraverts are comfortable speaking while they are still forming their thoughts. Introverted children may appreciate a few moments to gather their thoughts before participating.

One mother says, "When we pulled into our driveway after a two-week family vacation, my Extraverted son immediately ran down the street to see what was happening with his buddies. He was bored relating to the same four people. My Introverted son went to his room and shut the door. Doing everything as a foursome for two weeks had deprived him of the privacy he needs." Some people confuse Introversion with shyness. Keep in mind, according to psychologist Jerome Kagan of Harvard University, "Shy people are more likely to be Introverts, but Introverts are not all shy."[1]

One more caveat: When children turn into teenagers identifying their preferences may be a little confusing. Some mothers report that their Extraverted children start acting like Introverts at home, retreating to their rooms for privacy. Others are surprised to see their Introverted children spending so much time with peers. Adolescence is a time for your teen to begin separating from you and experimenting with new identities.

> ## Introverted Kids
>
> Most of the early development of Introverted children will be inward-oriented and somewhat hidden. They might not be able to put themselves "out there" like their Extraverted peers until a much older age. Many parents worry, most of the time unnecessarily, about their Introverted children fitting in with Extraverted norms. "My Introverted child dazzles me with his observations and insights," says one mother, "but he clams up in the classroom." Don't lose faith in an Introverted child who may simply be a "late bloomer." Introverted youngsters might not achieve maturity and competence in their Extraverted side until they are adults.

Sensing–Intuition

Sensing children are hands-on learners. Until they've had direct experience, it isn't quite real. They tend to be literal, needing accuracy and trusting the facts. If dad suggests his Sensing daughter was ten minutes late for dinner, she'll likely respond that she was only nine minutes late.

A Sensing fifth grader complained about a school assignment—he was to make up a fictional country, draw a map, and then answer questions based on his map. "To me this is a complete waste of time. It isn't real. How will they know if the answers are right or wrong? I'd rather work with a real country and real map." His Intuitive friend, on the other hand, loved the assignment and went all out creating a country of his dreams.

> Says one Intuitive mother, "When my ten-year-old Sensing daughter got pneumonia, she loved carefully sorting her medications and keeping track of which pills she takes every four, six, and eight hours. She did a more accurate job than I could."

Sensing children may prefer reading nonfiction, biographies, encyclopedias, game manuals, newspapers, and magazines over fiction. If a friend suggests turning a bus seat into a magic carpet, the Sensing child may respond, "There's no such thing."

Sensing children often take pleasure in little things—details on a miniature doll, putting on a favorite shirt still warm from the dryer, or the smell of a new spring morning.

Without as much concern for what's real, Intuitive children enjoy coming up with new ideas and imagining. They may relish making up a story from a picture or pretending the closet is a treasure cave.

"My Intuitive stepdaughter decided to publish a family newspaper, *The Tiddledy Winks News*, and had great fun writing stories for the first issue," reports one mother. "She later dropped it when her interest turned to another inspiration—starting a business creating greeting cards on the computer."

Intuitive children often prefer school assignments that let them be original, such as illustrating a poem, creating a board game, or choreographing a dance. Sometimes, however, they struggle with the practicalities and end up with something that falls short of the initial vision.

Intuitive children might not be aware of their surroundings or the here-and-now, going through the day like an "absent-minded professor" and forgetting such necessities as lunch or bus money. They tend to be book learners, focusing on the big picture and abstract concepts rather than needing as much direct experience and facts as Sensing children.

Thinking–Feeling

Thinking children ask lots of "how" and "why" questions. They need to know the reasons behind questions and requests, not to mention the logic of how things work. Teachers have to earn the Thinking child's respect through fair rules, impartial consequences, not playing favorites, and being knowledgeable. Motivated by achievement and competition, Thinking children tend to measure their performance by objective standards and accomplishments.

The Thinking child's interest in principles and truth can make him or her a good debater, assertively and objectively arguing a critical point. One grandmother told her Thinking grandchild she had to get her parents' permission if she wanted to stay the night. The girl responded, "Great! I love arguing with my parents."

Thinking children tend to show love through concrete actions and responsibility, rather than "mushy" talk. They may back off if others appear overly affectionate, and they may avoid or cut short discussions of feelings.

Though they do not intend to be unkind, their bluntness and often unawareness of feelings can sometimes offend or hurt. One Feeling mother relates this story: "While traveling on business in China, my husband called home to say hello. As I passed the phone to my Thinking son, I mentioned the call cost about $2 a minute. Then I over-heard him say to his dad, 'Why don't we hang up now and you give me the money you would have spent on my part of the phone call.' Without knowing type, I would have thought *how uncaring*, but instead I just laughed."

Feeling children are people-pleasers, seeking praise, feedback, and the feeling of being special. They are motivated by relationships and the desire to be helpful and well liked. Interested in getting along with others, they may avoid conflict. Most re-port an inability to work well in friction-filled situations. A friendly dinnertime debate may sound like fighting to a Feeling child and dampen his or her appetite.

For Feeling children, praising the deed is the same as praising the child. One Feel-ing child came home from softball practice saying the coach liked her. When asked why she thought so, she responded, "Because he said I was a good hitter."

The opposite is true as well. If Feeling children believe a teacher doesn't like them, they'll be distracted from the learning at hand. Feeling children need plenty of affec-tion, acceptance, and closeness to flourish.

Judging–Perceiving

Judging children need structure, limits, and routine to feel secure. When they wake up in the morning, they might ask mom or dad what the plan for the day is. They like to know what to expect and when.

Flexibility is hard for a Judging child. A preschooler may have a temper tantrum if activities don't go as planned or the baby-sitter fixes lunch differently than mother usually does. Transitions can be especially stressful, whether it's changing activities or welcoming a new sibling. Judging children often need preparation and extra time to adapt to changes.

Doing things the "right way" is important to Js. So they'll want to know the rules. Adults might be impressed with their responsibility and maturity, but friends consider them bossy if they try to make everyone adhere to rules or do things the right way.

Judging children are generally on time and organized. Deadlines are stressful, so they tend to work steadily to avoid a last-minute crisis. They prefer to finish their work before feeling free to play.

Perceiving children thrive on freedom and spontaneity. They don't like waking up to hear that the day is all planned for them. They prefer to go with the flow, doing what they want when they want and being open to opportunities as they arise.

The very routine that makes a Judging child feel secure can make a Perceiving child feel tied down. As one child asked, "When Justin drops by at 5:30 with a great new video game, why do we have to stop for dinner if I'm not hungry?"

Gifted at living in the moment and enjoying life as it happens, Perceiving children are naturals at trying new things and adapting to the unexpected. They are generally tolerant of others. Friends say they're fun-loving and laid back, but parents often worry about lack of follow-through and organization. Work and play go together, and they try to make their work fun (expect a water fight when they wash the car).

More process- than product-oriented, Perceiving children typically wait until the last minute to do school assignments or handle their responsibilities. Fast-approaching deadlines can produce a burst of energy, focus, and productivity. One ENTP thirteen-year-old boy explains, "It's more important to me to know I have the capacity to do an assignment than actually doing it. If I have one hour of homework, why does it matter if I do it first or last?"

Using Type in Parent-Teacher Conferences

Understanding my children's personality types has helped me be a better advocate for them in the classroom. At my son's third grade parent-teacher conference, for instance, the teacher complained about his inability to stand quietly with the other boys when the class lined up at the door for another activity. In my mind, this behavior was directly related to my son's preferences for Extraversion, Sensing, and Perceiving; he was most apt to show inappropriate behavior when structure and stillness were required.

First, I explained to the teacher Dan's need for action and movement and asked if she could provide more kinesthetic opportunities for Dan to burn off energy. Maybe she could ask Dan to lead a game of Simon Says or follow the leader with the kids while they waited for stragglers to join the line. The teacher was willing to give it a try.

Then, back home, I had a talk with Dan. His first response was, "It's not my fault." Knowing he was a Thinking type, I said, "Of course, it isn't *all* your fault. But what percent do you think *is* your fault?"

"About 60 percent," he answered.

"So let's just focus on the 60 percent that is under your control. What are three things you could do at school to improve your behavior during line-time?"

We tossed around ideas and finally arrived on a plan. We agreed that if he could follow the teacher's rules for three weeks he could have a reward. Perceiving children like to be rewarded with freedom. The reward he requested was a special dinner, made just for him, and he could decide whenever he wanted it. I laughed. Apparently abiding by my set times for family dinners and having to eat what was put in front of him made him feel restricted rather than secure. I agreed to his request, thinking I was getting off pretty easily. A month later, after a good report from his teacher, Dan requested his reward: homemade lasagna served at 10 p.m. I happily complied.

My other child is a Feeling type; her fourth grade teacher was a Thinking type. She held the children to high standards and tended to be short on praise. In fact, my daughter thought her teacher didn't like her. When I went for a parent-teacher conference, the teacher expressed concern about Jane's poor attitude and reluctance to participate. I explained to her teacher that some students are motivated by competition or accomplishing goals, but Jane was motivated by the relationship. She does her best work and tries to live up to expectations when she thinks the teacher likes her. I asked if she would be willing to try to improve her relationship with my daughter by having a brief personal interaction with her at least once a day. It could be a compliment ("That's a nice dress"), a question showing personal interest ("What did you do over the weekend?"), or a request for help ("Would you please take the attendance sheet to the office?"). Within a week or two, Jane was coming home happy and enthusiastic about school.

Sometimes a teacher with a different style than yours might be a bonus for your child. One ENTJ mother with an ENFP child realized her son did best with a teacher who was more touchy-feely and relaxed than she was. Instead of trying to impose her standards on the teacher, she consciously backed off and appreciated the teacher for giving her child something she was not able to give. Similarly, a mother may purposely hire an in-home childcare provider whose style complements and offsets the weaknesses of her own style.

Tips for Raising a Child with a Preference for . . .

Extraversion

1. Allow play and socializing after school and before bed or naptime. Extraverts need people time before starting homework and winding down time before falling asleep.

2. Make a conscious effort to hear about the Extravert's day when he or she comes home from preschool, football practice, a party, or summer job. They need talking time to process the events of the day.

3. When you need to discuss something important, try talking together while doing something—taking a walk or drive, planting a garden, or eating at a restaurant. Early on, my best talks with my young Extraverted son occurred while he was swinging. As a teenager, a late-night walk together helped him open up.

4. Include extended family, friends, and their families for family get-togethers. Young Extraverts enjoy social networks beyond their immediate family and the energy of other people in their homes. For them, more is usually merrier.

Introversion

1. Allow time alone after school, day care, or other activities. Introverts need privacy and downtime to regroup before doing homework or continuing with the next scheduled activity. In fact, bedtime or dinner might be a better time to check in with your Introverted child, rather than right after school. He or she will be better able to talk about the day having had some time alone to process it.

2. Instead of starting conversations with a question, invite an Introvert to listen to your thoughts first.

3. Realize silent companionship is relationship-building with Introverts. You don't have to constantly fill in quiet moments with talk.

4. Try written communications. Say what's important in a note. Have your young Introvert do the same—suggest he or she write you a letter. One family kept an open journal in the front hall, so members could jot down their thoughts and suggestions and respond to others' entries.

Sensing

1. Supplement directions with details, examples, and specific how-tos. A global directive like "research your report" will not produce note cards and a bibliography. And "clean your room" will not be as effective as "Empty your wastebasket, vacuum under the bed, put dirty clothes in the hamper." In the words of a ten-year-old ESTP girl: "When my mother tells me to clean up my room, I pick up

one piece of clothing and put it down the shoot. After all, she didn't say clean up everything in the room, so maybe one item will satisfy her."

2. Teach a Sensing child through hands-on, direct experiences. Provide real-life experiences to supplement or clarify book learning at school.

3. Engage the Sensing child's senses when making a point—let them taste, smell, and feel your message if you can. Ask him or her to repeat what you've said.

4. Realizing a Sensing child can get stuck in "what is," play the "what if" game for new ideas: "What if you miss the bus home, what can you do?" "What if you're locked out?" Debrief experiences: "What could you have done? If it happens next time. . . ."

Intuition

1. Expect bursts of productive energy and inspired activity followed by extended periods of doing nothing and showing no interest in much of anything.

2. When there's a project to be done, start with the big picture and don't offer too many details. Be able to answer questions about specifics as the project unfolds.

3. Know that an Intuitive is attracted to many new ideas and possibilities, but don't expect him or her to follow through on everything, whether it's activities or friends.

4. Give Intuitive children the time and space they need to play with ideas and dream, no matter how unrealistic or absurd. Wait until the initial inspiration cools before helping them be more realistic.

Thinking

1. Respect a Thinking child's need to know why by giving the reasons behind your requests and decisions. "Unload the dishwasher now because I want the kitchen cleaned up before cooking dinner." "I'm letting you borrow the car because I trust your judgment."

2. Ask for even the young Thinking child's help when problem-solving family issues, both large and small. When rules are broken, plans are changing, or be-

havior needs correcting, ask what he or she thinks would be fair or a reasonable solution.

3. Motivate with goals and objective rewards, such as points, prizes, or special privileges.

4. Provide opportunities for a Thinking child to practice independence and self-sufficiency.

Feeling

1. Realize a Feeling child is motivated by the relationship. He'll play his best softball if dad is the coach. She'll write her best story if she thinks the teacher likes her.

2. Appreciate and support a Feeling child's efforts to bring the family together and create happy times. Give plenty of praise, compliments, and positive feedback. Don't expect a Feeling child to know he or she did well or is loved without hearing it from others.

3. Meet a Feeling child's needs for dependency and closeness early on. Staying longer with a clingy preschooler may make separation easier in kindergarten.

4. When you want to correct behavior, sit close, hold his or her hand, and make sure he or she feels loved before you address the problem. Do it gently.

Judging

1. Provide household structure, even if it's just one or two routines a day, to help your Judging child feel grounded and comfortable.

2. Begin the day by telling your child about any plans, even if they are sketchy or still in process. "You have a piano lesson at 4:30, and I'll be at Aunt Mae's all afternoon."

3. Give a Judging child something to control to develop planning and organization skills rather than always following your plan. Do it his or her way, when appropriate.

4. Reward a Judging child with more responsibility and more authority.

Perceiving

1. Allow your Perceiving children free time after school to unwind. Be careful not to over-structure their time.

2. Factor playtime into any task. Perceiving children need time to explore and have fun while working. It may take twice as long as you think it should to complete a task.

3. Help them anticipate the day ahead. Ps live life "in the moment" and don't naturally plan ahead like Js. One father's solution to forgotten homework was to anticipate every class for the next day together with his daughter and put everything she needed in her backpack before bed. "First period is Reading, what do you need to bring?"

4. Limit their options when making choices. One mother let her child choose what to wear, but limited her choices to one drawer of T-shirts and sweatpants. Another learned to set time limits: "You have five minutes to choose the toy you want to buy."

Parenting Perceiving Kids in a Judging World

Raising a Perceiving child in a society that overvalues Judging attributes can be tricky, and sometimes even worrisome.

Around 75 percent of the mothers who attend my mothering styles programs have the preference for Judging. They have grounded their lives in purposefulness, plans, and "to do" lists. They feel responsible for guiding and shaping their children and who they become. Most Js don't understand or value the strengths of the P mindset and motivation. It feels foreign and undependable to them as a way to get through life, so it's difficult to honor or trust the Perceiving way for their children. One Perceiving mother summed up the P way like this: "I like to meander toward goals. But I end up accomplishing lots."

But even Perceiving parents sometimes worry about their P children. It's a Judging world out there, after all. They wonder, "How can I teach my child to meet external expectations without negating who he is?"

As type develops, these children learn through trial and error how to provide the right amount and type of structure they need to be effective and meet their own expectations in life. In the early years, it's appropriate for the parent to provide the structure and limits that are missing in the child's type make-up and keep expectations for J-type behavior modest. As children mature, parents can gradually withdraw support and expect them to regulate themselves on their own. It's important to help a child cope with Judging expectations without giving them the message that who they are is wrong.

Here are some additional tips to help you keep that balance:

- *Tidy-up together.* Setting a big mess in order can be overwhelming to a Perceiving child, not because of the physical effort but because it requires making lots of decisions: Where does this toy piece go? Should this paper be thrown away or saved? Is this shirt ready for the laundry or can I wear it again? You'll have more success (and even some fun and togetherness) cleaning side-by-side with your Perceiving child. You provide the model of sorting, ordering, and breaking the job into specific tasks. Let them do most of the labor. Ps are less inclined toward tidiness partly because it requires their nonpreference of Judging, but they also may prefer their disorderly room to an orderly one. Js need external order to function effectively but Ps can function well without it. One J mother says, "After a major spring clean, I asked my P son how he felt about his clean and orderly bedroom. He responded, 'Good, but unnecessary.' For me, it's the opposite. A tidy room is necessary and also good."

- *Forget chore charts and ask for help as needed.* In one family, a child had to do ten "deeds" to earn a weekly allowance. Whenever the dishwasher needed unloading or the table set, the mother would ask, "Who wants to earn a deed?" Usually, her Perceiving child would come running. But one Judging mother voices a common complaint: "Whenever I ask him to take out the garbage, he asks if he can do it later and then forgets. It takes more energy to keep the situation open and risk not getting it done than just doing it myself." A solution? Put it in writing. Try a note on his pillow that says, "Take out garbage before you go to bed."

- *Limit expectations of follow through to only the most important.* Perceiving children get pleasure from starting projects and sampling a variety of experiences—playing the piano, going to Brownies, ice skating, being with a new friend—without the expectation of finishing and sticking-to-it that Js assume. Parents don't want their children to grow up to be quitters, but it's inappropriate to expect P children to follow through on every beginning. Identify your minimum requirements for them and then expect follow-through in only those most important areas. One J mom says, "I expect her to catch the school bus every day, do homework on time, be prompt for dinner, and keep wet towels off the floor. But it's her choice about continuing with violin or softball."

- *Motivate Perceiving children through their other preferences—F, T, S, or N. Reward them with freedom.* Unlike Js, Ps aren't motivated by the joy of "getting it done." If you want them to do something, motivate them through their other preferences. FPs are motivated by the relationship. Tell them how it would make you happy, help you out, or let you be together. TPs are motivated by competency, independence, and fairness. Give them the reasons why, tasks that challenge, and an atmosphere of mutual respect. SPs want fun and variety. Make it into a game or an adventure. NPs love possibilities. Point out where the task could lead, put it into the context of the bigger picture.

- *Reward your Ps for a job well done and compliance to the schedule with blocks of freedom and a break from the routine.* One J mother motivated her P son to follow his teacher's classroom structure by letting him be the boss of how he spends Saturday. "It worked like a charm," she said. "He obeyed the teacher all week and then spent Saturday in his pajamas, eating pizza for breakfast and cereal for dinner."

- *Allow for productive failure.* All children have to learn how they work best to accomplish an assignment under a deadline. Letting them miss a deadline or fail early on might be the best way to help them find their own way of succeeding. Ps often prefer working under pressure, in a flurry of activity, and with a burst of energy. Procrastinating until the last minute is one way they create the burst of energy they need. Viewed from a J perspective, it seems stressful and wrong. But to a P it probably isn't. As a parent, you can work with children to determine what the last minute really is. If a report is due Monday, and Sunday is spent at Grandma's house, then the last-minute it needs to get done is Saturday night.

Is It Misbehavior or Personality?

Despite good intentions and type awareness, no one can know what's going on inside another person day in and day out.

One time I asked my son to vacuum our family room and reminded him that our new dog was afraid of the vacuum. When I heard the vacuum motor humming away in the next room, I assumed all was well. But when I walked in I couldn't believe my eyes. He was vacuuming the dog! After a few deep breaths, I regained my composure enough to ask him what in the world he was thinking. With a quivering lip, he explained his reasoning. If the dog was afraid of the vacuum and he vacuumed him, the dog would learn there was nothing to be afraid of. Because my son is an ESTP and learns best by direct experience, he assumed the dog did, too.

So when you've come to a negative conclusion about a child's behavior—"She's doing it to irritate me," or "He doesn't care"—take time to check it out. "This is how I'm interpreting your behavior. Is that correct? Or is there something else going on I should know about?" Often what parents consider misbehavior makes sense when the full story comes to light in the context of the child's personality type. You may discover that your child is simply acting according to his or her nature, not defying your authority or purposefully pushing your hot buttons. That understanding may help you relax and find win-win solutions to troublesome issues.

With less verbal or younger children, or simply to get another point of view, you might want to ask an adult who has personality preferences similar to your child to help you understand your child's perspective. Two of my friends have children who are INFJs like me. From time to time they've solicited my insights, asking, "Did you ever do this as a child?" I enjoy sharing my thoughts. Each of us is a type expert when it comes to how best to raise a child of our own type. Therefore, I encourage you to use friends and relatives with types similar to your child as resources. In fact, children benefit from seeing and interacting with adult models of their own preferences. If you and your spouse don't share your child's preferences, you might want them to spend some time with adults who do. It can help them validate and learn more mature expressions of their personality. It may also be reassuring to you. If a friend or an uncle is your child's type, and they turned out OK, chances are your child will too.

You're Grounded!

Two widely used disciplinary tactics, "time out" for younger children and "grounding" for teens and pre-teens, make sense from the perspective of type dynamics. Taking a breather from outside activities can help parents and children alike improve their good judgment. So stop regarding them as punishments, and think of them as tools to help restore and develop balance.

When my young son hit his sister or acted out-of-control, I would call a time out, for both of us. He would go to his room for fifteen minutes and I would go to mine. A time out gave me a few moments to gather my thoughts and look at what was happening from another perspective. My son, too, gained self-control and equilibrium by withdrawing for a while. When we came out of our rooms a few minutes later, it was as if we were two new people. I was filled with increased clarity on how to handle the situation and he was calmer and more rational.

As the children grew older, I gravitated to "grounding" as my favorite way to correct their behavior. If they ignored a curfew or pocketed a few dollars from our wallets, I figured they had become "ungrounded" from our family values and their own good judgment. I thought some time away from friends and activities, and more time alone and with the family, would help them become "grounded" again in their higher judgment and best selves.

In fact, there were a few times I'd overhear them tell their friends, "Sorry, but I'm grounded until Monday morning," even though I hadn't restricted them. As teen-aged EPs, pretending to be grounded allowed them to stay home without losing face. Later, as they matured, they learned to say no to peers more directly.

Differences and Similarities in Your Style and Theirs

Once you understand your child's personality type, as well as your own, it's natural to wonder about how your differences and similarities influence your parent-child interactions. The next chapter explains typical joys and pitfalls for each of the different parent-child combinations. I think you'll discover that many of the frictions in family relationships can be improved by taking a type perspective. In fact, you may end up appreciating the very qualities that used to drive you crazy.

Notes

1. Sandra Marquez, Mimi Murphy, Sora Song, and Cindy Waxer, *Time* magazine, April 4, 2005. p. 51.

chapter 11

· · · · · · · · · · · ·

Using Type to Make Sense of Parent-Children Interactions

Is your child a dreamer, while you value common sense? Are you eager to get out of the house but your child prefers to stay home? Does your child have a meltdown over unexpected changes, while you love surprises? Clashes like these are often due to parent-child personality differences.

Raising a child who has a very different mindset and approach to life can be a challenge, to say the least. Opportunities to misunderstand and misjudge each other abound. Even the smallest everyday events can cause mix-ups. For example, I dropped off my grade-school aged son, an ESTP, at the library one Saturday while I did some errands. We agreed I'd be back to pick him up at 1:00. I expected him to be waiting in the lobby, looking for my car, and running out as soon as I pulled up. As an INFJ child, that's what I would have done, so I naturally assumed he would do the same.

When I arrived, he was nowhere to be seen. I was surprised and confused. Did he lose track of time? Did he wander into some nearby shops? I parked the car and started searching for him, a little worried and a little angry. Finally, I located him among the stacks of books reading, without a care in the world. "It's past 1:00, why aren't you in the lobby looking for me?" I asked, perturbed.

"Oh, I thought 1:00 was just an estimate and you'd come find me when you were ready."

Without the perspective of type, I'd be thinking my son was irresponsible, inconsiderate, and maybe just plain mindless. My way was right, and his way was wrong. With the wisdom of personality type, however, I began to understand how our different mindsets had yielded very different expectations. As an ESTP, he gave me the flexibility he would have wanted in the same situation. It never occurred to *me* that he wouldn't be waiting in the lobby, and it never occurred to *him* that I was keeping myself to a tight schedule so I would be back at a set time.

It wasn't a question of wrong or right. Both approaches had merit. With an understanding of personality differences, I learned to make my expectations more explicit and we'd try to find a way that worked for both of us.

If we approached this ordinary situation with entirely different expectations, how differently are we apt to approach bigger issues, like communication, intimacy, and life goals? Raising a different type child requires more mindfulness, attention, and energy. Yet, you don't have to be completely opposite personalities for different expectations to cause problems between parents and children. Sometimes a difference on even one dichotomy can cause friction or flare-ups.

Lying . . . or Imagination?

Diane recalls listening to a call-in radio program that focused on parenting issues. A mom called in, distraught about her young child's habit of lying. "He's constantly making up stories that aren't true," the mom said. "I keep disciplining him for lying, but it doesn't seem to help. He needs to know the difference between reality and lies." As the mom talked more, it was clear that the "lies" were simply evidences of a very strong imagination.

Diane, an Intuitive type, couldn't help wincing. To her it was clear that here we had a mom with a very strong preference for Sensing and a child with a very strong imagination and preference for Intuition. If only the mom could understand that her little boy was not lying (as in, giving an untruthful answer to a direct question), but exercising his imagination.

Unfortunately, the "parenting expert" on the radio show also did not understand this distinction, and gave the mother advice on how to help her child discern reality.

As an Intuitive child who grew up among Sensing people and who felt misunderstood much of the time, Diane felt sympathy for the little boy, and hoped that somehow his imagination would not be stifled. Even though Intuitive children may prefer their rich fantasy life to reality, they seldom have trouble distinguishing between the two. A Sensing mom may not understand the need for the stories, but she doesn't have to feel threatened by them.

When Parents and Children Interact

Most misunderstandings, worry, and mistrust occur in families when a parent and child have different type preferences. When parent and child experience personality differences, parents often fear something is "wrong" with the child and find it difficult to be approving and nonjudgmental. The child's self-esteem may begin to suffer. Differences can produce feelings of superiority or inadequacy—"Either my way is right and his is wrong, or he's right and I'm wrong."

In a sense, a child with different type preferences represents the undeveloped or untrustworthy parts of our selves. Because their way wouldn't work for us, we think it isn't likely to work for them either.

When raising a child who is different, a parent must make an attempt to look for the strengths of a child's style and give him or her permission to be who he or she is meant to be. Parent and child can work toward accommodation and compromise when it's important. Keep in mind, however, that as the parent you are more mature (although sometimes it may not seem like that!) and your personality is more developed. So, you may be more capable of bending to the child's needs rather than the other way around.

Yet, be careful not to lose track of your own needs and style. A mother who is constantly bending over backward to meet the demands of her child is apt to lose her balance. Mutual respect and negotiation is the ideal.

When I first became a mother, I believed that good mothers meet their children's every need. So I gave my Extraverted-Sensing son the constant interaction and experience he wanted. We spent most of each day out-and-about, doing, talking, touching, looking, being with others, and going from one activity to another. After a while I began to feel like he was sucking the very life out of me. I'd do, go, interact beyond my natural limits, explode, and then feel guilty afterward. Type knowledge helped me learn to retreat to time by myself before I turned into the "Introverted mother from hell."

When parent and child share the same preferences, there is a special bond, understanding, and compatibility. Communications are usually easier. Still, parents must be warned about seeing their own weaknesses in their child. One Extraverted mother says, "My husband is less tolerant of Emily's Introversion than I am because his own Introversion has caused him pain in life. He can't accept himself, so it's hard for him to accept Emily." Some parents say they can be hypercritical with a child who seems to have the same shortcomings. They may try to fix or heal those problems in the child rather than in themselves. Yet, it is unrealistic to expect a child who is immature and still developing to perfect the limitations that you still struggle with as an adult.

There is also the danger of stepping on each other's toes or reinforcing weaknesses. An Intuitive-Feeling mother and daughter may each want to write the most creative toast for a niece's wedding. A Sensing-Thinking father and son might align themselves against a Feeling wife/mother who wants to discuss feelings.

Knowledge and use of personality type can help families move beyond power struggles, win-lose dynamics, and getting kids to "shape up." It can help parents create a family environment where differences are respected and each person is allowed to develop and follow his or her own path. The issue becomes: "You're that way, I'm this way, and we love each other. How are we going to work it out?" With an understanding of type, your task is to give your children the benefit of your experience, perspective, and skills without giving them the impression that their natural way is wrong or undependable. It can be a tricky balance at times, but one worth striving toward.

> "The most important thing I learned was to accept my Introverted child the way he is and don't impose my lifestyle on him." —*an Extraverted mother*

On the positive side, you may admire the ways your child is different from you: "Chris is so outgoing; I could never be so comfortable with people," or, "Stephanie is so imaginative, I don't know where she gets it."

Perhaps you will even learn from your children! Raising my opposite type son has taught me the value of an entirely different approach to life, which has enriched my own. For example, I tend to be a worrier. I worry about doing it right, getting it done on time, and the possibility of things going wrong. Through a Sensing-Perceiving example, Dan has modeled for me a more relaxed approach to uncertainty. One evening while we were out walking, he explained to me, "I know you worry. Sometimes I know it would be appropriate for me to worry too, but I just can't seem to get it going. Like now, I know you're worried that I've lost all my sweatshirts. But I think, *Why worry? I'm not cold tonight, and if I do get cold maybe one will turn up.*" Little by little, I began to imitate his ability to go with the flow and enjoy peace in the moment. In this way, you might discover that your challenging child is really a gift.

Your children will become their best selves when you turn down your Judging side ("I'm right; I'm in control") and turn up your Perceiving side (acceptance and understanding). Although it's true that we bring the wisdom of maturity to the parenting experience, no one knows what's best for another in every situation. Too many of us treat our children as projects to manage, control, and direct, or as problems to fix.

In many ways a child is like a seed: each one holds the innate potential to grow, flourish, and blossom in its unique way. There's no sense trying to shape a lily into a rose. Similarly, a parent's responsibility is like that of a gardener. Instead of trying to make a plant grow, the gardener tries to provide the right mix of soil, sun, water, and nutrients, then waits patiently for the flower to unfold.

Your child's personality develops through practice. To become the person he or she is meant to be, each child needs an opportunity within the family to express and use his or her preferences.

Extraverted Parent–Introverted Child

The Extraverted parent often questions what's wrong with an Introverted child. Worried that the young Introvert doesn't have enough friends, spends too much time alone, and isn't interested in joining groups or organized activities, the Extravert wonders if the child is depressed or suffering from a physical illness. Extraverted parents can wear themselves out trying to get an Introverted child to perk up, join in, and have a social life.

The Introverted child may feel her parents are too intrusive, pushy, and always "in my face." Hounding can make her feel inadequate. One Introverted adult tells how his Extraverted mother was so worried about his lack of friends that she considered adopting a child: "She saw it as a way of providing me with the company she thought I so desperately needed but couldn't get on my own. It made me feel like a real loser."

On the plus side, many Introverted children talk about how Extraverted parents are a help speaking for them in uncomfortable situations, teaching them how to meet people, and introducing them to new kids in the neighborhood.

Introverted Parent–Extraverted Child

When an Introverted parent raises an Extraverted child, it is often the parent who feels inadequate and energyless. An active preschooler who wants constant interaction with mom can push the Introvert beyond her limits to the point of suddenly exploding, surprising them both by her quick change of demeanor. Introverted parents may criticize older Extraverted children for what they consider "unnecessary talking," whether in the car or watching a movie.

Extraverted children often describe an Introverted parent as too distant. The parent may be physically present but so lost in his or her own thoughts that the child finds it hard to break through and get his or her attention. Extraverted children also report worrying about an Introverted parent's isolation. The child may feel torn when accepting a social invitation knowing it will leave mom at home alone. Extraverted children want their parents to have friends, belong, and be with them as part of a group.

On the plus side, Extraverted adults say they appreciate the distance and privacy their Introverted parent gave them during the teen years.

Sensing Parent–Intuitive Child

Sensing parents see an Intuitive child's dreamy, uneven ways and wonder how he will ever make it on his own. They may see their role as giving an Intuitive a dose of reality—calling attention to careless mistakes and asking detailed questions about how he intends to find the time to accomplish his big idea or pay for it.

S–N and Intelligence

Sensing and Intuitive types define intelligence differently. A Sensing mother may discount her Intuitive child's insights and grasp of major themes if a report is messy or full of typographical errors. Likewise, an Intuitive father may make a Sensing child feel slow if she can't follow his quick transitions of thought, needs more time to absorb facts, or remembers the details of a lesson while forgetting the main idea. As they grow, Intuitive children may be frustrated with parents who are too literal and conservative, and a Sensing child may find it difficult to trust parents' Intuitive leaps.

The Intuitive may misinterpret his Sensing parents' involvement as "throwing a bucket of cold water on all my ideas." While Sensing parents might diligently show their love by managing a child's physical needs, the young Intuitive may discount those efforts, not noticing what they've done or realizing how much time it takes. One Intuitive tells how she noticed a bathtub ring at college and assumed the water was different in her dorm than at home. She had been oblivious to the daily scrubbing her Sensing mother gave the tub.

On the positive side, Intuitive children say they are often overwhelmed by the practicalities of implementing an idea and value a Sensing parent's help—typing a story, sewing a Halloween costume, or purchasing ingredients for a surprise birthday cake.

Intuitive Parent–Sensing Child

Intuitive parents resist focusing on the practicalities of day-to-day living, causing some Sensing children to feel ungrounded and wonder who or what they can count on. Intuitive parents may discount a Sensing child's need for concrete, specific information. When a Sensing child asks what's for dinner, and the Intuitive mother says she hasn't come up with an idea, the child may feel shaky and insecure.

On the positive side, Sensing children often say they appreciate an Intuitive parent's imagination, particularly when they need help with school assignments that require originality and creativity.

> After a new snow, an Intuitive mother sent her four-year-old daughter out to shovel without making sure she wore boots. When she came in, her shoes were soaked. "Oh dear," the mother said, "I can't believe I forgot to put your boots on."
>
> "That's OK, mom," the child responded, "you're good at other things."

Thinking Parent–Feeling Child

Thinking parents often report being perplexed by a Feeling child's sensitivity. "How can I correct poor behavior when she bursts into tears over a look sideways?"

They may also be concerned that the Feeling child appears to need "unlimited" emotional support—too many compliments, too much personal attention, or too much comfort. Thinking parents find it hard to believe that a Feeling child's emotional needs are genuine rather than manipulative. They might try to toughen her up by telling her to stop crying or keep her feelings under control.

Feeling children sometimes do not feel loved enough by a Thinking parent. Because they crave affection, praise, and appreciation, they may miss dad or mom's Thinking expressions of caring—respect and space to practice independence.

On the positive side, Feeling children often say they find comfort in the way a Thinking parent helps in a difficult situation: getting behind the emotions to look at it objectively and figure out how to apply problem-solving skills.

Feeling Parent–Thinking Child

Feeling parents often describe a Thinking child as not being cuddly or chummy enough and say they feel rejected or attacked from time to time. "I go to give her a big hug and she backs away," says a Feeling mother.

Feeling parents sometimes misinterpret their Thinking child's emotional distance and objectivity as lack of caring or love. From the Thinking child's perspective, Feeling parents can be intrusive, asking too many personal questions and initiating conversations about feelings. Thinking children also say Feeling parents can be overly involved and protective, not giving them the room they need to challenge and practice self-reliance.

Sensitivity is another issue. Says one Thinking teenager, "I try to make a joke, tease him, or argue a point. But Dad takes it personally. I don't mean to hurt his feelings, but he's overly sensitive about everything."

On the plus side, Thinking children say that when they're mad or sad, Feeling parents seem to care. "My mother gives me the opportunity to talk about how I feel," says a Thinking teen. "By communicating my feelings, I'm better able to manage them."

Judging Parent–Perceiving Child

Judging parents often find Perceiving children exasperating: "I ask her to do a job and she gets sidetracked by something more interesting." "His room looks like a cyclone hit it." "She waits until the last minute to do homework." "He could be Number One in his class if he'd only apply himself."

Judging parents worry that their Perceiving child will not find her way in the world. They may try to "make" their Perceiving child more focused, more responsible, more organized, and more considerate. The result can be a power struggle between a parent trying to control and a child bent on resisting control and proving her way is fine.

From the child's point of view, a Judging parent's emphasis on structure, planning, and order is superfluous. The Perceiving child doesn't need it to feel secure and may in fact feel confined, limited, and unaccepted.

One Perceiving adult says, "As a child, I liked having a messy room and an easygoing relationship with my things. My piles were my friends. My parents never understood, but they were kind enough to shut my bedroom door and forget about it."

On the plus side, Perceiving children say they appreciate knowing what it takes to survive in a Judging world and having been "pushed" to develop many of those skills.

Battle of Wills

When Judging parents raise Judging children, the result is often a battle of wills. Judging parents want to exert maximum control over home life, leaving minimum, if any, space for Judging children to develop their own structure and exercise their own judgments. One Judging adult remembers, "As a child I desperately wanted to help my mother in the kitchen. But she wouldn't even let me load the dishwasher for fear I'd do it wrong. That made me feel powerless and resentful." Regardless of age, each Judging type in the family needs to have his or her own domain of control, whether it's one drawer in the kitchen, the family calendar, or a play area.

Perceiving Parent–Judging Child

When Perceiving parents raise a Judging child, they often feel put upon to make structure and plans when they don't feel the need. "My son wakes up each morning asking what's the plan for the day, and I don't have one," says a Perceiving mom.

Perceiving parents sometimes question what's wrong with a child so focused on boundaries and control. "Sure, I bought the boombox for my daughter to play CDs in her room. But I wish she'd lighten up and be more gracious about sharing when she comes home and finds me listening to it while I fix her dinner."

A Perceiving parent's casual approach can leave a Judging child feeling insecure and uncared for. He often wonders, "Is anyone in charge here? Or do I have to make the order and plans?" Sometimes a Judging child will try to organize a Perceiving parent by making to-do lists to be completed while he is at school or saying an activity begins fifteen minutes earlier than it does to be on time.

One Judging mother says, "When I was a child I had no bedtimes or curfews. I could do pretty much what I wanted. I doubted whether my parents really cared. If a friend called to make plans, I'd pretend to ask my parents if it was okay."

On the positive side, Judging children say they appreciate their Perceiving parents' help to find balance in life. They grow up knowing there's always fun to be had and that work can sometimes wait.

Using Type with Children: Ten Real-Life Examples

I asked parents how they have used type knowledge to be more effective with their children. Here are some of their answers.

Extraversion–Introversion

"My older son and I are big Extraverts," says one ENTJ mother. "We talk fast and enjoy dynamic discussions. My middle son, an Introvert, has a hard time breaking into our conversation. Sometimes he resorts to raising his hand. Type knowledge has taught me to consciously help him find an entry point by inviting his comments and giving him a turn to talk."

According to an ISTP mom: "Knowing type has helped reduce conflict between my two sons. Sometimes my Extraverted son stalks his Introverted brother, looking for someone to play with. I try to support the Introvert by reminding him that he might like to go to his room to read for a while. Otherwise, he gets overwhelmed and loses his temper. For my E child, sending him to his room is a punishment; for my I child it's a reward."

"At my house we're wild, noisy, and constantly on the go," says Helen, ESFP. "One of my children talks a blue streak. The other one keeps his thoughts to himself. I've learned that I need to slow down and find ways to connect with him one-on-one if I want to know what's on his mind."

Sensing–Intuition

An Intuitive mother was having problems getting her Sensing-Perceiving daughter to put away her toys before bedtime. Remembering that SPs like fun and action, the mother devised a "Treasure Hunt Game." She hid pennies under piles of toys and clothes. A half hour before bedtime, her daughter could play the game and discover the buried treasure, which could only be found as the room became uncluttered.

A Sensing mother was having difficulty getting her Intuitive son out the door, into the car, and on their way to preschool. One snowy January day, he was dawdling as usual and ignoring her "it's time to go" warnings. Remembering Intuitive types prefer enthusiastic and imaginative communication, she went outside and called to him: "Come, let's go for a ride in my snow chariot." He raced out the door and hopped in the snow-covered car with a smile on his face.

Thinking–Feeling

One Feeling mother says, "I've learned to ask my thinking child what he *thinks* about a situation, and my Feeling child what he *feels*."

A Thinking father was about to throw the Halloween jack o' lanterns into the garbage when his Feeling son began to cry. Before he knew type, he would have said, "There's nothing to cry about. Stop it!" But this time he asked his son why he was sad. His son told him that the pumpkin faces looked almost human to him, so much so that he had given them names. It seemed heartless to throw them away. The dad changed his approach. He gave the pumpkins a funeral, complete with a eulogy, backyard burial, and a grave marker. The dad succeeded in disposing of the rotten pumpkins and honoring his son's sensitive nature.

"Type has taught me how to express love more effectively to my two Feeling daughters," says an ENTP mother. "When Maggie wants a hug while I'm working at the computer, I've learned not to swat her away like a fly or tense up my body; I give her a hug. My own loving style is more clinical and dry. For example, I'm constantly clipping newspaper articles and sending them to Suzanne, my college daughter, but I may forget her birthday. I've learned to show love in different ways for different kids, even if it feels a little uncomfortable at times."

Judging–Perceiving

One ENTP mother said that type had helped her tremendously with her Judging daughter. "When my SJ daughter asks me what day it is, I'm not going to say, 'Honey, you're just a little kid; you don't need to know what day it is,' I'm going to tell her what day it is!"

An ESFJ mother says learning how to better motivate her children has been the most helpful. "One of my children is motivated by responsibility, the other, freedom. Whether it's getting kids to put away their clothes or do their homework, they get jazzed by different rewards."

Parenting in the Face of Cultural Pressures

Our culture and school systems overvalue Extraversion, Sensing, Thinking, and Judging and undervalue the opposites, except when it comes to girls (female = Feeling). That means children who have preferences for Introversion, Intuition, or Perceiving may grow up somewhat out of step with cultural expectations and need extra support and sensitivity from their parents. The same is true of Thinking girls and Feeling boys, who don't fit neatly into gender stereotypes.

A parent needs to make a conscious effort to understand and empower children who have minority preferences, encouraging them to develop and trust their gifts and wisdom. There may be times, however, when you feel out on a limb, especially when your friends' children seem to be following a more traditional path. Or you may end up defending your child's uniqueness to a closed-minded teacher while secretly harboring her same concerns.

Remember, according to Jung and Myers, a child's personality is inborn. Even if you consciously tried, you wouldn't be able to change your child's personality. Mothers who are constantly saying to their children "Be a different way" or "Don't be that way" need to accept the futility of that approach. Your child is a unique, wonderful person. As parents, our challenge is to understand our children for who they are and support them on their own individual paths. Remember you are in an inherent power position with your children. What you say and think about them is important. As an old folk saying goes, "We can't make them but we can break them."

chapter 12

It's a Family Affair

Often a clash between a parent and child will force the parents to look at the dynamics of the whole family system. But you don't have to wait for a problem to gain a better understanding of your family's unique dynamics. Did you know that every type speaks and listens in its own language? Or that different types respond to and express different caring styles?

Knowing your family's culture and each member's needs within it can head off some problems before they start. Personality type is widely used in business and organizations for team building, and it can be a powerful paradigm for understanding and building the family team as well. Many mothers say type has been a useful tool in helping their families become more nurturing, communicative, and appreciative of differences.

Penley's Parenting Pyramid

My approach to parenting and family relationships can be summed up with Penley's Parenting Pyramid. Just like the food pyramid that advocates fruits and vegetables as the foundation of a healthy diet, followed by grains and dairy, and then a sparing

Penley's Parenting Pyramid

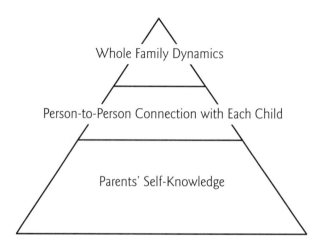

Whole Family Dynamics

Person-to-Person Connection with Each Child

Parents' Self-Knowledge

consumption of fats and sugars, my pyramid visually shows where to put your attention for healthy parenting.

At the foundation of the pyramid is the parents' self-awareness: *This is who I am and this is who I am not. This is where I stand and why. I manage my own stress, energy, and adult relationships. I am becoming the best person I can be.* Many family therapists agree that a parent's sense of self is the emotional and psychological foundation for the whole family. As a parent becomes more self-aware and strives to become a better person, the children in the family flourish and are free to become their best selves. Anything you can do to raise your own self-esteem directly influences the self-esteem and success of your child. By growing in your identity, you can improve the dynamics of the entire family and, ultimately, our society at large. After all, the life we live is our greatest creative act and our most important legacy.

The second tier is real person-to-person relationships with each child. To be successful, a parent must strive toward a relationship with each child that acknowledges separateness ("My child and I are not the same person. We have different natures and life paths."), respect ("Each of our approaches to life have pluses and minuses; I am your parent and authority, but eventually we will be equals."), and openness ("Here's what I think and feel; tell me what you think and feel."). As you can see, the framework of personality type is an asset in accomplishing each of these objectives. The quality of the connection between parent and child is more important than any particular parenting technique.

At the tip of the pyramid is mindfulness of the whole family's dynamics: *family culture, strengths and blind spots, differing needs for togetherness/autonomy, odd man out/special affinities, and cooperative parenting.* Sometimes when a problem arises with a child, the source of the problem lies elsewhere in the family. It might be a reflection of the parent's own issues. Therefore, to help a child who is having problems, you might have to take the focus off the child and turn it toward yourself.

Here's one example. A mother was alerted that her third-grade son was showing uneven math scores. On one quiz he'd do fine, but on the next he'd fail. His teacher showed her a list of his quiz scores ordered by date. As the mother looked over the list, she noticed that the dates of his poor grades coincided with the dates she had worked as a substitute teacher. She realized that the stress she felt being jarred awake by an early morning phone call to substitute and then rushing around to get herself and her children out the door on time had transferred to her son. On the mornings she substituted, he apparently arrived at school too anxious to concentrate. Instead of trying to "fix" her son's problem by, say, hiring a tutor, she focused on reducing her own anxiety about getting ready for work on a moment's notice. Ultimately, she realized substitute teaching didn't suit her because of her Judging preference. Changing her plans for the day on a dime required too much flexibility. She stopped substituting and began working full time as a nursery school teacher. Her predictable schedule and morning routine reduced her stress and allowed her son to focus on his schoolwork without worry.

However, it isn't always the mother's issues that impact the family. Sometimes a father's stress, whether due to his job, a sports injury, or his own parent's illness, may make everyone else in the family a little more tense and anxious. Or a child with special needs may affect the dynamics between the other children in the family. Therefore, it is sometimes helpful to look at the whole family and become savvier about its dynamics.

Family Culture

When a child is born, he or she enters a family culture of values, mindsets, traditions, and lifestyles—those of the parents and generations of grandparents and great grandparents.

Socioeconomic and ethnic norms play a role, as well. Yet it's important to recognize that the parents' type preferences are a significant determinant of the family's culture, too.

When a child's preferences match those of the family culture, parents often remark how easily he or she fits in and gets along with other family members. When a child's preferences differ from those of the parents, he or she may be regarded as challenging. A child who has a preference undervalued by other family members can begin to believe there is something wrong with him or her.

Of course, your family culture may be quite different from your next-door neighbor's. In fact, every family has a personality of its own. When I belonged to a baby-sitting co-op, I visited many different families' homes and followed their directions for taking care of their children. Some homes were orderly with rules posted on the refrigerator, freshly laundered pajamas, and set bedtime routines. Others were more relaxed with piles on the kitchen counter, snack dishes in the bedrooms, a mini-trampoline in the living room, and children who were free to go to bed when they wanted.

Like these families, your family has its own style and way of doing things, as well as having its own preferences for certain personality traits. The same behavior may be encouraged in one family and punished in another. For example, a child who speaks up for him or herself may be considered assertive in one family while another family might regard such behavior as disobedient.

Type knowledge can make parents more aware of the unique culture they are providing as well as offer some clues for healthier and more enjoyable family living.

Determining the personality type of your family's culture is easy if you know each member's personality type. Just tally up how many Es, Is, Ss, Ns, Ts, Fs, Js, and Ps in the family and identify the four-letter type that is the majority. It's as if you are determining the personality of the family as a whole. If there is a tie on a dichotomy, give the parents' types more weight because of their greater influence and authority. Here are three families as examples:

Family A

Mother, INFJ   Father, INFP   Son, ESTP   Daughter, ENFP
    2 E, 2 I, but the parents are Is, so = I
    1 S, 3 N = N
    1 T, 3 F = F
    1 J, 3 P = P

The family culture of this family can be described as INFP. This family provides a quiet haven where people can do their own thing in an atmosphere of acceptance and understanding. The family values sensitivity to each person's needs, feelings, and perceptions. They may spend time together watching movies, and everyone is typically in their own room by 9 p.m. reading. Studying the INFP mothering profile will yield more insights about the strengths and characteristics of this family culture.

INFP Family Culture

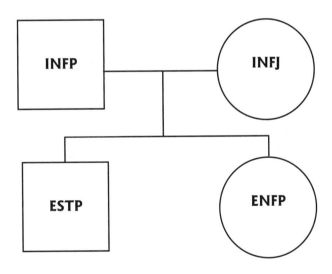

Family B

Mother, ENTP   Father, INTJ   Daughter, ENFP   Daughter, ESTP
    3 E, 1 I = E
    1 S, 3 N = N
    3 T, 1 F = T
    1 J, 3 P = P

This family's culture, ENTP, is action-oriented and energetic. They go places and do things, exploring all that life has to offer. Education, independence, and world travel are priorities. Again, refer to the ENTP mother profile to understand more about this family's strengths and characteristics.

ENTP Family Culture

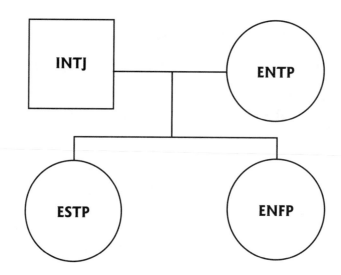

Family C

Mother, ENFJ   Father, ESTJ   Seven children

Daughter 1: ISTJ

Son 1: INTP

Daughter 2: ESFJ

Daughter 3: ESFJ

Daughter 4: ESFJ

Son 2: ISFJ

Daughter 5: ESFJ

6 E, 3 I = E
7 S, 2 N = S
3 T, 6 F = F
8 J, 1 P = J

ESFJ Family Culture

This ESFJ family does many things together: participating in sports, going to parties, enjoying good food, and discussing best buys. Now that the children are grown with children of their own, their extended family numbers thirty-one. They emphasize family traditions and have perfect attendance at get-togethers: a ten-day beach vacation each summer, an annual pig roast in October, as well as an Easter egg hunt, Thanksgiving dinner, and holiday cooking contests.

Families that Don't Fit the Formula

Let's look at one more family: Father INTP, Mother ESFJ, Daughter ESTJ, and Son INFP. According to my formula, this family is evenly split on every dichotomy. Even giving extra weight to the parents' preferences won't break the ties, because the parents are opposite types. In families like these, factors like ethnicity or which parent has the biggest presence in the home will likely be more influential than type in determining the family culture. In addition, more care may be required to avoid misunderstandings, power struggles, and miscommunications on a day-to-day basis. I mention this here just to remind you that type knowledge can't explain everything. Although using a type formula can yield insights, family relationships are often more complicated.

Blind Spots

In each of these wonderful families mentioned above, the family culture has strengths but also blind spots, gaps, and weaknesses. The first family, Family INFP, is somewhat of a loner family; they belong to few community organizations and keep their social circle small. In fact, when the daughter wanted to join a father-daughter activity and camping group, the father opted for the two of them to go on their own father-daughter excursion instead. This family culture might feel boring and isolating to Extraverted children.

Family ENTP is likely to downplay feelings and practicalities, and skimp on downtime. The ENTP mother says, "I worry that my ENFP daughter is too sensitive and my ESTP child is too in-the-moment."

In Family ESFJ there are lots of chiefs, which may result in power struggles and battles of will. So many EJs in a family may fight for airtime to get their ideas on the floor. The Ss are likely to squabble over a petty detail, such as who gets which bedroom or the order of events at holiday get-togethers. Within an ESFJ culture there's also a tendency for matters to get overly personal, with family members not respecting people's privacy and boundaries, and people perceiving slights where none were intended.

Odd Man Out

When looking at your family's dynamics, it's important to ask yourself who in the family is most different from the culture and the rest of the group. Without extra support and sensitivity, that individual may end up feeling out of sync, alienated, and lonely. It's likely that member will feel least nurtured and accepted in the family. One mother said that she felt so different from the rest of her family growing up that she was sure that she was adopted. However, the rest of the family might have their own issues with the "odd man out." They might be bothered by her differences, or resentful when she doesn't "get with the program." She might then become the lightning rod for the family's tension.

Let's look back at the three family examples. Who is odd man out in Family A? (By now you've probably guessed, this is my family.) Looking at this family diagram, I would consider my ESTP son to be odd man out. He is the only ST in the group, and differs on three letters from the family's INFP culture. However, when I asked him if he ever felt like odd man out, he said, "Mom, I'm not odd man out, you are!" He was focusing on the J-P difference and he is right about me being the only J in a family of Ps. Truth be told, we've both felt like the family's odd ducks at times.

How about Family B? The INTJ father is the most unlike the rest. He's the only Introvert and the only Judging type. His personality differences are amplified by being the only male among three females as well. It would be easy for him to feel like an outsider in the family, three against one. The EP females go, do, and interact, while IJ Dad prefers to stay home, alone. Without type awareness, it would be easy for him to feel cut off, and for the others to cut him off, causing resentment on everyone's part. Understanding dad's differing needs for interaction and spontaneity can lead to a workable compromise. Perhaps dad can commit to one family outing a week, or sometimes the family can join him in a quiet activity of his choosing.

In Family C, clearly the INTP son is the most unlike the rest of the family. In fact, his personality is exactly the opposite of the personality of the family culture. He was an observer in a family of high-volume Extraverts, a mastermind problem solver with all things mechanical among those more people-oriented, and a laid-back sibling surrounded by seven others fighting to be in charge.

Special Affinities

Just as some family members can feel left out, some members have special affinities to each other that can be partially explained by being type-alike. A mother will confide to me that one child is easier for her to love and spend time with than the other. Another will worry that her child seems to like being with her husband more than with her. When you analyze family dynamics through the lens of personality type, these special affinities sometimes make perfect sense.

In Family A, the ENFP daughter shares more letters in common with her INFP father than her INFJ mother. This may explain why the father and daughter are often aligned and share a close understanding. And although my son and I are totally different types, the fact that we are both at odds with the family culture has created a bond between us.

In Family B, the ENFP daughter and her father have a different dynamic. She is three letters different from her father and just one letter different from her mother. Chances are this ENFP daughter feels more affinity to the mother than the father. Also in Family B, the two daughters are each only one letter different from their mother and yet two letters different from each other. Given this type dynamic, I would predict that they each tend to be closer to their mother than to each other. Because the ENTP mother serves as a bridge between the ESTP and ENFP sisters, outings as a threesome are apt to work better than just the two sisters together.

In Family C, the N mother is likely to have a soft spot for her only N child, who may offer her a respite from the detailed communications of a Sensing household.

Too Much Alike

Once I discovered a family where the mother, father, and two daughters were all INFPs. Their family culture therefore was clearly INFP. However, just like a strong team, in every family all eight of the type bases need to be covered. When everyone in a family has the same type, someone must take responsibility for the preferences not represented. Often the missing preferences, in this case E, S, T, and J, will be divided up among the members based on varying abilities, inclinations, and interests. This is done, of course, without conscious awareness. For example, the youngest child may become the gregarious family clown (E) and the mother may fall into the role of SJ caretaker. Their types don't change, but the expression of their types might change to fill in the family's gaps.

Moreover, when two or more family members have the same type, individuals will likely develop other parts of themselves to differentiate. I consulted with a high school girl who guessed herself an INFJ, but had trouble accepting it once she discovered her mother's type was INFJ as well. As an adolescent, she felt it was important that she carve out a separate identity from her mother's—even if it meant denying her nature and acting like someone she isn't.

Gender Alert

When I analyze a family's make-up, another factor I consider is how gender expectations might figure into the dynamics. Typically parents over-identify with their same sex offspring and vice versa. If one of them has preferences counter to stereotypical gender roles, the relationship between them often has an extra layer. For example, in Family B, the mother prefers Thinking, and one of the daughters prefers Feeling. The mother might be pleased that her Feeling daughter won't feel out-of-step with feminine expectations like she does. Or she might have a hard time accepting a daughter who is more traditionally feminine. Similarly, the ESTJ father in Family C might feel uncomfortable about his ISFJ son's more sensitive ways. It's hard to predict how society's gender expectations might figure into family relationships, but it is a factor to consider when trying to understand relationship clashes and family triangles.

Changes in Dynamics

When new siblings are born or older children move away, the dynamics of the family change. When my ESTP son left for college, the rest of us noticed how quiet and relaxed our home became. The three remaining members were all NF's (INFJ, INFP, and ENFP), so the family had become more homogenous and relationships less challenging.

Sometimes family changes alter the predominant family culture, too. After a twelve-year gap, Family B added two new offspring, an ENFP daughter and an ENFJ son. When the older girls left for college, their new family looked like this:

Family B—Second Stage

Mother, ENTP   Father, INTJ   Daughter, ENFP   Son, ENFJ

The family culture of this second stage family unit is still clearly EN, but now there is an even split on T-F and J-P. The old triangle of ENTP mother–ENFP daughter–ESTP daughter has disappeared. Interestingly, the mother reports that the INTJ father is now much more involved with the family, especially with his son. This could be due to the father's own maturation, the addition of a male child, or the fact that he and his son have two letters in common, one more than he had with each of his three daughters.

Differing Needs for Closeness

In her book, *The Dance of Intimacy*, Harriet Lerner says that true intimacy is made up of two elements: connectedness (We) and separateness (I). Everyone has his or her own "recipe" for how much connection and how much separateness feels comfortable in intimate relationships. Some people crave more closeness and some want more space.

This propensity is determined by many factors: socioeconomic and ethnic norms (think *My Big Fat Greek Wedding* versus the Royal Family of Great Britain), past experience, gender, and age. For example, typically children require more personal space during the teenage years.

However, I believe our preferences for Extraversion-Introversion and Thinking-Feeling can also factor into our personal intimacy recipe. When looking at your family's dynamics, it is important to understand who might need more closeness to feel loved and cared about and who may need more space.

Let's consider the E-I dichotomy first. Extraverted types are outwardly focused and need connections with others to feel energized. They typically skew toward the "We" side of intimacy. Introverted types need time and space to focus inward. They feel most comfortable in relationships that honor personal space, individuality, and autonomy.

Thinking and Feeling differences also influence the amount of togetherness or separateness a person prefers. Thinking types need psychological distance from others in order to decide logically and objectively. Feeling types tend to go through life up-close and personal: "Tell me what you're really feeling or needing, so I can make a good decision for everybody involved." They are naturally drawn to closeness and connection with others.

So both Extraverts and Feeling types would tend toward the "We" end of the intimacy continuum, and Introverts and Thinking types would tend to be on the "I" end of intimacy. When Extraversion-Feeling and Introversion-Thinking are combined in a type these differences may be accentuated. Therefore, EF and IT types would tend to be at opposite ends of the "We/I" spectrum. The ET or IF types would fall more toward the middle. These types have an inherent balance (or conflict) between their needs for personal space (I or T) and togetherness (E or F) in intimacy.

Now let's factor in gender differences. Women typically seek more connection and men seek more independence. Therefore, EF females and IT males may be at the most extreme ends of the "We/I" continuum of intimacy. One ENFP woman told me this explained her marriage perfectly. Sometimes she felt she was literally chasing her INTP husband around the house, following him from room to room. She was trying to get a comfortable closeness and he was trying to get a comfortable distance. And after an intimate weekend getaway, the EF might expect the closeness to continue but the IT will likely be craving some space.

Similar differences can arise between parents and children. For example, the conflicting needs for emotional closeness and distance were a big factor in a relationship between an ISTJ mother and her ESFP daughter. Unless conscious effort is made to understand the other's caring style, the daughter may continually seek more closeness and interaction than the mother can comfortably provide. The daughter will likely interpret this as "I'm unlovable" and the mother will end up feeling inadequate or resentful, unable to meet her daughter's emotional needs.

Another example concerns telephone behavior among parents and their grown children. I know an adult ENFJ daughter and ESFJ mother who talk to each other on the phone every day. Another mother I know, an ENFP with an INTP son, often feels rejected because her son seldom picks up the phone to connect.

These differences also show up within friendship and social interactions. In a women's workshop on caring styles, I asked everyone to join hands and stand side-by-side in a circle. One by one I gave each person a big hug. Afterward I asked, "Who liked that?" and "Who hated it?" The IT types talked about tense stomachs, sweaty hands, and thoughts of escape. One ISTJ said, "I've learned to cope with hugs because just like jumping into a cold shower, you know it's going to be over soon. But holding hands is terrible because it goes on and on." The EF types typically said they loved the hugs and wondered why I don't do it more often. The ETs and the IFs were somewhere in the middle.

Learning to respect and honor your loved ones' differing needs for closeness and separateness is one way to better express how much you care. But a differing need for closeness is just one aspect of a person's caring style. Different types show and recognize love in different ways.

How Do I Love Thee?

There are a myriad of ways to communicate caring and love. But when another person has a different personality type, he or she may miss your message and end up feeling unloved. Knowing about type differences in caring styles can help you love others in ways they can recognize and receive messages of love that you might have not noticed before. As one ENTP mother says, "Understanding personality type hasn't made me more loving, but it has helped me appear more loving to each of my different type children. I've learned to express my love for each child more effectively." Another mother, an ENTJ, says, "My teenage son is an ISFJ and it's hard to find ways to connect. One day I surprised him and his girlfriend with cupcakes on their one-year anniversary. Without knowing his type, this never would have occurred to me. I was a little nervous he'd think it was too sappy, but to my surprise, it was a great success."

Often we treat people the way we'd like to be treated. Here's one example. "My husband had been on the road for business all week. I wanted him to know how happy I was to see him so I greeted him at the door with a kiss, asked him about his trip, and told him I'd made plans for us to go to the theater with friends on Saturday. His response was cool and critical. I was hurt." This woman has preferences for ENFP and was showing love through enthusiasm, physical affection, verbal sharing, and opportunities to have fun together. However, her husband, an INTJ, was more apt to feel put upon by her caring style than cared about. Being an Introverted Judging type, I suspect he would have preferred her giving him some space to unwind and a few minutes to make the transition from being away to being with her. "I wouldn't want people rushing at me after being out all day," says one Introverted Thinking type."When I come home I'm happy, but I don't need to express that outwardly."

Although Ts may care deeply, they may seem cool and detached to Fs. Thinking types tend to show and recognize love through respect for boundaries, independence, and fair treatment. Feeling types convey and recognize caring by a show of warmth, accessibility, and helpfulness.

Sensing and Intuition Differences

Most mothers make an effort to show love in traditional ways: providing good food, touching, giving cards or gifts, saying please and thank you, spending time together, listening and sharing, or saying "I love you." These approaches probably best fit Sensing-Feeling types. Sensing types express their love in concrete ways: a favorite dessert, a filled gas tank, or buying a special gift. Intuitive types more naturally express love by making plans, showing enthusiasm for ideas, sharing insights and dreams. Intuitive parents may downplay concrete expressions of love, and Sensing children may misinterpret this behavior as not caring. Intuitive children may take the Sensing parent's practical care for granted and still need appreciation of their ideas to feel loved.

Do Feeling and Thinking women experience intimacy differently?

In a workshop, we asked women to describe a moment of intimacy. Both Feeling and Thinking types mentioned the physical connection and emphasized communication. However, they differed on what kind of communication made them feel intimate with another. For Feeling women, sharing their concerns and innermost feelings is what does the trick. On the other hand, Thinking women say they want to engage in intellectually stimulating, head-to-head analysis. For Feeling women, intimacy is about being able to "mind read" each other's needs, showing reciprocal accommodation, giving undivided attention, and providing opportunities to talk without pressure to hurry up or get to the point. For Ts, it's about doing things together, treating the other with fairness and respect, and living up to responsibilities. Fs said the biggest romantic turn-on for them was a heartfelt sharing of concerns, feeling understood and nurtured. For Ts, it was a hearty debate about politics in the Middle East or the existence of Adam and Eve, or seeing the other handle some situation expertly and competently.

One mother reports, "When my ESTP daughter plays tennis with her dad, the point is playing tennis. When my ENFP daughter plays tennis with her dad, the point is building their relationship."

Judging and Perceiving Profiles of Caring

Is there a difference in how Judging and Perceiving mothers show they care? Although women may flex their own caring style to meet another's' needs, these are some common J-P tendencies:

Judging	Perceiving
doing things *for* their children	doing things *with* their children
following through	spontaneous play and surprises
setting limits	giving freedom
calling or contacting regularly	being available
directing behavior	accepting behavior
control	stimulation
commitment	adaptability and flexibility
self-sacrifice	making things fun
being on time	being with you in the moment

When Judging parents go beyond their natural inclinations to give Perceiving kids freedom and acceptance, they worry that they're not doing their job. To Perceiving children, it may feel like caring, but to Judging parents it feels like neglect. Remember: If Judging children are given too much freedom or Perceiving kids experience too much control, they will wonder if their parents care.

Women say J-P differences factor into friendships too. A Perceiving woman may call a Judging friend with a spur-of-the-moment invitation to do something together. If the J friend can't change her plans to respond, the P friend is likely to interpret this as not caring. Likewise, Judging women are apt to complain that their Perceiving friends don't care because they don't call to chat or make plans on a regular basis like they do. The same misunderstanding might occur between Extraverted and Introverted friends. Extraverts are more apt to initiate contact than their Introverted friends.

Communication Styles

Caring styles are closely related to communications styles. Understanding differences in communication styles is one more way type can be used to strengthen family relationships. What we say and what we hear are greatly affected by our types.

"Mommy, why did you say you wanted plastic bags instead of paper?" asked my young ENFP daughter during one trip to the grocery store. Knowing she has preferences for Intuitive-Feeling helped me interpret her question. Earlier that day, she had overheard my husband telling me why he preferred paper grocery bags. Therefore, I felt the real meaning behind her words was this: "Why aren't you doing what Daddy likes? Is there something wrong between you two?" I reassured her by explaining that although I might want to please Daddy in important matters, I preferred plastic bags and was sure he wouldn't mind. She seemed satisfied.

Had my ESTP child asked the same question I would have interpreted it differently. He would have been speaking in the Sensing-Thinking language, and I would have responded to him literally, without looking for hidden meanings. I would have told him the objective facts: both plastic and paper are recyclable; I can carry eight plastic bags but only two paper; and plastic takes up less room than paper to store.

Four Type Languages

There are four main type languages: Sensing, Intuition, Thinking, and Feeling. Your most fluent languages match your middle two letters.

My ENFP daughter and I both naturally speak and listen in the NF language.

With my ESTP son, it's a different story. His prime languages are Sensing and Thinking, which are my least fluent communication styles. Similarly, my first languages are his least fluent. To communicate we have to find some common ground. Someone has to learn to speak the language of the other. In relationships this shift often happens unconsciously. When it doesn't, there's apt to be lots of irritation about misinterpreted messages. For example, when he was younger, I asked my son to help me out by going into the basement and putting a load of clothes in the dryer. Later, when I unloaded the dryer, I realized there had been a glitch in our communications. I assumed he'd transfer the load of wet clothes waiting in the washer to the dryer. Instead, he had loaded the dryer with laundry from the basket of dirty clothes waiting to be washed!

I had spoken in the broad generalities of Intuition and he had listened with the literal ears of Sensing. To communicate more effectively, I needed to rephrase my message in the language of his type.

Given personality differences, how do you talk most effectively with different types?

Speak Sensing with Specifics

With Sensing types, be factual and direct—say who, what, where, when, and how. Back up any request with practical data and information about previous experience. Be specific and proceed one step at a time. Describe a situation first in concrete terms before expressing feelings about it or trying to solve it. If it's really important, have them say it back to you to engage more of their senses and check for gaps.

For example, I might have said to my son, instead: "Go to the basement, take all the wet clothes out of the washer and put them in the dryer. Close the door of the dryer tightly—it won't work unless it's totally shut. Turn the white dial in the upper right to 60 minutes. Press the silver button to the left to start the dryer. You'll hear the clothes tumbling."

When listening to Sensing types, try to take in the facts, specifics, and rich descriptions without interrupting, looking for hidden messages, or rushing to get to the point.

Talking in Intuition Is Wonderful!

When speaking to Intuitive types, be enthusiastic and imaginative! Point out interesting possibilities and relate the issue at hand to the big picture or the future. Define the task broadly, giving just a few details to start, but be available to answer specific questions as they come up. Leave room for them to add their own ideas and come up with new solutions.

For example, you might say to your child: "Did you know there's a hungry fire-breathing dragon living in our dryer? Could you go feed him some wet laundry? If you need help figuring out how to do it, ask me for more details. I'll be fixing you a special reward for your bravery."

When listening, allow time for their random flow of ideas and leaps from one possibility to another before focusing on practicalities. Intuitive types tend to speak indirectly, so listen for the real meaning behind their words. Simple words can represent complicated thoughts and complicated words may mean something quite simple.

Make Sense with Thinking Types

When talking to Thinking types

1. Start with the bottom line first

2. Stay cool and calm

3. Be brief

4. Be direct

5. Be logical

6. Tell the reasons why

7. List the pros and cons, including feelings as facts to be weighed in the decision

8. Appeal to their need for challenge, competence, and fairness

9. Involve them in problem solving

For example: "I want you to help me with the laundry because I have a lot to get done today. Do you think you can figure out how to work the clothes dryer? You're getting older and I think you are capable of more responsibility."

When listening, allow opportunity for complaining and "conversational criticism." Try not to interpret comments as criticisms or criticisms as personal attacks. Stay calm and reasonable, acknowledging the logic in their reasoning. Feel free to objectively debate a point or request adequate evidence.

Feeling Language Feels Good

The language of Feeling is personal and friendly with the intent of making people feel comfortable, valued, and special. With Feeling types, take time to lay a groundwork of

Giving Negative Feedback to Feeling Types

When you need to say something difficult to a sensitive child, spouse, or worker, here are several steps you can take to increase the likelihood of positive outcomes.

Pick a comfortable time and environment, perhaps over a cup of coffee or during a walk. Start your message with assurance about your relationship. With children you can sit close or hold a hand. Next, preface your comments with a statement of intent and expected response, "What I'm going to say may be hard for you to hear, but it is not my intent to hurt your feelings or make you angry. I'd like you to just listen first without responding. You can tell me what you think at the end, or take more time if you need it. That's O.K." This allows Feeling types to prepare themselves by putting up some protective armor and provides the space they may need to respond more objectively.

Balance negative feedback by saying some important positives up front. "I like the way you do A and B. I need to talk to you about C. . . . " Try to present the problem as logically as possible. Some people use this model: First, describe the situation (Sensing), then say what you think (Thinking), what you feel (Feeling), and end with what course of action you want (J-P). It's easier for Feeling types to absorb criticism that makes sense to them rather than something that seems like a personal attack.

Feeling types typically want to please or help, so provide suggestions for better ways to meet a need: "It would please me more if you did D" or "Next time, I need you to do D." End your conversation by referring to the positive continuation of your relationship, "I love having you as my daughter," "I'm here if you want to talk about it later," or "Are there any hard feelings we need to resolve?"

good will and connect person-to-person before getting to the point. Say how the idea helps or affects people. Feel free to use flowery words, such as, "I'd love it if . . ." or "You're the best!" To change behavior, express need and admiration instead of criticism.

For example: "Sweetheart, I'm the luckiest mom to have such a helpful son. How would you like to do me a big favor? My legs ache from going up and down the basement steps doing the laundry. You could really make me happy by putting some clothes in the dryer. I'll give you ten thank-you hugs for your help!"

When listening to Feeling types, be alert to nonverbal cues. Even simple statements can be loaded with values, hopes, and fears. When Feeling types are required to give negative feedback or say no, they may speak indirectly or not at all.

After the laundry snafu with my son, I rephrased my request in the four different languages and asked him which one he would have preferred. He surprised me by choosing the Feeling version. That was a reminder to me of the universal appeal of the Feeling language with young children, before their types are fully developed. If you don't know your child's type, therefore, start with Feeling communication style. However, I believe with my ESTP son, the Sensing version would have had the best chance of producing the desired result of wet, not dry, clothes in the dryer.

Translating your message into the other person's communication style will increase your communication effectiveness, especially when you're attempting to communicate something important or when your usual way of speaking isn't producing the result you want. Careful communications as well as flexible, caring styles can help build relationships. You can create a more loving, supportive, and happier family by being mindful of your family's culture and the individual differences within it. But remember, taking care of your own issues first has a dramatic effect on your family's well being.

Part 3

Putting It All Together for You

"I am what I am."

—Popeye

· · · · · · · · · · · · · ·

chapter 13

How to Recharge Your Batteries

By the time my children were six and three, I was on the verge of burnout.

I had this idea that I would "do" mothering for five years and then resume my former life when my children headed off to kindergarten. I must have unconsciously approached mothering with a sprinter mentality—give it your all and go great guns because it's only a short distance.

Six years into it, motherhood was looking more like a marathon. To go the distance, I had to switch to a more long-term strategy. The key to that was learning how to maintain my energy on a regular basis.

I knew that meant meeting my own needs. However, I didn't know what I needed. It was only after learning about personality type that I was able to identify my needs.

Each of us finds different aspects of mothering draining and has unique ways of recharging. Your personality type can be your guide as you devise a "daily nutrition plan" for your psychic energy—what gives you energy, and what to avoid.

Following are some suggestions for ways each particular preference might recharge. The recommendations for your four preferences will most likely appeal to you, but because you use all eight preferences, the suggestions for your nonpreferences might sound attractive, too. So go ahead, be kind to the letters in your type, but indulge your opposite letters once in a while whenever it feels right. Remember, type is just one way of thinking about your uniqueness.

Personal Energy Management

Extraversion: Adult conversation, action, variety. Extraverted mothers are energized by conversation and interaction—going out to lunch with friends, playing on a softball team, or attending parties and group events. To keep energized, they may need to chat with a friend on the phone or listen to talk radio as they change diapers or clean up the kitchen. Manning the PTA booth at the Farmers Market, joining the church choir, or inviting couples over for pizza are all ways she can keep fresh.

Some Extraverted mothers think they must be Introverted because they, too, sometimes crave a break from their hectic schedules. These days, all of us are too busy and most likely overloaded. Even Extraverts sometimes need to get away from people and action to feed their spirits.

Introversion: Privacy and time alone. "Time alone to recharge" is what's most important for Introverted moms. Some solitude each day is a necessity, not an indulgence that can be put off until later.

If I spend too much time interacting with others, I feel my energy dwindling, my brain shriveling, and my judgment becoming shaky and ungrounded. To revive myself, I need to slip back into the cool waters of solitude.

When my children were underfoot, I found taking thirty to sixty minutes each afternoon alone in my bedroom would decrease my yelling by 95 percent. There were times when I was so mentally exhausted that I spent my thirty minutes simply staring at the ceiling. If I squandered my time-out because there were PTA phone calls to make or dishes to wash, I would inevitably explode before I got the kids tucked into bed for the night. Drained by a constant external focus, Introverted moms go through the day dangerously low on energy.

It takes some creativity and self-discipline to feed yourself the solitude you need in order to do your best. Some mothers say they get up early or stay up late to have the house to themselves. One mother journals for thirty minutes and then takes a twenty-five-minute walk first thing in the morning. "If I've had my hour of solitude first thing,

I can make it through the rest of the day with all the external demands," she says. Another mom checks herself into a local hotel with a stack of books for the weekend at least twice a year. The tactic I used was telling my bounding seven-year-old son, "Mommy's gas tank is empty. The only way she can fill it up is by time alone in her room. I've set this timer for thirty minutes. You need to play or read by yourself until you hear it go off."

Sensing: Feeding the five senses.   If you are a Sensing type who focuses on details and the concrete things around you, then being in your office cubicle or bungalow day after day, surrounded by the same old knickknacks, throw pillows, and wallpaper can become stifling.

Sensing types need new sensory stimulation to stay fresh—skiing down a snow-covered mountain in the icy air, planting bulbs in moist fragrant earth, or fingering bolts of printed designer fabrics. Museums, amusement parks, forests, and gardens are examples of good places to feed the five senses. But perhaps the shopping center is the most accessible lift to the senses. Elaborate window decorations, attention-getting displays, and fresh merchandise are all designed to seduce shoppers. For a Sensing type, a day at the mall can be a quick energy fix. If you can't find a baby-sitter, browsing through glossy catalogues and colorful magazine photographs might also do the trick. One woman said she kept old *Victoria* magazines around to "remind me that not everything in the world is plastic."

Intuition: New ideas, perspectives, dreams.   Anything new and original is like candy to Intuitive types. It gives them the energy they need to deal with the mundane aspects of childcare and homemaking. Taking a class, reading a book, or talking with an interesting person all feed Intuition. As one mother said, "At the end of the day, I'm exhausted from doing the laundry and making the meals, but when I've taken a French class or gone to a movie I feel more alive."

To maintain their energy, Intuitive types need time to dream, imagine, and entertain possibilities. "Sometimes I need a break from reality and go on a visit to la-la land," says Margaret. "I've read all the volumes of Harry Potter. I couldn't interest my teenagers so I read it on my own." Another Intuitive mother took a class on goddess mythology at the women's center, just the thing she needed to recharge.

Thinking: Objective validation of competence.　　The primary way Thinking mothers fuel their energy and self-esteem is through objective and concrete validation of their competence: promotions, raises, bonuses, good grades, and awards keep them pumped up. Unfortunately, within the subjective and personal realm of mothering these are in short supply. So Thinking mothers typically look to employment and volunteer opportunities outside the home for their energy boost: exceeding sales objectives at work, spearheading the fund-raising for the hospital, or managing the church budget.

Thinking mothers typically gravitate toward the money and leadership positions in volunteer organizations. One Thinking mom explained, "Money is important and it isn't subjective. Making a financial goal is my kind of warm fuzzy. I *know* I did a good job."

Another Thinking mom says, "I used to feel superior to my mother's friends who went out to lunch and gossiped together. Then I realized that being PTA president was my indulgence. I recharge my batteries by proving my competency."

Feeling: A break from others' needs.　　Feeling mothers are distracted by the needs of the people around them. Constantly tuning in to feelings and anticipating requirements, they may respond, give, and accommodate until they are completely depleted. To keep themselves from burning out they need time away from other people's needs.

Often a physical separation is necessary: leaving the house, shutting the door, or going away for the weekend. Yet most Feeling moms find it hard to pull away because they are so connected to their children and are always doing for them. However, it is often a great gift to remove yourself from the family dynamics and let your partner and children have their own direct relationship. When Feeling moms take a break from caretaking, it is usually a win-win situation. She comes back recharged; the kids practice their independence; dad gains experience as primary caretaker and gets to know his children better.

Vicky, an Extraverted Feeling mom, says, "Because I sometimes crave time alone I thought that meant I was an Introvert. But now I see it isn't the quiet I need, it's time away from other people's needs that recharges me. I energize by going to a movie or sitting in a coffee shop with no one to please but myself."

Feeling mothers who work outside the home in nursing or social service may think they are getting a temporary break from family demands. But tending to the needs of their clients may drain them in the same way mothering does.

Judging: A place or project to organize, control, and complete.   When childrearing gets hectic, Judging moms need order and completion to regain balance and energy. I remember one grade school holiday both my son and daughter invited friends over to play. I sat in the living room calmly doing needlepoint as the children cavorted around me. Making every neat stitch and finishing each row gave me a sense of control that counterbalanced the commotion of six silly kids.

Emily, a Judging mom, says, "My home office is my haven. I have my files alphabetized, my calendar up to date with appointments, and my in and out baskets organized; everything is just the way I like it. It's the one place I don't have to be flexible."

Perceiving: Freedom from a tight schedule.   Although all types of mothers do badly when they are over-scheduled, too much juggling can squeeze the very life from Perceiving moms. Drained by getting children off to school on time, sticking to homework schedules, and meetings at work, they need long blocks of hangout time to recharge. "When I turn over the daily calendar and see nothing but white space, I know it's going to be a good day," says one Perceiving mother.

"I'm as happy as the kids when school's out for the summer," says Marci, a Perceiving mom. "I need freedom from the school year schedule. One day we're still in our pajamas at noon. The next day we're off early for a day at the beach. If the kids are having a good time somewhere, there's no reason we can't stay longer."

Irene says, "I love Little League season because I'm freed from my husband's expectation of a set family dinnertime. The kids need to get to the field by 4:30 p.m. and games aren't over until 8:00, so we eat what we want whenever we're hungry."

What Are Your Stressors and Energy Robbers?

Knowing your personality type can help you let go of the need to do and be everything. Saying no to what we find lifeless and unsatisfying makes us happier. As an Intuitive, if I spend every day on Sensing tasks, I rob the world of my unique gifts and myself of the joy of using my gifts.

Capitalizing on the Energy of Others

When you need an energy boost, think not only of activities that might recharge you, but people who might provide the energy balance you need. We are drawn to people whose energy makes us feel good. If we need a lift and some excitement perhaps we'll seek out an ENP. If we need to calm down and feel grounded an ISJ will likely hit the spot.

Whenever we are forced to overuse our nonpreferences we become stressed out, exhausted, and feel less successful. Knowing what drains us can help us avoid or minimize the parts of mothering we find most stressing and unfulfilling.

Stop the Busyness—and Have More Fun

As we were leaving yoga class one day, another mother told me, "During relaxation at the end of class, I heard a voice inside my head say, *What gives you the right to feel so relaxed? Just who do you think you are?* It made me feel guilty for not being busy."

When I talk about energy management I want to make it very clear that I'm not talking about how to get more energy just so you can become busier or get more things done. Our society is caught up in constant, often mindless activity and productivity that seems to keep us from fully enjoying our lives or our children.

If you've tried to slow down and stop the busyness in your own life and haven't succeeded very well, don't be too hard on yourself. It isn't just you; it's all of us. As a culture, we know a lot about activity and doing and know very little about reflection and just being.

Getting a handle on busyness is critical to enjoying life as a mom. As I've tried to enjoy my life more fully, I've risked letting go of constant busyness to discover what lies beyond. I've learned that making room for peace and joy doesn't sabotage productivity. It actually improves it.

Busyness ≠ Productivity

Packed up and ready to move into our new house, I pushed myself to vacuum our old apartment, wanting to leave it tidy. My husband was working a crossword puzzle. "Can't you do something productive?" I asked. He calmly replied, "Janet, you're frantically busy, but the vacuum hose isn't even connected to the motor." I glanced over my shoulder, and to my embarassment, saw that he was right.

Often it's good to pause to consider whether our actions are necessary and connected to what really matters, or a crafty distraction from addressing more significant issues. For instance, sometimes busyness stems from trying to prove our value. In our masculine-oriented world, being born female and making children a priority can create doubt deep inside about our self-worth. What if we gave up trying to prove our value? Would we be a lot less busy? It takes courage and support, but nothing is more powerful than claiming your worth based on who you are instead of what you accomplish.

How to Stop the Busyness

The old-fashioned way to stop is to get sick. The body in its wisdom says, *I'll help you out by doing what the mind doesn't know how to do*. Nature knows about the value of stopping. Every winter, nature stops its busyness to catch its breath, put down deeper roots, gather energy for a new season of growth. Nature knows what we fail to acknowledge—nothing can constantly be blooming.

Sometimes we treat ourselves more like machines than living beings. Attempting to produce more and go faster is a sure route to burnout. The impossible expectations that are put upon mothers—to give and give—already sets us up for depletion. To add to that the expectation of producing more and more is a recipe for disaster. We feel happier with a cycle of rest and activity, expansion and integration.

I encourage you to consciously go against our culture and embrace a different pace as a mother. I encourage you to manage your energy based on your personality type, and also on the inner wisdom that knows, deep inside, when to slow down or even stop.

Yea for Play!

In my interviews with mothers, I discovered that Judging moms were experts at getting things done, but universally struggled to enjoy their children and their lives as much as they thought they should. Being a J myself, I began to think if I didn't change my lifestyle my tombstone would read, "Never has someone accomplished so much and enjoyed it so little." To Js, motherhood is the ultimate responsibility, so if they are having fun they think they must be shirking their responsibilities.

Yet having fun is a great energy booster and stress-reliever. Genuine fun is always spontaneous; it can't be forced or scheduled. It bubbles up and embraces you when you let go. So add more fun to your life by consciously making a space for it and breaking your own rules once in a while. Yes, you can serve ice cream for breakfast! Leave your bed unmade! Have some fun and your children will love you for it! (Especially if they are Perceiving children.)

The Biggest Energy Booster—or Robber—of All

Now that you've identified your energizers and energy robbers, it's time to turn to what can be either the biggest time robber, or energizer, of them all: commitments outside of the home. Whether paid or unpaid, work can either complement your mothering or sabotage it. In the next chapter, we'll explore how your knowledge of your type will help you make the choices that are right for you.

chapter 14

Balancing Family with Outside Commitments

For most women, being a mother means more than taking care of children. Most mothers are involved with outside commitments that are separate from and in addition to their parental role—paid employment or volunteer projects. Whether these commitments round you out or stress you out depends in large measure upon whether what you do outside the home complements or sabotages your responsibilities as a mother.

Knowing your personality type can help you make more workable choices about outside commitments in four important ways:

- Feeling more comfortable and confident in your work/family decisions.

- Understanding the whys of your potential work/family conflicts.

- Identifying work and volunteer situations that fit you best. (Several type and career resources are listed in the back of this book.)

- Alerting you to outside commitments that would drain you in the same ways mothering does.

To Work or Not to Work?

No one is quite certain of the long-term consequences of various work/family decisions. This can leave a mom feeling shaky about the path she has chosen—no matter which one it is. Type knowledge can help you make a stand for yourself on what work option suits you best, and help you be more accepting of other women's choices.

For example, Susan, ESFJ, says, "Motherhood opened the door to my passion. I've always loved home and children and never saw myself in the work world. Type helped me understand my needs and empowered me to say it's OK to be a full-time stay-at-home mother; this is right for me." On the other hand, Pat, ENTJ, says, "With my own style and values, I'd rather be working than shopping or making my house beautiful. I may always have a little guilt about not always being available to my children, but I think I'm a better mother working than I would have been staying home."

According to my research, all three employment options—full-time employment, part-time employment, and stay-at-home full time—are represented among all sixteen types of mothers. Still, some slight Thinking-Feeling differences did emerge. Thinking moms tend to be OK about leaving a small child in the care of a competent caregiver. Caretaking of little ones draws heavily on SF skills, and therefore T mothers may feel less of a match with those tasks. Combine this with how much the work world values Thinking skills, especially the leadership of TJ types, and it is easy to understand why Thinking moms in general, and TJ moms in particular, might gravitate toward continuing their jobs. Later, when the children start becoming more rational, Thinking mothers may reevaluate their work/family balance and decide to become more involved at home so they can make their special contribution.

Feeling mothers, on the other hand, may feel young children need their "mommies" regardless of the quality of childcare and feel compelled to stay home. Later, when their children are more mature, they may feel more comfortable working outside the home.

So keep in mind over the childrearing years, a mother's employment status may change several times. I myself have worked part-time, full-time, and have also been a stay-at-home mother. Every situation has had its inherent pluses and minuses, and each type may choose to stay at home or work outside the home for different reasons.

THE WHYS BEHIND OUR WORK CHOICES

	What Stay-at-Home Mothers Say	*What Working Mothers Say*
ENFP	"Being an at-home mom is the best job I've ever had—it fits my skills, it's challenging, I feel like I'm really living life! When I worked, there was no time for fun."	"I love being a feminine role model for my kids, someone who really loves her job and has fun at it."
ENFJ	"Child-rearing is the most important job in the world, no matter what anyone thinks. When mothers work, kids lose a sense of their importance."	"I need a sense of identity separate from my children and the fulfillment of making a meaningful contribution in the world."
ENTP	"I am more competent than most childcare providers, plus I love the autonomy of being at home. Work accentuates a natural inclination to pull away from a family focus."	"I like work—the responsibilities, decision-making, leadership—and I'm good at it."
ENTJ	"Being at home helps me slow down and learn about my domestic side. When I worked, I got overly immersed and found it hard to switch gears to my children's pace."	"Work is me! I love my job and I'm good at what I do."
ISTJ	Being there physically alleviates guilt over not being there emotionally. When I worked, I was tired all the time."	"Earning a living is an integral part of real life; I like modeling the work ethic for my children."
ISFJ	"No one knows my children's needs and works to meet those needs like I do."	"My work provides a concrete structure for my life and enhances my self-respect."
ESFJ	"My kids need me, why leave them so I can go help someone else?"	"Work enables me to model for my children my values of hard work, persistence, contributing to the community, and a woman having something for herself. At home, instead of pats on the back, I get another load of dirty dishes."

POTENTIAL WORK/FAMILY CONFLICTS
BY PERSONALITY PREFERENCE

	Why I want to work outside the home	*Why I want to stay home full time with children*
Extraversion	"I need to be with people. I'm too isolated at home."	"I want to focus my greatest energy on my children and family."
Introversion	"I need blocks of solitude to concentrate, without distractions and interruptions."	"I don't have enough energy for home and work. I don't feel like I can 'do it all.'"
Sensing	"I need the opportunity to use my skills and be connected to the reality of the world."	"No one can take care of my children's basic needs and physically be there for them like I can."
Intuition	"I need exposure to new ideas and perspectives."	"No one can develop my child's potential like I can."
Thinking	"I need objective validation of my competence, a sense of accomplishment and achievement."	"Parenting is my highest priority. I don't want to miss all the once-in-a-lifetime opportunities."
Feeling	"I need to be valued and appreciated. Also, working outside the home gives me a more objective viewpoint about my children."	"Parenting is the greatest kind of intimacy. My kids need me, and I don't want to separate from them constantly."
Judging	"I need something I can control and complete."	"I need maximum control over home life."
Perceiving	"I need the stimulation and variety work provides."	"Work involves too much juggling, structuring, and living with a schedule."

Although personality type is limited in predicting a mother's work behavior, it is more helpful in understanding the *whys* of her decision.

As you read the comments in the previous two charts, which did you resonate with? If you feel conflicted, well, welcome to the club! Perhaps nothing causes so much ambivalence in a mom as trying to find a workable balance between employment and family. I hope that at least seeing the issues in black and white will help you know what will fit you best at this point in your life, as you weigh all the factors involved.

The Importance of Fit

Whether working outside the home works for you will depend in large measure on whether or not the employment situation fits your personality type. A mismatch between work and personality type can cause stress, fatigue, and feelings of inadequacy for anyone. Yet this is probably even truer for mothers. Most mothers come home to a "second shift" of additional family and household responsibilities and say there just isn't enough free time to adequately recharge after work.

That's why it's so crucial to find a job that fits who you are. Your work should complement your mothering by providing an outlet for the things you don't do or can't get at home. In that situation, the job can be an energizer that enables you to be a better mother.

Even if a job fit you well before you became a mother, you may find that things change once you have the baby. Motherhood adds responsibilities that can unbalance what you've worked out before having children.

For example, before children I worked as an account manager at an advertising agency. Every day I stretched my INFJ preferences to meet the demands of an ENFP job. Without children, I could come home and recharge my batteries with lots of time alone. But when I became a mother, the flexibility and people interaction required to deal with changeable clients and an active two-year-old required too much EP for my type. Had a career counselor been able to explain why it was such a struggle to combine my work situation with my mothering style, I might have been guided to a career that didn't drain me in the same ways mothering did.

An ESTJ mother tells a comparable story: "Before children, I loved being a therapist. Now that I'm a mother, I struggle to listen and empathize with my clients at work after being emotionally supportive of my children day after day at home. I secretly

A Feeling-Judging mother of two preschoolers was feeling drained by her job as a bedside nurse in ways she had never experienced before. With the support of her family, she decided to try a modest job change, rather than a sweeping career move. She improved her work/family balance by going to work as an office manager for doctors in private practice. Taking care of schedules, ordering supplies, and occasionally helping with patient care at work was a better balance to the emotional drains of caring for small children at home.

wish I could help my clients balance their checkbooks instead."

Feeling women experience similar issues. Many are typically drawn to the helping professions—nursing, teaching, community service. After becoming a mother, however, the Feeling woman may find herself overextended in the Feeling dimension of her jobs. She's caring for the needs of others at work and then coming home to care for the needs of children and family. This can lead to burnout.

Understanding your personality type can help you make adjustments needed for a better blending of work and family balance. If you currently feel a need to find more of a balance, remember this: the "mother" job is the one you can't quit. You'll increase your success of balancing work and family by choosing a work situation that considers the struggles of your mothering style and doesn't drain you in the same ways.

Volunteering

Even if you stay at home to mother your children full-time, you may find yourself pressured and overcommitted. It's easy to say yes to all the people who call upon you for help because, "after all, you don't have a job."

The trick is to use volunteerism as an outlet to express your personality type that mothering does not provide. Or, at least, to match your type to the task at hand. Just as with a job, a mismatch can lead to misery. Even worse, it can compromise your mothering.

After I quit working full time, I thought that part of being a good mother was volunteering. And what could be more "good" than teaching Sunday school? I wanted my children to get an introduction to religious tradition, the Sunday school program was manned by volunteers, and therefore, I felt obligated to support the program by volunteering. My kids were six and three.

Though I believed in what I was doing, nevertheless every time I taught Sunday school I would come home and scream at my kids. It was an enormous hassle to get myself and the children nicely dressed and out the door on time each Sunday. Then I had to throw myself into a group of active little kids, try to get them to finish a craft assignment in an orderly manner, teach a lesson, deal with my own child being jealous that I was paying attention to the other kids or acting up as a poor reflection on me. It was all too much. By the time I left the church, I was so exhausted and over-extended that I couldn't get my children out the door fast enough to let down my Church Lady façade and yell at them for bickering with each other.

When I discovered I was an Introvert, and an INFJ, it all made sense.

Teaching Sunday school drained me in exactly the same way being a mother did—too much people interaction and group commotion, too many details and practical tasks, too many people with conflicting needs to please, too much trying to bring order out of chaos. One of the first things knowing my type taught me was to stop doing it.

I began to ask the questions, How can I volunteer in a way that suits me? How can I choose things that supplement and enhance my mothering instead of detract?

This may be easier to do for some types than others. Because the preferences for E, S, F, and J are the most frequent for women, there seem to be lots of opportunities for volunteering that use those preferences—meetings, group projects, potluck meals, bake sales, room mother, lunch room volunteer. There are fewer opportunities for I, N, T, and P. Yet you can find them if you know what you're looking for: thinking of program ideas for your parenting organization, writing the church newsletter, one-on-one tutoring, and perhaps revamping the School Board's strategy plan. Knowing your type can help you pick and choose volunteer assignments more carefully, and be happier with the results. For example, one ENTP friend said that knowing her type helped her understand and accept that she made a great last-minute substitute, but hated having something on her schedule on a regular basis.

Making decisions based on your type can also rid you of the guilt of not doing what doesn't suit you. Remind yourself that others actually like doing what you hate to do. Yet occasionally, you might consider choosing a volunteer commitment that lets you play and experiment with different identities. I was surprised to see an INTP mother I knew flipping hotcakes at a Boy Scout Pancake Breakfast fund-raiser. As she put a stack on my plate, she smiled and said, "This is so not-me that I actually find it fun!"

Top Twelve Stress Busters

To sum up many of the points discussed in this book, here is a master list of my favorite tips. They should help you evaluate which outside commitments to take on, get a handle on stress, and enjoy your life more. Some may be more appropriate for you than others. Again, let your wisdom guide you.

1. *Exercise your self-knowledge muscle regularly.* Most experts agree that this is the most critical step for controlling stress and burnout. Exercise your "Who am I? What do I want?" muscle every day. Just like all muscles, it grows strong with use. Exercising your "I" muscle means honoring your preferences. It means allowing yourself "being" time—freedom from the busyness of your life, the time pressures, and the pressures to produce (even if you're a J).

2. *Keep your gas tank filled.* Now that you've identified your energy robbers, make sure you make time for regular energy replenishing, whether it's staring out the window as you sip a cup of coffee, or putting on your red shoes and heading downtown for an evening of dancing. A mature mother will become her own gauge and make sure she is living well within her emotional and physical limits.

3. *Use high octane lead-free premium, not economy, in your gas tank.* What we take in emotionally and spiritually directly affects what is available for our children. If you are consuming a diet of stress at work, nightly news about how bad the world is, and busyness to the point of tears, you can end up starving your children. And they, in turn, will become even more demanding.

   But if you feed yourself on uplifting books, music, art, intimate friendships, satisfying work, education, exercise, and spiritual practices, you will be able to offer your children more.

4. *Turn down the volume on control and responsibility and turn up the volume on learning and letting go.* A retreat leader once gave this advice, "To avoid burnout, the first thing you should do each morning is resign as director of the universe." When stress and a sense of inadequacy weaken our inside world, we compensate by controlling people and things in the world around us. This only leads to disappointment and makes us feel like failures. That's why time management, with its premise to exert more control over what's going on, is not the answer to

mother stress. After being a parent for only a day, we realize how little control we actually have over our children and our schedules. We must practice seeing our children as promises unfolding, just as we are, and not as projects or possessions to control.

5. *Listen to your body.* Even exercise gurus who used to say "no pain, no gain" and "go for the burn" are now advising to "listen to your body," "know your limits," and you'll accomplish just as much. So if your shoulders start aching or you get a cold, stop. Take a break—for maybe fifteen minutes, maybe fifteen days. Don't say, "I'll stop when I finish this," or do one more thing. Your body can keep you balanced. Act on its messages instead of overriding them.

6. *Be realistic about your things-to-do list.* The year I decided to stop the busyness, I paid very close attention to my "to-do" lists. I realized I was often totally unrealistic about what I could actually accomplish (a pitfall especially common to Intuitive types). One list of things I intended to do on a particular Saturday ended up taking six weeks to accomplish! I began a regular discipline of cutting back, of focusing *first* on the things that would feed me most, and on any other things that absolutely needed to get done. Then I tried to delegate or let go of everything else.

7. *Clean out your commitment closet regularly, and give something away to "Goodwill."* When I used to give away old clothes, I would debate with myself about how much wear was still in them. I'd figure that if there was another Great Depression, perhaps I'd like to have this dress. So I would save it.

   But later I became more ruthless. If I don't really like it anymore, or if I can survive without it, away it goes (never to be missed). I hope it will go to someone who will enjoy and use it more than I. It's the same with our commitments such as Sunday school teacher, alumni secretary, or marketing consultant. Each commitment should be periodically reviewed in a ruthless way—"Is it still important to me? Do I still enjoy it? Does it still fit?" and if it's a little tired in any of these areas, away it should go.

   Sometimes we think we're indispensable. We ask, "Who will do it if I don't?" It's easy to feel "everything must be done by me, and only me, or it won't get done." One mother agonized over whether to accept a volunteer position. She wanted to do it, but wasn't sure she had the time. When she finally said no, the person trying to recruit her said, "Oh, that's fine. I sensed your hesitation, so I asked So-and-So, and she said she'd be delighted to do it."

Experiment with taking the risk of not doing everything. Pass on commitments that don't fit you to someone who might like them more. You don't have to know who they are being passed on to. Just have faith that the task will be right for someone. And if perchance no one makes the commitment her own, so be it. Maybe this year there will be no balloon launch or Valentine's party. The world will not end, and perhaps a few mothers will end up a tiny bit more relaxed and loving of their children because of it.

8. *Make a cheat sheet on ways to say no in your own style.* Just as you are cleaning out your current commitments, new opportunities will pop up. People will ask you to take on various projects. You need a comfortable way to say no to those commitments that don't meet your criteria. Often we get over-committed simply because saying yes is a knee-jerk reaction, and we haven't developed a comfortable style for saying no when it's appropriate.

I have found that giving an immediate, plain, and direct no is too hard for me. It's easier for me to first give myself some breathing room: "Can I call you back on that? This is a really busy time and I want to make sure I am not over-committing." I am also more comfortable with a temporary no: "I would like to help but it will have to be next time. I cannot take on any new projects right now." I like a selective no as well: "That job just doesn't suit me, but could I help in another way?" or "Field trips are not my thing. Could I bring cookies instead?"

Another of my favorite ways of saying no is: "You know, it just isn't going to work for me right now." Avoid saying, "I'm sorry" or "I can't" if it isn't true. There's no need to negate yourself just because you want to say no instead of yes.

9. *Ask for help.* For some of us, "h-e-l-p" is the ultimate four-letter word; somehow we want to give the impression that we have it all together and don't need help. Just like saying no, asking for help is sometimes an underdeveloped skill that feels awkward and almost impossible at first. Because of the awkwardness, it seems simpler to just continue doing things all by yourself. But if you make a point of asking for help regularly, you become more polished with practice. If you are worried about toilet training your firstborn, ask a mother who already trained two of her own to be your tutor and support. If you need more than a Saturday evening with your spouse to rekindle romance, exchange children for weekend sleepovers with someone who has similar needs.

10. *Turn your expectations into ideals, not rigid standards.* High expectations are most motivating if viewed as goals in the process of taking shape. Expectations are debilitating when used as rigid standards of measuring where things stand now. For example, a mother who wants her children to eat a well-balanced diet and makes that a rigid standard for each meal can turn pleasurable mealtimes into a battleground. But by viewing that expectation as an ideal to strive toward, she can focus her efforts in the right direction and ultimately come very close to attaining her goal. So keep your high expectations, but add a healthy dose

> ## When to Say No
>
> Think about when it's hardest to say no. When is it easiest? Is it harder or easier in person? On the phone? Through a note? When it's someone you know or a stranger? (When I have to say no, I cross my fingers that when I call I'll get an answering machine. That's my easiest way.) Is there any other circumstance that makes it easier or harder for you?
>
> Consider saying no whenever:
>
> • it doesn't feel right.
>
> • it detracts from your own sense of well-being.
>
> • the timing is wrong.
>
> • you feel you have been giving too much and not getting enough back.
>
> Say yes only to what is good, healthy, and natural for you.

of patience and respect for the evolution that's necessary to keep your expectations realistic.

11. *Do not procrastinate fun.* Many of us live by the ethic, "You play when your work is done." In mothering, where the responsibilities are never-ending, this perspective leads to *no fun.* It may also lead to losing touch with what *is* fun for you. A life without fun is usually full of resentment.

   Learn to play first, even if it goes against your nature. Make an inventory of what brings you genuine pleasure and enjoyment, and then add one of those things to the beginning of your "things to do" list each day.

12. *Adopt a different yardstick to evaluate your productivity.* The world defines productivity largely in terms of conventional masculine standards. Consciously redefine your standard of success to fit your current values, beliefs, and life experiences. I feel successful every time I write a friend an encouraging note, correct my child's behavior with compassion and calm, or serve a family meal that is attractive, nutritious, and delicious.

The Bottom Line

For mothers with children at home, the bottom line and guiding principle should always be, "What enhances my mothering and my life?" Of course, earning an income and contributing to the family finances can be a big boost, too. The more you can make choices that truly empower you to be the best person you can be, the more satisfying mothering will be for you. And, of course, the better mother you will be.

· · · · · · · · · · · · ·

chapter 15

Becoming Your Best You

MOTHERHOOD CHANGES YOU. I'VE HEARD IT TIME AFTER TIME, "BEFORE I WAS A mother I was *that* way (thinner, freer, more confident, more accomplished) and now that I'm a mother I'm *this* way (wearier, wiser, more or less structured, more loving and accepting)," with many different variations.

In this book, I've given you the tools to be yourself in motherhood. But being yourself is a deepening and expanding process, rather than a static and limiting concept. According to Jung and Myers, *what* you are—your type—never changes. Either you're an apple or an orange. But *who* you are within that type never stops changing.

Motherhood, fueled by the perspective of type, can be a catalyst for your own personal growth. By meeting the challenges and demands of motherhood, many women, including myself, have healed childhood wounds, become truer to themselves, grown in character and wisdom, and become a better person all around.

Much has been written about how the child changes and grows. Very little has been written about how the mother changes and grows alongside her child. All the while we are changing diapers and making peanut butter sandwiches, another drama is unfolding—the drama of our becoming more complete, and completely ourselves. Having children is life changing. Part of our job as mothers is to cooperate with the process.

That's not to say it's an easy process. Not at all. In fact, over the last decades, motherhood has become increasingly stressful, out of balance, and intense for many mothers. Although these challenges can be solved on a number of levels, empowering mothers with a stronger sense of self and fostering their personal growth is one important part of the solution. Self-knowledge is important for success in any job or any relationship. That makes it doubly important in mothering, which is part job and part relationship. Motherhood is a coming-of-age process, a boot camp for becoming a stronger, more realistic and more compassionate you.

Swiss-Cheese Parenting

Before having children, many mothers considered themselves to be on top of their game—confident, capable, and successful. Yet there's nothing like mothering to rock your world and bring your inadequacies out of the closet and into your awareness. Underneath our "got it all together" personas, unbeknownst to even ourselves, we are often full of holes.

Over the years I've come to think of this phenomenon as "Swiss-cheese parenting." We bring all of our wounds and self-misconceptions to the job of childrearing, right alongside our open hearts and best intentions.

Where do these holes come from? The answer is as individual as the person. But for the most part, based on insights from both my own journey and the stories of many other women, I've discovered three primary sources: misconceptions from your own imperfect childhood, having a personality that makes you feel out of step with cultural expectations, and the problem of being a female in a world still based largely on patriarchal values and standards.

In our attempts to be perfect parents, we often ignore the wounds and cut off the empty or broken places. But the experience of mothering can help us move from "holes to whole" if we let it. Having a brand new baby is like turning over a new leaf on life. You want to avoid the mistakes your parents made with you and do mothering better than it has ever been done before. In fact, when you begin the job of parenting your child on some level you are also re-parenting yourself, filling in the gaps of your own childhood. Being a mother is a chance to become the mother you always wanted.

This re-parenting can take on many faces. Some are fun. I loved cotton candy as a child and never got enough. So at carnivals and amusement parks I was quick to treat my children to a pink cloud of fluff. Over time, I realized it was *my* need for cotton candy I was trying to fulfill, not theirs. They much preferred licorice strings and snow cones. Finally, on my forty-ninth birthday I rented a cotton candy machine and invited my friends over for a cotton candy party. The adult-me meeting the unmet need of the child-me created a surge of pure joy.

But sometimes the process of re-parenting means dealing with the "tough stuff" that comes up. Often our children's development will trigger our own unfinished business. Mothering made me aware of how I constantly over-extended myself and ignored my personal energy limits. I had to finally come to terms with my need for solitude and depth, a slower pace, and the shame of being different from the Extraverts around me. I saw my perfectionism more clearly and began to examine its roots. I also learned how I unconsciously structured my life and expectations so that I was constantly re-inflicting myself with the hurts of my childhood.

Type knowledge itself can sometimes function as a re-parenting tool. Understanding the strengths and uniqueness of my type provided the validation and acceptance I'd craved growing up. Many other women echo the same sentiment. If you felt misunderstood by your parents, the framework of personality type can offer you understanding. If you felt unappreciated growing up, type affirms your innate value as a person.

Susan, an ESFJ raised in a Thinking family, says she was never allowed to express her feelings at home. "My mother would say, 'Don't be sad' or 'How could you be angry?' I learned to stuff my feelings so as not to displease my mother. It was hurtful." As an adult, learning about type has helped her reclaim her gifts as a Feeling type. Now as a mother, she makes a point of letting her children feel what they feel without consequences.

Pat, ENTJ, was raised by an ESFP mother who seemed to value sociability and light-heartedness above all. "I grew up believing my more serious and analytical approach to life was wrong," she says. "But when I learned about the characteristics of my type, I finally felt validated for who I am."

Of course, some mothers begin motherhood with huge holes. Perhaps their parents were alcoholic, mentally ill, or physically and psychologically abusive. In my mind, nothing is more important than intentionally not passing on the negative legacy you might have inherited. It takes a lot of self-awareness and self-discipline to end a cycle of mistreatment. Although undoing an unhealthy heritage may get very little recognition, those who have the courage and determination to do it make an incredible contribution to their children and society.

I met an INTP mother who, before children, had worked as a corporate attorney. She'd been abused as a child, and although many of her peers continued their careers while childrearing, she could not. Breaking free from her parents' patterns took all the energy and mindfulness she could muster. Sometimes she lamented her loss in status from being a lawyer to "just a mom." "When people ask me what I do for a living," she says, "I feel like saying, 'I don't abuse my kids,' because that's the real truth. It doesn't look like much but it takes everything I have." These special mothers are unsung heroes, as deserving of a Medal of Honor or honorary Ph.D. as any soldier or scholar.

As you focus on being a good mother to your children, remember to be a good mother to yourself, too. As you get to know your vulnerabilities learn to embrace them with compassion and acceptance. You are a human being, after all. Whatever progress we make in healing our own wounds and filling our empty places frees our children to live fuller, less encumbered lives.

Making Peace with Your Own Mother

After your personality type, how you were mothered may be the next most important influence on your mothering style. Our mothers are our models; we remember how it was for us growing up and we want to replicate the good parts and undo the bad parts. Our mothers also shaped us into the people we are. To be more mindful in mothering, we have to be more mindful of our own mothers—who they were, what they did, how they affected us, and how they still affect us. This is a rich and complex area, and in this section we can only scratch the surface.

The mother/daughter relationship is a one-of-a-kind relationship. We assume mothers and daughters will have a special bond and feel like kindred spirits. There's a certain oneness and connection that can be either nurturing and supportive, or intrusive and negating. Sometimes it's hard for either to know where one person begins and the other ends. Most of us seek a special closeness with our mothers and also a separate identity.

When mother and daughter are different, they may feel at odds. The relationship falls short of expectations and this can lead to mother-blaming or self-blaming. A mother may interpret a daughter's different way as a personal put-down even though the daughter is simply being herself. It's easy for one or the other to end up feeling "wrong" about who she is. We begin to define ourselves in a negative way—"I'm not" or "I can't"—instead of "I am" or "I can."

When we become mothers ourselves, we often see our mothers with different eyes. We gain more empathy and understanding, and see her as more of a peer than an authority. Type can help undo feelings of wrongness that originated from the mother/daughter relationship and also give us a lens to increase our acceptance and appreciation for our mothers. As we grow in self-compassion, we are likely to extend that compassion to our mothers and vice versa.

If you haven't already, make a guess of your mother's personality type and read her profile in Chapters 6 or 7. That should give you a greater understanding of her mothering style versus yours. If your mother is willing, I encourage you to share with her the information in this book and use it as a springboard to discuss your differences in an impartial and objective way. Over the years, some workshop participants have come back a second time with their mothers so they could learn this information together. Invariably, the older generation says, "I wish I'd known about this when my children were little." I remember an ENFJ participant with her INTJ mother. Within the safety of the workshop environment, the ENFJ talked about not getting the praise and closeness she desired from her mother and the INTJ talked about how her daughter's social life seemed frivolous and overwhelming at times.

Looking back on your childhood, what are three strengths you most appreciate about your mother's mothering style? What are three things she didn't do well in raising you, her weaknesses? What's one way you are *like* your mother as a parent? What is one way you are *different* from your mother as a parent?

As simple as these questions are, they are powerful in demonstrating that your mother is a mixed bag, just as you and all mothers are. As wonderful as she was, she had shortcomings. Or as awful as she seemed, she had strengths.

Pat, ENTJ, says of her ESFP mother, "My mother's values and priorities sometimes seemed dumb or confusing to me. Growing up, I considered her a deficient and disappointing mother. Now I see she and I were just different. Yet she had a positive influence on my life. Because she thought all kinds of people were fun I think I learned to be more open-minded about different sorts of people."

The last two questions deal with issues of connection and separateness. It's important to realize that although you might resemble your mother in some ways, you are a separate person. You don't have to fear becoming your mother, because you couldn't even if you wanted to. An ISTJ mother raised by an ESFJ says she and her mother are both perfectionists, but she sets more boundaries to protect her time and space than her mother did. An INTJ mother raised by an ISFP says they both give their children plenty of space, but the INTJ is more proactive and intentional about creating her child's future. An ENFP raised by an ESFJ says they both are active and social, but the ENFP is more comfortable verbalizing her feelings.

Quiet the Comparing Mind

It isn't just comparisons to your own mother that can shape your expectations or shake your confidence; it's comparisons to the mother next door and the one down the street, too. Look around at any playgroup and you'll see differences in how other women handle hitting, sharing, or feeding, for example. These differences are simply differences. But if you are feeling a little shaky about your own approach, then you might take the differences personally and interpret them as implicit criticisms. At least that's what I so often did. My comparing mind would notice a difference, and it would set off an inner dialogue: *If her way is right, then my way is wrong. Uh-oh, I'm a bad mother.* Or *If my way is right, then hers is wrong. She's a bad mother.* Part of the growth in mothering is dealing with self-doubt and feelings of wrongness in a way that doesn't negate either you or the other.

Personality type helps us get beyond a core cultural belief that there is one right way to do anything, one standard of worth and success. The truth of nature is diversity. We live in a world that expresses life in a trillion different ways: a million different species of plants and animals, hundreds of different ethnicities and races, thousands of different beliefs about our relationship to the divine, and billions of different human life paths and stories. Instead of one right way there are many right ways, each befitting of a particular situation and objective.

When I talk with a mother who feels like a bad mother because she made a mistake or didn't live up to an ideal, I soothe her with this thought: *You are your child's mother because of who you* are, *not because of who you're* not. Personality type helps quiet the comparing mind and keep you centered in your own truth. Both are essential for growing into the best you.

Developing Your Own Wisdom

> "Sometimes I get down on myself and think my children would have better manners if Aunt Nancy raised them. Then I stop and remind myself although that might be true, I provide my children with lots that Aunt Nancy doesn't."—*Pat, ENTJ*

Experts, books, and well-meaning friends and family can provide new information, perspectives, and skills for "better" mothering. But they can never be a replacement for your own wisdom. To be a good mother and do your best by your children, you must find your own way rather than follow or copy someone else's way. You have to give yourself room to act from your best judgment and then learn from your mistakes.

My son, Dan, loved to baby-sit for a little boy who lived down the street. While talking with the boy's parents one day, I learned that during one baby-sitting stint Dan had entertained the boy by setting on fire some old plastic action figures in the alley. I was shocked and made a beeline home to admonish him about the dangers. "Just one drop of that melted plastic would have badly burned either of you," I said. "Use good judgment!"

"But how does one use good judgment if they don't have it?" he asked earnestly. His question gave me pause.

My wisdom about the dangers of melted plastic came from firsthand experience. I had once bought synthetic rope from the hardware store to make a jump rope for my daughter. While cauterizing the frayed ends at the gas stove burner, a drop of melted goop landed on my finger. I still have the scar. My son hadn't had that experience, so how could he know?

Developing good judgment—I like to call it wisdom—takes time and real-life experiences. It is a process that can't be rushed. We think and we act (not necessarily in that order) and we learn. Looking outside for quick answers stalls the development of our own authority.

Understanding your personality type in mothering can give you the confidence to act from your own perceptions and judgments so you can become stronger and wiser for your children, yourself, and society in general. Your judgment will be wisest if you consciously use Sensing, Intuition, Thinking, and Feeling in decision-making: get the facts, generate options and possibilities, and determine what you think, how you feel, and what you want. One of my greatest wishes is for mothers to begin to act from their own judgment and authority and show us how our world can become more life sustaining for everyone.

From outside appearances, Susan, an ESFJ, seems like a traditional mother. She's a stay-at-home mom with two daughters, a husband, and a lovely home in the suburbs. Yet on the inside, her thinking is far less traditional. She learned about personality type eleven years ago and believes it has helped her develop an uncommon wisdom. "I used to think I was responsible for creating polite, socially acceptable, well-rounded children. Now I know I am only responsible for creating an environment where they can become who they're meant to be. Personality type helps me understand the *why* of others' behavior and that has positive ramifications for every aspect of life. I can make better decisions, handle interpersonal issues with more savvy, and am more apt to give people the benefit of the doubt. I've widened my range of acceptable behavior for my children and myself. It's freeing!"

Pat, ENTJ, has worked full time as a school administrator since her two adopted children, now 15 and 17, were youngsters. She says, "Having children forces a crystallization of your values and priorities. You have to figure out who you are and what you want to impart to your children. Knowing personality type gives you the wisdom and courage to take a stand for yourself and your own beliefs. I used to think my job was to protect my children from difficulties and heartbreak. Now I think my job is to help them deal with life's challenges rather than avoid them. That's the only way to develop character and confidence."

Reframing Your Struggles

Learning to embrace challenges is good advice for mothers as well. In talking to hundreds of mothers over the years, I know for certain that every mother struggles. And every mother is surprised at how hard mothering is compared to what she expected.

But here's the irony of it all: Acknowledging—even surrendering to—the fact that mothering is hard will actually lessen your struggles. Like it or not, much of mothering is about wrestling with the challenges that arise. Even when you're not sure what action to take or which choice to make, you generally have to do something. Doing nothing carries its own ramifications.

Looking back on my childrearing years, it seems as if I struggled every step of the way. I interpreted my struggling as a sign that I wasn't good enough. Yet now that I have the perspective of a veteran mom, I think that there are certain struggles that *can't* be avoided in mothering, such as sleepless nights with a newborn or an older child getting sick the day you're leaving for vacation. And there are others that *shouldn't* be avoided in mothering—how to meet your child's needs without negating your own, when to take charge and when to let go, how to balance getting things done with building relationships or having fun. Struggles like these serve as stepping-stones to self-development. It is through these struggles that a mother defines who she is and becomes the mother she wants to be.

Even the best mothers don't have all the answers. Nobody does. When you become a mother you're a beginner. New mothers hold a mental picture of how

---

Good Intentions Count

In the business world, performance and the bottom line are what matter. But in mothering, good intentions count. I frequently remind mothers that they are doing the best they can. You may not get every situation right, but if your core intention is to do what's best for your child, your love will come shining through. On some level, children sense the love behind your actions, and this helps erase the effects of your mistakes. One mother told this story, "Once I was berating myself for punishing my five-year-old daughter, so I asked her, 'You know I love you, don't you?' 'Yes, I know,' she answered. 'I've looked into your eyes and seen your heart.'" Another mother, after a particularly bad day with her young ADD son, would tiptoe into his room at night while he was sleeping. In the quiet darkness, she apologized for losing her temper and poured out her heart to him. Although he was sound asleep, she felt connected to him on a deep and healing level.

---

good they want to be, but struggle because they lack the experience and know-how necessary to do it. I read somewhere that it takes ten years and ten thousand hours of practice to become an expert at anything. Motherhood is unique among endeavors because it is constantly changing. Just when you master babyhood, your children become toddlers. At the point when you finally feel comfortable with raising young children, your offspring knock you off balance by turning into teenagers.

When our children show us their messy finger paintings we ooh and ahh in admiration and say, "Good job!" We know from our own experience that, with practice and time, they will become more and more competent at picture making. So we give them the room and encouragement they need to develop. Wouldn't it be wonderful if we could treat ourselves the same way?

Motherhood in 3-D

If you take just a little time to reflect on it, it's obvious that there is more to mothering than meets the eye. Although we might not always consciously realize it, our ordinary experiences of making lunches, clipping fingernails, and remembering school permission slips have a deeper significance. Raising children is an invitation to participate in the most sacred mysteries of life. For many women, being a mother is a catalyst for re-evaluating childhood concepts of God and awakened spirituality.

By spiritual, I don't mean religious. Even women who don't claim a religious affiliation or are uncomfortable with the G-word will admit that there is a transcendent and transforming side to motherhood. Some even call it sacred.

For me, motherhood is a lot like a picture in a Magic Eye book or poster. Perhaps you've seen them. On the surface these stereograms are pictures of chaotic and colorful designs that seem to have no form or center at all. But if you relax your focus, look *through* the surface picture, and give yourself a few moments, a hidden three-dimensional image will take shape. When I focus on this deeper reality, in these picture books and also in motherhood, I feel a sense of awe and delight. And once a hidden reality is discovered, you begin to look for it and expect it.

There seems to be a very human need for proof of a deeper significance and higher power in life. For many of us, giving birth, receiving a precious child through adoption, or the intense love we have for our children is proof of the magic beneath the surface of life.

Soon after my husband and I had started trying to conceive our second child, I was doing the weekly grocery shopping. As I remember, I was in the soft drink aisle scanning the shelves of cola and root beer, looking for something without calories or caffeine. Suddenly—like an effervescent bubble rising to the surface—I became aware of conception. Whereas before I had only experienced myself, on some energy level, there was now the buzz of a second life beginning inside, the essence of another entity within.

I paused for a moment to absorb this happy surprise. The experience felt so significant I hardly knew what to do. I considered reporting it to the customer service counter. Maybe they would make an all-store intercom announcement, "Conception now taking place in aisle four; frozen shrimp on sale in aisle five." Eventually, I simply smiled to myself as I grabbed my six-pack of soda and pushed my cart down the next aisle. Yet inside of me began an inner dialogue about the big issues: What is life? Is there such a thing as a soul? From where did this new being come? This experience was a catalyst to my own spiritual awakening.

In talking to mothers of all different faiths and non-faiths, I've discovered transcendent experiences like these pop up frequently in childrearing, often when we least expect it. Motherhood is a human journey, to be sure, but it also can be a spiritual journey if we are open to it.

One woman says, "There are moments of extreme happiness and contentment in my role as mother. It can happen shampooing hair or making soup. A spark goes off in my brain. I am connecting in a deep way with the essence of mother—all nurturing, all comforting, all accepting. I feel a sense of communion and kinship with all the generations of mothers who have come before me. Yet, I can do the same things and not get that special feeling. For me, the sacredness of mothering is the opportunity to connect with this archetype of the Divine mother."

Other mothers talk about being shaped through the process of raising a child. As one woman says, "We are here to lead them, but ultimately they lead you. And you don't really know where."

Mothers may feel tied down with children. Yet many say that children have a grounding effect, too, which helps keep them centered in the here-and-now.

Still others talk about how raising children gave meaning and higher purpose to their lives. One mother says, "We yearn to be indispensable in this world, and in this job we are." And another, "We give our children life and they give us a reason for living." Finally, mothers talk about wanting to pass on to their children a spiritual legacy: "As we parent, we model the emotional outline of God. It's a sacred responsibility."

However, some mothers become frustrated when day-to-day demands seem to cancel out the magic of mothering, leaving them feeling flat or empty. From my own experience, I have found that whenever the material and the spiritual seem to compete for our attention, the material wins out—at least in the short run. However, eventually the spiritual dimension of mothering re-emerges and remains eternal.

Personality type is used in the spiritual realm as well as the business realm, because the simple process of being true to yourself has spiritual significance. The model of personality type echoes the inherent individuality and unity of existence. Each of us has been gifted with unique strengths, and the world seems to work best when everyone lives freely from their unique gifts. I've also heard this: Each of us has one piece of the truth. If we want to know the whole truth, we have to be open to the truths of others.

Even if you don't formally meditate, pray, or worship, getting closer to your own truth and living from your center is a spiritual practice.

Feminine Grounding

Part of your truth as a mother, and as a person, is being a female in what is still largely a man's world. Despite heartening progress, our society continues to regard women and femininity with ambivalence. In some ways, nothing is more wonderful, more beautiful, more attractive, or more enchanting. In other respects, the feminine is devalued, diminished, and regarded with disdain and even aggression. As women, many of us internalize that ambivalence. Therefore, our feminine side can be a source of both self-love and self-hate.

For me, the experience of becoming a mother was like coming out as a woman. Until I got pregnant, I could hide my womanhood when it served my purposes. In graduate school and at work, I could compete with men, play their games, and pretend to be just like them. Then I became a mother, and the ruse was up. When business clients called me at home the baby would start making baby noises in the background and I would cringe. A part of me was embarrassed to be a diaper-changing, breast-leaking, tied-down mother in a world that values power, control, and independence.

Carl Jung believed that each person has a masculine side and a feminine side—the anima and the animus. So when I talk of masculine and feminine I am talking beyond male and female. Many women carry inside of them a masculine side that criticizes their feminine ways and values. This masculine voice may tell us that we are stupid, weak, and inferior; that we "throw like a girl." Motherhood, infused with both the passive power of creating new life and the active power of a mother bear protecting her cubs, can help us cultivate our inner authority as women and build resistance to all that is anti-woman or does not enhance life.

Living inside a woman's body shapes our reality. Our experiences of monthly menses, gestation, and nursing, in all their glorious messiness and unpredictability, likely make us more connected and more yielding to the natural cycles of life. Tending our children's growth day to day reinforces that connection and brings us closer to both our own vulnerability and our own power.

The traditionally masculine model of power is characterized by domination, control, mastery, competition, winning over others, superiority, and a hierarchical system. Feminine power is less about force and more about the power of life, love, creativity, and letting go. Empowered femininity provides balance in the world, and serves to keep masculine power in check.

What Is Success?

Empowering your feminine side may require redefining your personal criteria of success. The culture's general measure of "success" is based more on a business model (which is largely masculine) than a personal or feminine model. The business model emphasizes big, money, public recognition, extraordinary, initiating, doing, and accomplishing. Using this yardstick to measure the value of what we do as mothers will only end up making us feel unsuccessful. We may compensate by being overly busy with schedules and to-dos. "How have you been?" a friend asks. "Busy," we answer. In that one word we attempt to legitimize our worth.

Forget the business model of success! For that matter, forget the busyness model of success, too. Each of us needs to come up with our own yardstick for success in mothering and in life—one based on our values as a mother, a woman, and a person. One that honors the small, everyday, private, spontaneous, and inwardly significant acts of life. We need to give ourselves credit for things like closeness to family and friends, fostering independence, helping others, making beauty, enjoying life, loving fully, showing kindness, tenderness, and compassion. We need to reclaim our strengths and use them to make this a better world.

Mothers Are VIPs

Sometimes we get mixed messages about the importance of mothering. On the one hand, people will go to great lengths, physically and financially, to bear or adopt children. On the other, compared to more prestigious professions, mothering can seem second rate.

Yet even in these times of unprecedented opportunities and professional successes for women with children, probably no desire goes deeper—nor is a more powerful and motivating force—than the desire to be a good mother. Being a good mother touches women's deepest needs for intimacy, competency, and generativity. And raising a child is incredibly important; it determines the quantity and quality of the next crop of humanity.

Every time I lead a mothers group I'm touched again by how noble and persistent mothers are in doing whatever it takes to be a good mother. To get to one typical meeting, a woman had to wrestle her two-year-old out of his pajamas, into the car, and up the stairs to the baby-sitting room. ("He's big for his age," she says, "so it takes a lot of muscle.") Another had to listen to the wails of a three-year-old who was unhappy to be left in the nursery. Should she let her cry and disturb the group? Or let her daughter sit on her lap and intrude on the other mothers' precious child-free time? Still another had to cancel at the last minute because one of her twins had a high fever. Just carving out a few hours for learning and conversation can be a major undertaking for mothers of small children. Yet their efforts are seldom acknowledged except perhaps among each other.

I remember giving a seminar to a group of mothers and one woman lay on the floor the whole three hours. She was confined to bed rest at this stage of her pregnancy but she didn't want to miss the workshop. I had to wonder: in the same situation would a man be this determined? Yet this gallant mother is more likely to feel inept about not being able to carry her pregnancy normally than to feel heroic about putting her ego aside and persevering despite obstacles.

Mothers are society's unsung heroes. In fact, I think mothers are "peace-time soldiers." As mothers we can do more than raise a flag, write our congressman, or send a check to bring about peace and justice. We live in a world of differences. Starting in the cradle we can make an indelible mark on how our children react to differences, how open are their hearts, how respectful are their actions. We can plant the seed of respect for others in our hearts, in our homes, and in our communities. We can teach our children that differences are good and are nothing to fear.

How do we do this? By example, primarily. By how well we accept and appreciate our own differences and those of our children, partners, and neighbors. The stronger you are in your own self-valuing and self-acceptance, the more you believe in the rightness of many ways, the less you feel that someone being different is a negation of you—the less you'll have to defend yourself or attack another, in your thoughts, words, or actions. Person by person, this is the way to create a kinder and gentler community. People don't need our fear-based judgment; they need our blessings.

Pablo Picasso said, "My mother told me, 'If you are a soldier, you will become a general. If you are a monk, you will become the Pope.' Instead, I was a painter, and became Picasso."

The world says you can become whatever you want. Perhaps you wanted to become a lawyer, or doctor, or scholar, or scientist, or artist.

Perhaps you were a lawyer, doctor, scholar, scientist, or artist, before you had children. Or maybe you haven't yet fulfilled your dream.

Either way, you became a mother. I hope that someday you will be able to say, "Instead I was a mother, and became my best self."

I believe Jung said that women would transform the world simply by being their own true selves. My mission with this book is to inspire and empower you to be your truest and best self. Individual transformation yields social transformation. The world needs your voice, your piece of the truth, your individuality, and your womanhood. The children need you! Be brave. Be yourself. Become the best you. And know, in your heart, that your children will surely follow.

Frequently Asked Questions

Can my type change over time?

According to Jung/Myers-Briggs theory, the answer is no. The *expression* of your type may change over time due to age, development, and environmental influences, but your "true" type is innate and doesn't change from birth to death. For example, if someone is born a "daisy," we'd expect them to change from a tiny brown seed to a green sprout and then to a full flowering plant. We'd also expect a daisy in a garden with just the right amount of sun and water to look different than a daisy growing between the cracks of a concrete sidewalk. However, we would never expect a daisy to suddenly turn into a lily.

One other important point: What you guess your type to be can be influenced by temporary fluctuations in life situations. I hear people say, "When I took the MBTI instrument the first time I came out a J. Then five years later I took it again and came out a P. It was interesting to know my type has changed!" But according to this theory that is incorrect. Either you are a true J that has been recently developing your P side or you are a true P who is finally letting yourself be who she really is. Your true type doesn't change, although its expression may, as each of us grows toward greater wholeness.

I'm in the middle on one of the dichotomies; doesn't that mean I'm more balanced?

Balance, according to Isabel Myers, is having a clear and well-developed use of your preferences, plus the ability to use your nonpreferences when a situation requires it. She never advocated being equally adept at both aspects of a dichotomy. Being in the middle of a dichotomy may also be due to an internal conflict or inadequate development.

Do similarities or differences make for more marital satisfaction?

Most research on type and marriage suggests that marital satisfaction is not determined by the number of preferences shared between the couple. Yet, Tieger and Barron-Tieger, in researching their book *Just Your Type*, discovered that couples' ratings on marital communication were correlated to their ratings for marital satisfaction. When a couple's types are very different, good communication can require more effort and be a challenge.

Are people with the exact same type the most compatible?

People who share the same four letters often have an uncommon understanding. However, their relationship may lack chemistry or spark. At large workshops, I break the participants into type-alike groups of six to ten women. The women usually describe the experience as validating and relaxing. We don't realize how much energy we spend every day accommodating and reacting to people's differences. But after a while some of the types, ISFJs for example, ask to return to a mixed-type group. They need the spark of an Extraverted or Intuitive type to keep things interesting. Sometimes too much similarity can become boring or unbalanced.

I think I was a different type before I had children. Is that possible?

As mentioned previously, mothering stretches you in many ways. To meet the demands of childrearing you might become more J or P, or more F, for example. But just because you are developing new parts of yourself doesn't mean your core type has changed.

Can I be a different type mother to each of my children?

Once again, it is likely a case of stretching and flexing to meet the demands of a particular situation or to be more effective with a specific person rather than changing your type. My preference is Feeling, and my son prefers Thinking. When I ask him to unload the dishwasher, I stretch my natural style to give him the reasons why: 1) It's time for me to prepare dinner; 2) The dirty dishes on the counter are in my way; 3) Before I can put the dirty dishes in the dishwasher it needs to be unloaded from yesterday. Although I am communicating in a Thinking way, it doesn't mean I'm a Thinking type.

Is there something that every type mother has in common?

Although my research has focused primarily on mothering style differences, there seem to be at least three things every type mother has in common. First, no mother thinks she has enough patience with her children. Different mothers are patient about different things; one might lose it over a cup of milk spilling and another over having to give long explanations. But each mother we interviewed felt short on patience. Second, every mother could use a hand with housework. Those with a high cleanliness quotient need help maintaining their strict standards, and the more relaxed housekeepers get overwhelmed by the basics. Third, all mothers do badly when over-scheduled. The DayTimer crowd and the go-with-the-flow types may differ in how much is too much, but once they hit their limit, they both report turning into "Gestapo Mom."

How does type affect discipline styles?

In my research, I found discipline to be a fuzzy area. I anticipated clear T-F type differences, but they were not as apparent as expected. Discipline seems to be greatly influenced by how the mother was raised and current cultural biases. However, we did find that Js tended to have more rules than Ps. Ts seemed to be better able to stay cool, calm, and objective when enforcing rules, and Fs tended to be pushovers or turn into ogres. Ts gravitated to logical consequences and cause and effect to teach and correct behavior. Fs gravitated toward cooperation, give-and-take, and responsibility to the parent/child relationship as a way of shaping behavior.

What is the difference between temperament and personality type?

In layman's terms they are the same. Each refers to an innate propensity toward different mindsets and traits. Within type theory, however, the terms have slightly different meanings. David Keirsey used the Myers-Briggs system to identify four basic temperaments: SJ—Guardian, SP—Artisan, NT—Rational, and NF—Idealist. People within each of these temperaments share many of the same core values, needs, and life themes.

Does one of my middle two letters play a stronger role than the other?

The theory of type dynamics says each type has a dominant psychological process that serves as the leader and an auxiliary process that serves as its helper. One of your middle two letters is your leader and the other is your helper. ESTJ, ISTP, ENTJ, and INTP are led by Thinking. ESFJ, ISFP, ENFJ, and INFP are led by Feeling. ISFJ, ESFP, ISTJ, and ESTP are led by Sensing. INTJ, ENTP, INFJ, and ENFP are led by Intuition.

Where can I take the Myers-Briggs Type Indicator instrument?

If you would like to take the Myers-Briggs Type Indictor instrument to confirm or clarify your type, contact us at www.motherstyles.com. We will help you find a qualified professional who will administer the instrument and give you appropriate person-to-person feedback. Other resources are the Center for Applications of Psychological Type (www.capt.org) and Association of Psychological Type (www.aptcentral.org).

Resources

Children and Parenting

Lawrence, Gordon D. *People Types and Tiger Stripes: A Practical Guide to Learning Styles*. Gainesville, FL: Center for Applications of Psychological Type, 1993.

Meisgeier, Charles, and Constance Meisgeier. *Parents' Guide to Type*. Palo Alto, CA: Consulting Psychologists Press, 1989.

Murphy, Elizabeth. *The Developing Child: Using Jungian Type to Understand Children*. Palo Alto, CA: Consulting Psychologists Press, 1993.

Neff, LaVonne. *One of a Kind*. Gainesville, FL: Center for Applications of Psychological Type, 1988.

Scanlon, Susan. *KidTypes*. Alexandria, VA: The Type Reporter, 1993.

_____. *Relax, Mom, You're Doing a Great Job*. Alexandria, VA: The Type Reporter, 1991.

Tieger, Paul D., and Barbara Barron-Tieger. *Nurture by Nature*. Boston: Little, Brown and Company, 1997.

Marriage/Couples

Kroeger, Otto, and Janet Thuesen. *16 Ways to Love Your Lover*. New York: Delacorte Press, 1994.

Lerner, Harriet. *The Dance of Intimacy*. New York: HarperCollins, 1990.

Tieger, Paul D., and Barbara Barron-Tieger. *Just Your Type*. Boston: Little, Brown and Company, 2000.

Work/Careers

Hirsh, Sandra K., and Jean M. Kummerow. *Introduction to Type® in Organizations*. Palo Alto, CA: Consulting Psychologists Press, 1987.

Tieger, Paul D., and Barbara Barron-Tieger. *Do What You Are*. Boston: Little, Brown and Company, 1992.

General

Keirsey, David, and Marilyn Bates. *Please Understand Me*. Del Mar, CA: Prometheus Nemesis Book Company, 1978, 1984.

Kroeger, Otto, and Janet Thuesen. *Type Talk*. New York: Delacorte Press, 1988.

Laney, Marti Olsen. *The Introvert Advantage*. New York: Workman Publishing, 2002.

Martin, Charles R., Ph.D. Revised by Allen L. Hammer, Ph.D. *Estimated Frequencies of the Types in the United States Population*. Gainesville, FL: Center for Applications of Psychological Type, 1996, 2003.

Myers, Isabel Briggs. *Introduction to Type®*. Palo Alto, CA: Consulting Psychologists Press, 1993.

Myers, Isabel Briggs, and Mary H. McCaulley, Naomi L. Quenk, and Allen L. Hammer. *MBTI Manual—A Guide to the Development and Use of the Myers-Briggs Type Indicator*, Third Edition. Palo Alto, CA: Consulting Psychologists Press, 1998.

Myers, Isabel Briggs, with Peter B. Myers. *Gifts Differing*. Palo Alto, CA: Davies-Black, 1993.

Pearman, Roger R., and Sarah C. Albritton. *I'm Not Crazy, I'm Just Not You*. Palo Alto, CA: Davies-Black, 1997.

Organizations

MotherStyles.com
Register for Mom's Circle, connect with mothers who are like you, and learn from those who are different. More helpful information. Seminar and presentation schedules. Complementary materials: Parenting style presentation illustrations, M.O.M.S. video/DVD, audio tapes/CD—*How to Put More Fun in Your Mothering*, *Reclaiming the Sacred Side of Mothering*, and *Is It Misbehavior or Personality?*

16Types.com
www.16Types.com
Website for books, materials, training.

Association for Psychological Type (APT)
P.O. Box 10058
Gaithersburg, MD 20898-10058
800-847-9943
www.aptinternational.org
Membership organization of type users, training, conferences, journals.

The Center for Applications of Psychological Type (CAPT)
2815 NW 13th Street
Suite 401 Gainesville, FL 32609
800-777-2278
www.CAPT.org
Research, training, books, materials, MBTI distribution, and on-line administration.

Consulting Psychologists Press (CPP)
CPP and Davies-Black® Publishing
1055 Joaquin Road, 2nd Floor
Mountain View, CA 94043
800-624-1765
www.CPP-DB.com
Publisher and distributor of the Myers-Briggs Type Indicator instrument, books, materials,
    and training.

PersonalityType.com
Paul Tieger and Barbara Barron-Tieger
800-YOUR-TYPE
www.PersonalityType.com
Website for the authors of *Nurture by Nature*, *Do What You Are*, and *Just Your Type*.

The Type Reporter
11314 Chapel Road
Fairfax, VA 22039
703-764-5370
www.typereporter.com
A psychological type-based periodical, published several times a year. Back issues contain arti-
    cles about applying type to everyday issues.

Type Resources
36 Pauline Road
Louisville, KY 40206
800-456-6284
www.type-resources.com
Books, materials, training.

Acknowledgments

This book was a long time in the making, and it would never have come into being without the helping hands and thoughts of others.

I most want to thank two remarkable women, both named Diane, who were instrumental in the writing and development of this book.

Diane Eble is the *MotherStyles* collaborator and, with ten prior published books, an accomplished author in her own right. She was gracious enough to lend her gifts and experience to the writing of this book. Consolidating almost two decades of my presentations, observations, research, and participant comments was a daunting task, much like assembling a ten-thousand-piece jigsaw puzzle. Diane's steadfast commitment, vision, and nurturing collaboration guided the book from concept to soft cover.

Diane Stephens is the co-author of *The M.O.M.S. Handbook*, my self-published workbook that has been used as a take-home resource in seminars and classes since 1995. She and I interviewed type-alike groups of mothers in order to develop the profiles in this book. Throughout the development of Mothers of Many Styles, Diane balanced my perspective with her more Extraverted and objective point of view, and her advice and expertise were invaluable.

In turn, Diane and Diane have each been there for me along the way, whenever I needed a sympathetic ear to listen or a hand to hold.

I also want to express my gratitude to Isabel Myers and her mother Katharine Briggs for making Jung's theory of psychological types more useful and accessible. The story of two women making a breakthrough contribution while raising children, keeping house, and working at their kitchen table has been an inspiration to me. Mary McCaulley, the former director of the Center for Applications of Psychological Type, once told me Isabel Myers and I shared a common dream: If parents knew type, it would change the world. There have been times along the way when I relied on the spirit of Myers to spur me on.

I also want to thank the many professionals who have built on Jung's and Myers's work to create a rich body of type knowledge from which I could learn. Among them are Binnie Ferrand, Elizabeth Murphy, and Susan Scanlon. Ferrand is the professional who introduced me to personality type. A retired kindergarten teacher, she co-led my first mothering seminars and has been there with advice, encouragement, and insights throughout the development of my work with mothers. I think of her as the god-mother of M.O.M.S. Murphy is the pioneer in applying type to children. All the while I was deepening my expertise on mothering styles, she was deepening her understanding of type with children. Her work has been a valuable complement to my own. And Scanlon, the editor of *The Type Reporter*, has the gift of simplifying type theory, making it come alive through the voices of real people, and applying it to everyday issues. She saw the value of my type application to mothers early on and has provided years of friendship and support.

I also want to thank Jamelyn Johnson, the longtime coordinator of Research Services at the Center for Applications of Psychological Type (CAPT), who promptly and kindly answered many questions.

I want to thank the women who generously contributed their time to read and comment on portions of this text prior to publication: Suzanne Brue, Katie Compernolle, Stephanie Denson, Marsha Serling Goldberg, Barbara Heyn, Riza Kapora, Catherine Lockhart, Liz Martin, Lisa Mastain, Laurel O-Sullivan, Helen Schaeffer, Nancy Wagner, Anna Whitcomb, and Sarah Zeldman. I want also to acknowledge the special contribution of Ann Baucus, Carolyn Brocksmith, Marka Bruhl, Debbie Burns, Rene Goldstein, Julie Hays, Katie Hildebrand, Judy Luken-Johnson, Margaret McIntyre, Teresa Melcher, Carol Meylan, Kelly Morgan, Bette Papke, Mary Robbins, Amy Whittcamper, and Carol Zsolnay, as well as the hundreds of mothers who contributed their stories in workshops and interviews.

I want to thank fellow author, Patricia Butler; my literary agent, Joelle Delbourgo; and my editor, Marnie Cochran, all of whom recognized the value of *MotherStyles* at first sight.

Last but not least, I would like to thank my children, Dan and Jane, and my husband, Steve, who were such good sports about my using them as examples throughout the book.